Bringing Race to the Table:

Exploring Racism in the Pagan Community

Bringing Race to the Table:

Exploring Racism in the Pagan Community

Edited by Crystal Blanton, Taylor Ellwood,
and Brandy Williams

Megalithica Books
Stafford England

Bringing Race to the Table: Exploring Racism in the Pagan Community
Edited by Crystal Blanton, Taylor Ellwood, and Brandy Williams
© 2015 First edition

Editors: Crystal Blanton, Taylor Ellwood, and Brandy Williams
Copy Editor: Leni Austine
Layout: Taylor Ellwood
Cover Design: Isis Sousa

ISBN: 978-1-905713-98-1
MB0172

A Megalithica Books Publication
An imprint of Immanion Press

info@immanion-press.com
http://www.immanion-press.com

Dedication

A special moment of honor to those who have lost their lives in this struggle. This book is dedicated to those who have been killed, incarcerated, profiled or harmed unjustly in a society that is struggling to unravel years of racism and oppression. We dedicate this book to the young Black men and women who were unarmed and killed by law enforcement during the time this book was being created. This book is dedicated to the protestors, the warriors, the organizers and the social change agents who are actively shedding light on the problems that continue to thrive in our community, and demanding attention onto these issues. This book is also dedicated to the healers that are working to bring love, healing and acknowledgement to the pain of racism in today's world, and healing to the historical pain of our ancestors on all sides.

May this book support the idea of growth, love, and honor. May our love of equity fuel personal growth and knowledge so that we can make changes in the systems that create such pain among one another. And may we learnt to better honor one another.

Table of Contents

Being an Ally

Introduction

Crystal Blanton, Taylor Ellwood and Brandy Williams

The social construction of race has always brought about challenges within society. This legacy of race has been one of complexity and has created some intense debate in many different communities. The modern Pagan community has not been exempt from the ongoing discussions of diversity and race, and these conversations have become more important as the community continues to grow.

In the construction of this book, the editing team has looked for many ways to bring these conversations to the "table" in a way that is insightful and supportive to the growing need to bridge conversations that are inclusive to all people. The Eurocentric foundation of modern Paganism has not always been one that has felt safe for people of color, or for those who want it to support the increasing diversity within the growing community.

The first section of Bringing Race to the Table features the voices and stories of people of color that are a part of our community. The experiences of people of color working within the spiritual foundation of Paganism while navigating racial challenges brings insightful information to the conversation of inclusivity. The authors in this section bring stories of beauty and struggle while working through issues of appropriation, discomfort, isolation and assumptions.

The second section explores racism in history and mythology. The authors in this section show how systemic racism is not a recent development, but something which has been part of history, as well as how it shows up in contemporary counter cultural movements.

The third section features the voices and stories of allies to people of color as well as advice to those allies from people of color. Becoming an ally is a journey that examines racism as it shows up in the life of the ally and the people around the ally, as well as what the ally will actually do to respond to racism. The authors in this section share stories of their journeys to become allies as well as advice on how to honor people of color and be supportive without being intrusive.

BRINGING THE ANCESTORS TO THE TABLE

Heaven Walker

IN THE EAST, PLACE OF NEW BEGINNINGS, KNOWLEDGE, AND THE SUNRISE.WE CALL YOU MAYA ANGELOU. WE INVOKE YOUR WISE WORDS, YOUR ELOQUENCE, YOUR WISDOM, YOUR CREATIVITY. GUIDE OUR SPEECH AS WE COMMUNICATE OUR HEARTS AND MINDS AND ENGAGE IN THIS SACRED DIALOG.

IN THE SOUTH, PLACE OF PASSION, WILL, MANIFESTATION, AND TRANSFORMATION.......WE CALL YOU ROSA PARKS. WE INVOKE YOUR STRENGTH TO BRAVELY STAND UP FOR WHAT IS RIGHT IN THE FACE OF ADVERSITY, TO INSIST ON BEING HEARD AND TO INSIST ON THE AFFIRMATION OF OUR HUMANITY.

IN THE WEST,PLACE OF HEALING, MAGIC, AND DARING.....WE CALL YOU MARTIN LUTHER KING JR. WE INVOKE YOUR POWERS OF PEACEFUL PROTEST, OF RAISING AWARENESS, OF STEADFAST VISION AND BRAVERY.

IN THE NORTH, PLACE OF INTEGRATION, STRENGTH, AND GROUNDED ACTION....WE CALL YOU HARRIET TUBMAN, WHO LED SO MANY TO FREEDOM THROUGH THE UNDERGROUND RAILROAD. GUIDE US AS WE SEEK THE FREEDOM FROM PREJUDICE AS WE ATTEMPT TO FORGE NEW PATHS TOGETHER PEACEFULLY.

AND IN THE CENTER....THE PLACE OF THE AKASHA WHERE ALL ELEMENTS COMBINE......THE PLACE BETWEEN THE WORLDS, THAT CHANGES ALL WORLDS, WE JOIN HANDS, BREATHE DEEPLY, OPEN OUR HEARTS AND EMBARK ON THIS SACRED JOURNEY TOGETHER IN PERFECT LOVE AND PERFECT TRUST. AND SO IT IS!

Understanding the Definition of Racism and its Power in Our Community

Crystal Blanton

Racism: a word with several definitions, and multiple interpretations. It is a loaded word and often misunderstood, giving rise to potential discussions that are hurtful, exhausting and often avoided. The implications and interpretations that happen when people talk about race within any community leads to a state of tension that is not always helpful in promoting change, mostly because defenses shut the conversation down instead of exploring the impact on our community and within the culture. This is not specific to the Pagan community, although it applies to it and other types of communities.

What I have come to understand in my experiences, and within my studies, is that people do not understand what racism, prejudice, privilege, microaggressions, cognitive dissonance or intersectionality mean. This lends to more assumptions about the integrity of individual people when these conversations happen, instead of looking at the systemic structures in place that promote inequity among different groups of people. The real conversations are not happening because we are too busy fighting this imaginary war of who is and who is not racist.

In order to have constructive discussions about how racism affects the Pagan community, and people of color within the Pagan community, we have to decode some of the definitions for the words we are using to illustrate the method of harm. There is no way to identify what we are looking at if we do not know what we are looking for; and without clear targets for corrective action, we are spinning wheels without the ability to find solutions.

The question becomes, what is racism and how does racism impact the social construct of the Pagan community?

According to the Merriam-Webster dictionary, the definition of racism is the "poor treatment of or violence against people because of their race, and the belief that some races of people are better than others". It goes on to give a "full definition" of racism as "a belief that race is the primary determinant of human traits and capacities, and that racial differences produce an inherent superiority of a particular race, racial prejudice or discrimination."

This definition applies to an individual interpretation of racism based on feelings of superiority due to racial characteristics, but it does not address more macro levels of racism and what that means outside of a micro or individual example of beliefs. Within the study of the social sciences, the definition of racism has been expanded to include structural, institutional, political, and macro level racism, and the damage of these racial caste systems. The tides began to change with academic definitions about 1970, when several individuals began to correlate racism on structural levels with that of power. Dr. Delmo Della-Dora defined racism in her paper 'What Curriculum Leaders Can Do About Racism' by stating, "Racism is different from racial prejudice, hatred, or discrimination. Racism involves having the power to carry out systematic discriminatory practices through the major institutions of our society" (Della-Dora1970). This coincides with Dr. Pat A. Bidol's definition in 1970 from 'Developing New Perspectives on Race' that "Power + Prejudice = Racism" (Bidol 1970). While Bidol has gotten a fair amount of criticism from people who do not agree with her interpretation of what racism is, she is not the only one who challenges the standard definition to include structural and institutional levels of racism.

In 1973, the National Education Association expressed the following in regards to the power and racism conversation, "In the United States at present, only whites can be racists, since whites dominate and control the institutions that create and enforce American cultural norms and values . . . Blacks and other Third World peoples do not have access to the power to enforce any prejudices they may have, so they cannot, by definition, be racists" (National Education Association 1973).

The varying definitions and explanations of racism gives us pause to contemplate how racism itself has evolved, and how our understanding of the impact of racism in varying different factions of society has expanded. As systemic racism, institutionalized racism, and aversive racism come on the scene, we can see how these definitions are important. Racism is not, nor never has been, just about a person's prejudice regarding differences in race, or a group of people. Racism as a system has more of an individual, societal, and structural impact on the lives of racial minorities than just another person's opinion. There will always be people who are prejudiced, or even racist, but structures that promote racism have the potential to cause much more damage than any individual can.

In the piece 'What is Institutional Racism,' Professor Vernellia Randall talks about some of the differences between individual, institutional and systemic racism; surprisingly, not everyone is aware that there is a difference at all. "Racism is both overt and covert, and it takes three closely related forms: individual, institutional, and systemic. Individual racism consists of overt acts by individuals that cause death, injury, destruction of property, or denial of services or opportunity. Institutional racism is more subtle but no less destructive. Institutional racism involves policies, practices, and procedures of institutions that have a disproportionately negative effect on racial minorities' access to and quality of goods, services, and opportunities. Systemic racism is the basis of individual and institutional racism; it is the value system that is embedded in a society that supports and allows discrimination" (Randall 2008).

It is important, when assessing the dynamics of any community, to remember that any faction of our society is still a part of the greater society. The Pagan community is but a microcosm of the macro issues within society, leaving us to ask questions about how the value system within our community might support or allow for discrimination. And remember, this is not always answered by looking at the covert examples, but also by exploring the ways that ignoring racism within our community enables it to continue. These are hard questions, and asking them will help us examine what it would mean to embrace true ethnic diversity.

When we ask ourselves why there are not more Black people, or any other ethnic minority practitioners, involved within the greater Pagan community, we have to be willing to explore these very issues in-depth.

Identification of the new ways that modern forms of racism have mutated are telling within this context, and is often something missed in circles of well-meaning individuals. The overt forms of racism that we are accustomed to identifying in society have continued to decline, giving the illusion that racism is no longer one of the prominent issues within the United States. Nothing could be further from the truth. Racism continues to transform and present itself within ways that are more viable within the structure of our modern day communities. Institutional, systemic and aversive racism are some of the newest ways that racism and racist tendencies are manifested.

When we look at systems of racism that have become a part of the fabric of American value structures, we begin to see that racism is not just about someone saying they do not like Black people, but about the ways that society conditions us to think, and the way that our biases and preferences are cultivated. When we see this as a part of the problem, we understand that aversive racism is not about someone's good or bad intentions; it is about the most covert of biases becoming so ingrained as normal thoughts that even the person does not see it as racist. Often aversive racism is passed off as personal preference. Preferences are hard to categorize as strictly right or wrong, hence lending to the confusion of what is and what is not racism.

Aversive racism can often translate as microaggressions to people of color. DW Sue is one of the people credited with bringing the discussion of microaggression to the forefront of social studies about race. In 2007, the American Psychologist published *Racial Microaggressions in Everyday Life; Implications for Clinical Practice*, where Sue states, "Racial microaggressions are brief and commonplace daily verbal, behavioral, or environmental indignities, whether intentional or unintentional, that communicate hostile, derogatory, or negative racial slights and insults toward people of color. Perpetrators of microaggressions are often unaware that they engage in such communications when they interact with racial/ethnic minorities" (Sue 2007). Again, it is important to point out that those who are the perpetrators of microaggressions often do not see what they are doing or saying as harmful towards another person, and yet the harm that happens to people of color during these daily exchanges are detrimental to their ability to truly integrate into society.

"You are Wiccan? You must work with the Egyptian Gods...."

Microaggressions are commonplace for people of color, but this concept is often ignored within the Pagan community, relying on the belief that no one within the community would purposefully alienate someone because of their race. In reality, some of the comments I have heard within our community from other people of color range from overt to aversive racism, with a host of microaggressions to boot.

"It isn't like there is racism anymore, we have a Black president now".

From strange, questioning looks when someone walks into circle, to asking a Hispanic practitioner if she was the maid at a Pagan event, all of these types of interactions happen within our community. People of color often are put in positions within the Modern Pagan community to speak on behalf of their minority ethnic group, becoming the unofficial ambassador for the community to connect with those of other races. Assumptions and questions about differences in our cultural make-up can serve to further marginalize people of color, especially when there are only one or two present.

The fundamental assumption that we are attempting to integrate into a community that is not ours is the root of all these microaggressions. Eurocentric construction of the Pagan community lends to a structure that coincides with greater society, making Caucasian the default, the overculture. This structure automatically "others" people of color, and defines a system of privilege that makes Eurocentric thought the primary consideration, while all others are compared against that which is already in place. Much like it is within greater society, the name of the game is about how we fit into what is in place, not how things fit with all of us included as a part of the whole. This community structure is a microaggression in itself from a systemic perspective.

"I am not sure what we are supposed to do to make those people feel more comfortable".

Racialist Paganism is only one example of how systemic racism works, and creates an overculture that locks out people of color solely based on race. I was recently told that I could not join a specific group of Heathen practitioners because I was not of European descent. When I challenged that, and actually concluded that I was, I was told I still could not participate because I was not of "primary European descent". When asked how that is measured, I was not given an answer that was consistent among those who would apply. In the end, I concluded that looks would be the determining factor of whether someone was of primary European descent, and although I would not qualify, my son would because of his sandy hair and blue eyes. These experiences reinforce and retrigger transgenerational trauma of the racism, violence, and harm done generations past and in the present. Understanding that Black people, for example, live in a world full of individual, community, and systemic hostilities because of their race, can give a bit more understanding of why this type of conversation might be hurtful for someone like me. We must ask ourselves how these interactions reinforce the culture that people of color are not welcome within our Pagan community and that our actual heritage is not honored within some Pagan circles. Genetically I might have more European DNA in me than African and yet I am not white enough for some circles.

"Why wouldn't you want to work with your own ancestors in an African tradition?"

There is a certain amount of cognitive dissonance that exists within the United States as a part of the fabric of our culture. As a country that has such a violent history, and the backbone of our successes built at the hands of others, cognitive dissonance has become an integral part of preserving our sense of humanity. It has become one of the most important survival skills we have within the US in order to continue life as we know it, and feel like we are good people in the process.

So what is cognitive dissonance and how does this apply?

Theories of Cognitive Dissonance initially came on the scene when the psychologist Leon Festinger proposed a theory about the person's need to create an internal balance between conflicting thoughts, beliefs and behaviors. This theory really points out something that we have seen individually with humans, but also within our society: the need to decrease the internal conflict, decreasing the amount of uncomfortable feelings brought about when actions do not match ethical or self identifying elements. In order for people to remain in alignment with who they say they are, they have to dismiss, justify, or rationalize behavior that would prove otherwise.

In society, we can see cognitive dissonance in the way we discuss how we have come to occupy this land. How are we good, religious folk when we kill, hunt, and annihilate a whole race of people who were living here first? How are we good, God fearing Christians when we buy, sell, trade, rape, kill, and enslave Africans as chattel slaves here in the United States? How are we a nation that is the land of the free, the home of the brave, when we have conflicting beliefs about social Darwinism and policies that define who are the worthy and who are not? These questions push us to question the American culture that encourages a sense of distance between our actions and our beliefs. The outcome in our society has been tragic. American culture encourages unnatural separations to protect ourselves from feeling this cognitive dissonance, making the process of feeling good more important than dealing with the internal and moral conflicts that make us uncomfortable. It is our natural response to cognitive dissonance to need it to be resolved.

This carries over into the Pagan community because it is an extension of the greater society. We, as Pagans, are just as responsible for what happens in greater society as we are for what happens within the Pagan community. There is no separation, and we cannot pretend that our spirituality makes us decent people if we are not out there fighting to make things right in areas of inequity for people of color.

We justify away what makes us uncomfortable. We also excuse rules, prejudices and guidelines that eliminate the participation of people of color. Then the community ignores the lack of black and brown faces in our circles or conventions, excusing it away instead of exploring it. Another means to remove the uncomfortable feeling that comes up by ignoring the reality that our community is not truly diverse.

It is my belief that the lack of understanding around what racism is, how racism appears within community, how people of color experience microaggressions, and how we continue the pattern of cognitive dissonance as a means to decrease uncomfortable feelings about how our actions support divisiveness within the community, perpetuate this state of ignorance around the existing social structure of privilege within the modern Paganism. If the mainstream within Paganism is not cognizant of the effects of racism in the overculture, and does not become active in promoting a culture of change that is inclusive of people of color, then we should be honest that diversity is not our goal. The road forward in an inclusive community would have to start with an honest evaluation of how our actions are causing intentional and often unintentional harm by setting a culture that is not welcoming or embracing of those who do not fall within the walls of our Eurocentric overculture.

What deities do we embrace that are from minority cultures? How are our practices relevant to those who are from different cultural experiences? How do we assess worth of other practitioners in ways that are empathetic of their cultural values, and how do we bring those value sets into our communities? How do our assumptions and biases create barriers for others to be included in our spiritual practices? How does our community accept, value, or welcome differences in practice, thoughts, culture, or experience?

The ability to access our own community culture would have to include honest personal reflection, but just as important, honest reflection of systemic community structures and guidelines. Remember, racism is not just an individual issue, but it is a structural issue that has the power to affect more than just one individual. This is not about judgment of who is bad and who is good; it is about removing the levels of cognitive dissonance that protect us from seeing that we actively continue racism and thus cause harm within this very community towards people of color.

Just because harm may not be intentional, it does not make it less harmful. When we ignore that the problem exists, we are not eradicating the issue, we are perpetuating it. Listening to the energy, the stories, the concerns, and the needs of those who feel marginalized in this community, by this community, would be a powerful place to start.

People of Color's Experience of Racism

Between the Worlds

Reluctant Spider

First, I take a breath and check with the divinity in me and ask, "What needs to be said?" Then, once again, holding what arose from the still place, I begin. Someone once told me that in an African worldview I am the embodiment and manifestation of all who came before me. I now also see a second message that can be directed at any individual: it is my job to share the divine vision of my life, as Rumi said, "a separate and unique way of seeing and knowing and saying that knowledge." It is getting habitually easier to live this mission, but it didn't start this way. I came from many places of privilege and opportunity that are not accessible to all peoples. My African American family raised me as a part of a military, middle socio economic class with way more than they had had. I grew up in a loving and supportive household with two parents, older siblings, music lessons, choir performances, plays and sports. I spent summers with grandparents learning how to crochet and be a black Christian of the praising, singing, clapping and eating good variety. It wasn't odd to see the Matriarchs in Afro-centric regalia and E'vry Voice lifted and Sang at family reunions. It wasn't only preached but actively modeled, black was beautiful and women were power.

But Black in the Midwest in the United States also had other realities. I knew I would be the only black girl in my orchestra, dance studio, or honors English class. I had a natural knack for language and developed an educated non-regional dialect English, quickly aware of disparate perceptions around ability and people of color. I was conscious that my good grades, awards and achievements through my traditional schooling years reflected not just myself and family but every person who looked like me. Basically, if you were looking for people of color, it was much more in line with the norm to look at the bottom rather than the top. When I climbed any metaphorical mountain, I was very aware of all the eyes watching. It didn't stop in high school and college. As I got older I would be the only black employee hired in a supervisory role or the first manager of color. After I had achieved some success, more people of color would follow into the organization. To a certain extent this meant I accidentally represented African American people and communities. This is neither fair nor correct as we all know someone we emphatically do not want to represent our version of humanity, culture nor country but this is what routinely happens to people of color in America. So even when I tried to push these considerations further back in my mind, there were some things that I did take on with conscious intent to improve "race" relations in America. For better or worse, my success, failure or acceptance has rarely been mine alone. Looking back, that portion of my life could be summed up with the phrase, "plays well with others." I was learning how to move within what our over-culture often considers success: corporate, suburban and middle class. I still prefer to build bridges and create openings rather than division and was fairly content with my contributions to the "Cause" of race relations in America. At the same time as stepping more fully into my Pagan self (of the eclectic wiccanish variety in the 90's), I realized two things. One, I was falling in love with a white man that had been my best friend since the 7th grade. Two, I was avoiding anything stereotypically African or African Diasporic in my practice. I decided to go with my heart with the man who went on to become my husband (although both of our families had to get used to the idea), but continued to struggle indecisively with the second. Being Black and a non-Christian/Muslim was already going plenty against my familial norms. So as I deepened in my Craft I expanded my "plays well with others" to "prays well with others." At first I wanted to learn vocabulary and practices that not only held power and meaning to me but would also be easy to share with others so things like Wheel of the Year, lunar cycles and tarot readings came into my practice. I read anything I could find online and in bookstores. However, just like most things in my life, it appeared I was frequently the only person of color represented. Isis was more often than not Greek and Oshun was just another love goddess. I looked past the white privilege filled images and tried to find the places of shared interest as I always had. I frequently would find myself going silent or pulling my presence back. Singing and clapping was too

24

uncomfortable for my former WASP Pagan friends. (I soon discovered ex-evangelicals to be better at this and darn fine energy workers.) I noticed my dancing around bonfires would immediately draw highly sexualized attention, so the serpent song my body wanted to sing got toned down and also eased the evil eyes that I was getting from formerly friendly Pagan women as they fought to hold their partner's attention away from my body.

As I grew in confidence, experience and self-gnosis, I realized that the song of my family and blood, wherever we came from and mixed on these American shores would not sit comfortably in the religious/spiritual community I'd just found. Sure there were some things that couldn't be changed or kept kept at home like my natural hair and adornments, the way I dressed, my body and voice. Those physical things were the legacy of my heritage broadcast and shining through me each moment of every day whether or not I intended to bring them along. But I wondered, what about life long dreams of walking with a bow-carrying brown-skinned hunter with dread locks along a beach at night to observe the crescent moon? Nope. It was many years before I spoke of Him and someone called Him Ochosi. I now call him, a wise and loving confidant, like an uncle, mi Tío.

Shared images and egregores are powerful carriers of social norms and culture and I had been shown in hundreds of ways that these parts of me were not in the common language of Pagan community. I did a little experiment by way of Google Images early in 2014. I did searches on certain terms and, after noticing a disturbing trend, began to count how many images I went through before I found something that reflected back an image like what appeared in my bathroom mirror. My first term was "Goddess." It was 21 images before I got to a person of color - a Native American. At 23 I saw a Hindi image. It was 35 images before I found someone whose skin reminded me of chocolate, though her nose was a little pointy, her lips not quite full and this sea goddess image had bright green eyes. It was 65 images before I got to a beautiful tree nymph with a green leafy afro, yellow flower gracing either side of her face and streaks of color tracing 3 lines on her cheeks. At 101 I got excited that I saw another... except that it was the exact same image as the one I saw at number 35. I stopped looking at 200 when I hadn't seen any others. I saw Hindi images that were photos or drawings of images from their rich religious culture. I saw Egyptian iconography every once in a while, but they all had European features.

Terms like "Black", "African,""African American", "Latina" paired with "Goddess" was heavily populated with the faces of celebrities and sexualized models. "White Goddess" immediately returned me to the postures, poses and Graeco-draped dresses we've expected to see in books and media when one thinks "Goddess" in America. I noted there was a decent saturation of Buddhist/Hindi images at this point along with the cover of Robert Graves, "The White Goddess." Perhaps I was stacking the deck too much. What about "Goddess, Pagan?" Zero results returned for any image of color (in the harsh polarized American way of seeing things). Even the little lonesome one from the original search was out. Wait, what was that one? Nope. It was another pale skinned Graeco Isis (not to knock Her, that's my Bud). I was too disheartened to continue to Google masculine terms of spirit/divinity. Just like "flesh colored" band-aids and "nude" panty hose/lipstick, the status quo wasn't talking to or about me, as if after 14 years in the Craft I was invisible. I learned quickly not to take it personally and have even been known to say "This book cover with a pale busty thin blue-eyed young woman with long flowing honey colored hair streaming out into the moonlight, I'm just not their target market." But I rarely was the target market, so I learned to ignore a lot. What I could not ignore was magick bubbling in my blood. Soon after the beginning of my Feri training, I could no longer ignore the rumblings of ancestors I carried forward. Though books only held brief fear-laced warnings ("Don't mess with that stuff"), I began to have shocking visits from those often called Orisha or LWA. I got goose bumps when I discovered I'd dreamed of and come in contact with Beings similar to those in Santeria called "Los Guerreros," pretty much in order. I struggled with my Altar, daily experiences with the Morrighan, Isis and Shiva in the company of Elleggua, Damballah, Obatala, Ogun and Ochosi. Maman Brigitte comes to me and tells me the tough lessons like my great aunt does, just in French or some kind of Creole that I can only understand in dreams. Freda speaks English on behalf of Damballah, Elleggua speaks whatever the hell he feels like, mixing in Spanish, French and English with images, feelings and sounds that are sometimes too big for my ears. I agonized, feeling lost or disrespectful (or worse - culturally appropriating!) being neither the type of Pagan I encountered in my wider community nor at home amongst most of the Diasporic/African Consciousness communities. Finally, I flat out voiced all of my worries to a grinning Elleggua who simply laughed. No One who I was building relationships with was there by accident and if They didn't like the company They would leave.

I was treating everything with respect, doing my best to research what was needful when my experiences were overwhelming my rational mind, achieving better understanding of what was being shared with me and wasn't mis-representing myself as something I wasn't. I was a Witch and trusted in my path, so if this was going to be par for my course then I should probably get used to it. I was the only one at my Altar with a problem. Finally I realized the only way to move forward was to sit down and just enjoy the company. But suddenly I was face to face with the strain that had been quietly building. I wasn't like everyone else and, though the individualistic Aries in me loved it, being so different felt dangerous and alienating. There is no gentle way for me to disassociate the fear and impact of racism on this stalling of my religious and spiritual journey. I had spent so much time trying to normalize and share similarities that I had accidentally stifled my own authenticity. I chose to wear a hat rather than a head wrap to not stand out or not dance around bonfires for fear of being over sexualized. The delicate balance of being a bridge had taken its toll. I could not be blind to the fact that 1996-2014 hadn't revealed myself reflected back in the megalith of Google's database. If I didn't know better, I'd think I was invisible. By the time the death of Mike Brown in August 2014 in Ferguson rocked the metro St Louis, MO area, national and international news, my fragile structure tipped and came crashing down. It felt like everything I'd quietly modeled had failed. The places of suppression and sacrifice weren't working.

The reality of being a part of any minority group is that actions of any member doubly impact the others, once as a human being in shared society and again as public opinion tries to gauge "normal." This applies as easily to people of color in day to day life as it does within beloved religious community, usually at an unconscious level. I have recently decided that keeping my voice low and my spiritual practice private was not shifting images (as easily seen in the megalith of the Google Image database) consciously or unconsciously the way I had hoped. I mention this also to provide opportunities to those within minority communities and those wishing to be allies. While not living a life inauthentic to who you are, if ever questioning how best to proceed, check what you are assisting to normalize. I realized I wasn't assisting in ways I truly needed reflected back. I turned inward to integrate the neglected pieces of myself back into a whole worthy of my ancestors, the American as well as the more romanticized French and African lines.

I'm a walker between worlds, literally, metaphorically and culturally. Some of us are more suited and, dare I say, "destined," to become a devotee to a specific deity. Once I thought my path would be like this with Isis as she was my first Patron, when I assumed a Pagan needed a Patron. Instead She set me outward and onward to claim my particular place as a Witch. My family, my life, and my preferences are not by chance and it took me a while to see it. My particular blend can be an aid to responsible eclecticism and finding appropriate intersections with cultures outside of those of our birth.

After hesitantly reading yet another over the top rant about cultural appropriation, I realized it's a tricky subject and I'll readily admit this is for selfish reasons. Some may say the hard line/simplistic view is "if you're not the right color/born in the country/didn't learn it from your family/ethnic group" equals cultural appropriation. That would make the vast majority of Pagans we know (self-included) stuck in the religion of their birth or forced to accept this tough label of being an appropriator. I think that's horse shit. I've already appropriated this weird soup of American culture, though my ancestors were from elsewhere and forcibly "invited" to these shores. I wasn't raised in a particular tribe/group etc., in Africa - which is a whole freaking continent of very different cultures, languages and practices. I have inherited whatever made it across the

Atlantic. This also leaves me with a few awkward questions about "racial" purity and what to do with those who do not come from one particular ethnic/cultural group (you know, like a bunch of us, again, self included). I ponder the majority of folks I know who are beautiful mutts with African heritage, but little to no direct family links to most of the Diasporic practices that they are living. And yet it calls to us. Either our blood begins to resonate or the ancestors we don't even know are willing to let us in, but there is a link to something greater than ourselves because more and more of us find it. Sometimes that link leads folks into something Euro-centric, from the Diaspora, back to the Continent or elsewhere and it is all valid. In this confusing mix it's very difficult to tell who's "properly prepared" outside of more and more complex and convoluted direct initiatory lineage and even then we continue to argue about that amongst ourselves. So my current boundaries around appropriation, learning and curiosity center around respect.

Here's a real life example of where I stand.

I enjoy languages. Languages hold cultural secrets in plain sight but only if a person takes the time to step inside deeply enough. I'm a student of the Spanish language and have been attempting improve my fluency since my first day of Spanish class in the ninth grade. The teacher walked in and did us a huge favor. He immediately began speaking in the target language. We were confused and woefully unprepared but by the end of the class we were introducing ourselves and each other in sounds once foreign to us. As a part of this, one of the first things we did was to pick a name that is more culturally appropriate in the target language. It's a chance to try it on, become this person who can intuitively speak and identify the sounds that may seem alien to our American English ears and being. Not unlike the "magical names" some folks in magical communities take, we step into the person we want to become.

What is culture appropriation vs culture exchange? Others will have better definitions than I do but the point that I wish to emphasize circles around taking the time to try to step inside the culture and identity, shepherded inside by someone who is already on the inside to help. Taking a name is an opportunity to become something, not a fashion statement. Taking the name "Nacho" and laughing hysterically every time you say it because it sounds funny (like so many of my class mates did) is part of the well trod path of cultural appropriation. So is the idea of taking on a Spanish sounding name and suddenly becoming a Latina. It doesn't really work that way. Just like initiation, the Tribe has to welcome you in as one of their own because they recognize you have become so like them and so trusted that it seems foolish not to recognize this part of themselves in you. When I stepped into my high school Spanish I choose Esperanza out of a list of possible names in our textbooks. Esperanza, the noun form of the verb esperar which can mean "to hope." I said it aloud and recognized my new future Self as a Spanish speaker, a person who hopes. I stepped into hope and became Esperanza as I faithfully did my homework. Though my vocabulary was (and still) elementary, I have loved the Spanish language from the first time it came from my mouth. I read my Spanish book and homework aloud, cultivating the lilt and cadence that at times felt intuitive. It had to get into my mouth, go into myself until it felt familial. Nonetheless, I recognize my Spanish as book-learned with no homeland, no particular spirit of place that other "hispanoblantes nativos" (native Spanish speakers) can ask "¿De donde eres?" and identify where my "family is from." I still keep studying, practicing and making big mistakes. But there are times with long time loving friends when I don't sound too bad and am welcomed to the table of the "Tribe." This honorary "Latina card" can be taken away just as quickly if I don't respect and represent it well, it is born of mutual love. But none of this intermingling can happen if I wasn't curious and didn't have an opportunity to learn because I wasn't born in a culture/ethnic group that spoke Spanish.

The reason for this trip down memory lane is that a decade later, spirits showed up in dream, trance and meditation and began trying to communicate in three languages, English, Spanish and French, even though my home household only speaks English and only one side of the family tree speaks of ties to French Huguenots. My ongoing relationship with Spanish and my African blood are two obvious ties to these Spirits that walk with me along my path.

By shutting down cultural pluralism and culture exchange because of the threat of cultural appropriation, we not only lose the possibility but also fall danger to demonizing the "other." Though I have discovered that forced or willing assimilating can be to the detriment of the individual, I find it dangerous when we separate too far apart that we don't get to remind each other that we're both human. Exploitation definitely happens and communities are well within their rights to decide who to share their own traditions with. Unfortunately it is also very difficult and heartbreaking to re-conceal a secret that has gotten out. Minority groups of all types have the right and task to bask in not only our own culture/ethnic group with healthy pride but also learning to cultivate respectful curiosity for others as well. I continue to believe that honesty is our biggest way to keep it respectful; no need to make up a grandmother who was the HPS in an unbroken line of Witches in order to validate their own witchcraft. Just be a witch. Live like one today. But if you want to be a Santera there are certain things you should know, study with someone who is already an initiated Santera, surround yourself with the community until it leaks from your pores and they accept you as one of their own. Perhaps then, you'll be offered and accept initiation and then will be recognized as a Santera. I do believe we should protect initiatory paths, but not all cultural things around them can, and from what I see, could ever be locked in. The initiates were products of and supporters of the non-initiated community so there are bound to be overlaps. We should say no to fakers and it is ok to require honesty to do business or enter relationship with one another because good quality is being able to back up your claims.

Honesty for me means I own my blood, what I know of it and what I don't. Honesty means stepping in to meet other cultures with respect and curiosity, asking questions and realizing that I may not get answers. I remember a group I was in, which focused around us being African American Pagans. We went out to eat at a Kenyan restaurant and I will never forget overhearing a group of Kenyan friends and the owner chatting at the bar near closing time. They were playfully arguing about something and the female owner behind the bar laughed and quieted the group by saying, "Alright, when the others leave, we'll have a Kenyan convention and figure this out." The "others" were us, the other brown-skinned folks in the large corner table laughing and discussing how our far flung culture impacted our spirituality. We weren't one of them, we were something else. And once again I was reminded of walking between the worlds in an uncertain place in middle America, the mixed off-spring of the Diaspora.

I've learned to play and pray well with others. I listen to messages of blood and dream. I walk in my body, in this time and place. I breathe deeply and let all the pieces of myself Align again and again to reaffirm what needs to be said and done next.

Then, I live another day among others trying to do the same.

Ashe, Beauties.

Works Cited

Source: CD: I Want Burning, Coleman Barks
"Moses & the Shepard" - translation of Jalal ad-Din Muhammad
    Rumi
Publisher: Sounds True, Incorporated; Unabridged edition (April
    2001)

When the Goddess is Brown:
Towards a Hermeneutics of Reparations

Lou Florez

"I knew what it was like to be haunted by the ghost of a self one wished to be, but only half-sensed"-Audre Lorde

Magic at its core is about agency, the agency within us all to transmute and transform the world while simultaneously being transfigured in the process. This capacity to revision and recast creation into a more poignant form, a form in which we can live the biggest versions of ourselves and our lives is our divine birthright and mandate. Paganism and the raft of magic is more than its rituals and symbols, it is the remembering and reintegration process through which we activate our innate potential and power to manifest the world as we see it.

When we cast circle and evoke our spiritual allies, guardians, and guides we stand in the liminal, the threshold between what is and what can be in its multiplicity of forms, shapes, and possibilities. The liminal demands of us a vulnerability, a nakedness before Spirit that holds the continuity and continuum of our narratives- our triumphs, passions, joys, and sorrows- in the ever churning cauldron in which existence comes into and out of being. As we stand within the circle we learn how to fully stand within ourselves as whole beings. These ghosts, spectral mirages of regrets and unclaimed opportunities are divested of their power and capacity to torment, because they are given voice and are welcomed as part of ourselves. We allow them the place they need to inform us of who we are and what we wish to become but have forgotten. In that moment they are transformed from the haunted specter into the guides in the journey of our becoming. This is the promise of Paganism which captivated me as teenager and continues to hold me in its sway.

As my personal practice has matured and the opportunities to engage in communal celebrations expanded, I noticed that that something was missing from my experience of transformation. I realized that the image that I saw reflected back at me was not my own, was not based upon divinities that looked or acted like me, but instead made me feel marginalized and excluded in content, reflection, and motivations. As a man of color, as a working class queer man, where were my gods, where were my symbols? What I have found instead are the vestiges of unaddressed privilege and silence which perpetuates the overarching monolithic narrative of "sameness," and "whiteness" through the discourse of the goddess, the craft, and all that it can be. While I honor the work that my foremothers, mentors, and elders have accomplished in order to strip away patriarchy, and rebirth a liberating practice of gender inclusivity, and personal empowerment, there are still many of us who are left standing outside of the circle waiting to be honored and recognized as part of the human and divine continuum.

Racism, Sexism, and Capitalism are some of the tools through which colonization has been enacted and continues to be perpetuated worldwide. They form interlocking systems of oppression, which divorce the individual from their respective place within humanity, and finally negate the agency of body, mind and spirit, which we all have a right to enact. Not only does oppression cause irreparable harm to its targets, but these systems damage the perpetrators as well, by restricting and suppressing the full breadth and depth of human expression through the creation of the subject and the "other." This "other" serves as a placeholder for the collective amalgamation of qualities that are seen as inferior and by their very nature, less than human. The fear of contamination by the other is so great, that one has to distance oneself through appearance, behaviors and physical locations in which the other is encountered. It is as if this "otherness" were a disease that could be caught. Little boys and men are taught to toughen up because of fears of being feminine, the owning and middle classes are taught to manage and control production and labor for fear of being part of the wretched poor, and Europeans and those of European ancestry are taught the myth of "whiteness" as way of distancing themselves from the brown body. While these are just a few examples of the enculturation process which maintains stratification and colonization, my point is that on both sides of the divide a severing occurs that splits the connective reflection of one person from another.

Iconoclasm: Smashing the Icon of "Whiteness" Within Goddess Theology

One of the issues that I had to face as I made the conversion from Catholicism into Witchcraft was that I had baggage from Christianity that needed unpacking. Whether it was the notion of sin, shame of the body, a guilt complex a mile long, or the image of god as male, I made a decisive and intentional commitment to not only replace the image of divinity from male to female, but the content of my theology. After all if nothing else changed besides the gender of god, how was it any different than having Jesus in a dress?

Part of the evolution of this work over the last several years has been to take the commitment further by not only engaging the question of gender, but also looking at the implicit assumptions that are inherent in Pagan theologies around race, class, and ability both within ritual contexts, as well as, in the pedagogical cannon itself (what we choose to teach, how we choose to teach it, and how it is taught). How do we encounter a Goddess that is not only reflective of our physical form, but of our inward experiences and motivations?

One misconception that I see perpetuated consistently within community when dealing with the subject of race within the Craft is the notion that divinity sees no color. My response is that the divine sees and feels all, but without the value judgments, without creating power differentials based upon some presupposed hierarchy. Secondly, and more importantly, is the fact that this response is a reaction of spiritually bypassing the issue of race completely, due to the privilege that the party giving this response allows for them to exist without having to confront it on a daily basis. After all, if it were not for the insidious nature of sexism, patriarchy and misogyny, the reclamation of the goddess would not have been necessary.

Another misconception that I would like to interrupt is the idea that the numerous aspects and faces of the divine can be divorced from their historical and cultural signification. The myth of "whiteness" has been deployed not only as method for dehumanizing the brown body, but as brainwashing narrative that intentionally seeks to forget the multicultural and multiethnic heritages of Europe. If we factually confront world history, we will encounter a land imbued with distinctive cultural identities and ways of seeing the world, which are vastly different from our own. These worlds are the birthplaces of our divinities, and create the vessels for engaging the expansive vastness in which the mysteries of the divine unfold themselves. It is time to move past the universalized archetypes of the mother, maiden, crone, warrior, lover, and experience the fullness of each goddess and god as a subject unto themselves.

Embodied subjectivity is of the utmost importance in our spiritual practices because it demands that we fully immerse ourselves into the world that that these beings both arose from, and continue to exist within. It is about understanding the subtle nuances of the varied cultural scripts, power dynamics, and the roles that these deities filled not only within the traditions themselves, but within the lives of the individuals who worshiped them. When we displace them from their cultural landscape, we turn them into objects, commodities, which can be used, traded and discarded at will. They no longer have the agency or power to liberate, instead they turn into tools to further disenfranchise and disempower.

Towards a Hermeneutics of Reparations

How do we as individuals, and as a community begin this work? We begin by making reparations in our theologies by investigating the sites of genocide, invisibility, silence, and fracture that have occurred due to colonization. We engage a hermeneutics of repair that demands a reinterpretation of not only the signs, and symbols of the Craft, but also of the language through which these interpretations are ascribed meaning and significance. Which of the stories of our divinities have been deemed important and which aspects have been diminished or ignored, in order to suit the prevailing powers? How do we hold the nuances of their historical narratives in time and location against our personal relationships with them? My claim is not that I have the answers to any of these questions, but that it is important to continue asking them.

It does not matter whether we are talking about Paganism or Earth-based spiritual traditions worldwide; colonization has pervasively, and intentionally, misshaped how we see the Earth and affected our relationship with her. It has in many instances decimated communities, devastated our stories and demonized our traditions. It is up to us to ensure that this time around all of ourselves, and our bodies, have a place at the table.

Beautiful Black, Wondering White, and Shady Grey: Racism in the Pagan World

Lilith Dorsey

It's 2014 when I write this, and I wish the word racism had no meaning or true relevance anymore, unfortunately it has more meanings and manifestations than ever before. I have been active in the Pagan community for over two decades as a vendor, lecturer and ritualist. If I'm honest I started coming because I was looking for some kind of spiritual home. A sacred community of like-minded and open individuals who would understand if I wanted to recycle my garbage, dance half-naked around a campfire, or hug a lonely tree. I am a Voodoo priestess, as well as an initiated Santeria and Haitian Vodou practitioner. I also have degrees in Anthropology and Cinema and Television Studies. I have dedicated most of my life to making sure my religions are represented accurately and respectfully. I just wanted to let you know where I was coming from spiritually and academically. Personally I think it is also important to note I am also bi-racial, my parents were married within the first month that interracial marriages were made legal in New York State. Experience colors existence, and these have been my paths.

In the early years of Pagan festivals and events, which started to really take off in the mid to late 1980's, there were always crazy hushed whispers, someone was going to shut us down, they didn't like our kind, you can't do that here. Many events banned drumming, or campfires, or recorded music. I was left seriously scratching my head. Now I will admit I like to push the envelope. I led the first ever Voodoo Suspension ritual with people hanging from hooks, and my spiritual house and I facilitated the first Voodoo Zombie Silent Rave (because no one wants to interact with others at a ritual anyway.) Voodoo is prime ground for stereotype anyway, due to myth and media. But I never expected some of the behavior I have encountered. It makes me sad, and angry. People hate out of fear or ignorance, and in the beginning I think we all thought it would improve with time.

A few years ago there was the incredibly bizarre time I got called a racist in my own campsite at an event. It's a long strange story...and then she threatened to cut me, but I will do my best to tell the short version here. I was presenting at one of the largest Pagan festivals in the Northeast, an event I have attended since it began. It was late in the evening and a young woman attempted to set up her campsite near mine. Now there would not have been a problem really except exactly where she was planning to drive in a tent stake was where the water lines for that entire section of the camp were located. I gently attempted to explain this to her, and offered to help her find another place to camp. Did I say it was dark out? She proceeded to mutter to herself, phoned a friend saying loudly that she was going to "cut a bitch" and then ended up at a nearby camp loudly complaining about "that racist Lilith." This is the part of the story where I mention I'm from Brooklyn. We even have a t-shirt Our Crack Whores Can Beat Up Your Crack Whores. I wouldn't out right hit someone at an event though, unless they hit me first, and then who knows what could happen.

This definitely has to be one of the most difficult situations I have ever had to navigate. I handled it as best I could both as a priestess and long standing member of the community there. I did my best to explain that I fought for years to have Pagan events like that one be a place where people of color would feel welcome and at home. Luckily that community supported me in return. When the woman in question refused to apologize, another African-American presenter told her that she was making "us all look like cheap niggas and she should get on her knees and thank me for the work I had done over the years." My words to her were much more gentle, but I understand why this woman responded this way and I'm sort of glad someone other than myself told her off.

These days people accuse me of reverse racism on my own social media pages. Some people are clearly crazy. Robert Anton Wilson told me once that people only engage in conversation to hear themselves talk. I know attacking a Voodoo priestess is a bit like starting a fight with the biggest guy in the prison, people do it to make themselves look better. My own feelings about racism in the Pagan community and more specifically in my area of expertise New Orleans Voodoo, Haitian Vodou and Cuban Santeria or Lukumi, are complicated. Let me start by saying I firmly believe that anyone and everyone should be allowed to practice whatever religion they want. Some of the earliest signs of human life were in Africa, and it makes sense that all humans would be interested in the religious practices that sprang from there. In my own spiritual house we welcome anyone who wants to attend with an open mind and heart. I have spiritual godchildren and students of all races, and I have the utmost love and respect for them. There can be a problem however when people of color are excluded from these sacred practices by either accident or design. Then it could be all too easy to forget our origins.

In many ways this is the same argument many Jazz and Blues musicians had when more socially acceptable bands covered their music, without payment or respect and became millionaires. History is full of lost heroes, heroines, and pioneers. It is in that spirit that I write this and everything else in the hope of making a positive change for the future.

One specific racist comment directed toward me showed up on a piece about why I hate black history month. The lines that I believe the reader was offended at were these:

"I saw someone's status the other day and it was simply "It's Black History month, beware the White Walkers." I have not stopped smirking. Now I am a regular viewer of Fox News, only because that makes me smirk too, and the other day they featured a talking middle class Caucasian head telling me how great Black history month is. You can see why the "White Walker" analogy is funny, cause it's true. "

Now, there is much more to what I wrote about Black History month, how as a whole it's formulaic and exclusionary, and you can read more on my blog Voodoo Universe. I also frequently get accused of being "angry." I am. I'm tired of lies and prejudice and the rest. My misguided naivete of decades past made me believe that a community that had been persecuted like witches and Pagans have, would be welcoming to Voodoo practitioners like myself. That has rarely been the case. Sometimes it was just bad jokes, like the festival organizer that liked to give all the Voodoo and Santeria presenters rubber chickens. More often it was the hushed rumors that they were going to mess with us. I've had altars destroyed, merchandise stolen, and wacko performers try to steal my religion, without any knowledge or initiation. These are ancient traditions, required study and dedication. It's hurtful to me that these unfortunate things happen, and it's hurtful that my religion also takes the blame or gets an accusatory pointy finger when anything goes wrong.

What my children and godchildren see and experience as racism is very different than when I was growing up. They are about diversity, inclusion, and pride. They are the victims of assumption and decades of poor behavior. I'd like to tell you I didn't hear of someone calling The Black Eyed Peas "Nigger" music at a Pagan event. I'd like to tell you my daughter never had to deal with people like this, but it wouldn't be true. If anything she is probably party to even more negativity because she is light skinned and people say things in front of her that they would be ashamed to voice in the presence of a darker skinned person. Unfortunately there are no easy solutions. The more we search for answers the more questions we seem to find.

Can people consume without usurping? Can people who say they "don't see color," truly see heritage? Will Voodoo ever move past tired tropes of jungle drums and lasciviousness? There are a lot of issues here, and obviously everyone's unique experience "colors" their attitude. It is my sincere hope that people will do their best to open their minds, seek accurate and respectful information provided by initiated practitioners in the religion, rather than snake oil salesman, hucksters, and dementors.

Native Appropriation

Janet Callahan

For many minorities, no matter whether its race, religion, sexual orientation or any other facet of who you are, it's often expected that you, as a single person, will represent the views of everyone else who shares your minority status. So let me begin by stating that I only represent myself – my beliefs, my viewpoints, and my experiences. I am, depending on your politics, either an enrolled member of the Oglala Sioux Tribe or a citizen of the Oglala Lakota Nation. It is a fact of life for Natives in the United States that they are expected to prove their enrollment and the percentage Indian they are (often referred to as blood quantum – literally, what fraction of "full blooded" Indian) – much like a pedigreed show dog, and unlike any other minority in the United States (or almost anywhere else, really). This is nearly opposite of the experience of Blacks in this country, who have a history of "one drop" of African blood making them still Black, no matter their cultural history.

Essentially, I am the vision that military minds of the 1800s had in their heads when they said, "Kill the Indian to save the man," the vision that tore children away from their families to live and learn in (usually abusive) church-based boarding schools, and justified this blood quantum idea. I am of mixed race (and thanks to my very light-skinned mostly German father, I'm assumed to be "white" wherever I go). I'm educated, upper middle class, and gainfully employed. I do not follow the traditional hunter-gatherer ways of my Native ancestors – I don't even live on the reservation, and have been there only to visit. My grandmother lives there, in her childhood home, and she and my mother both own land there, for which they get miniscule "rent" payments from the government program that leases such lands to ranchers – Indians, after all, are like children, and not capable of managing their own resources. I'm not Christian...but in the grand scheme of things, I suspect I still would rate higher on the scale used to judge worth in those days, since it's often clear to me that I do so now.

Growing up I learned many things about many different tribes, in an attempt to be able to answer the questions that are often posed (remember, everyone assumes that if you're an Indian, you know everything about all Indians). One important thing I learned is that when you look into history, there's almost nothing that's consistent across all tribes. In fact, while there has, over the last 30 years or so, been the development of "powwow culture" (a sort of melting pot over-culture that is the rule in large public pow wows and at urban Indian center events), and while there's always been sharing between neighboring tribes, it's been a more organic sort of sharing rather than something purchased or taken without understanding any of the cultural context of the things that are shared.

Another thing that has become very clear to me over the years is that the words we use matter. Talking about traditional Native concepts using Native languages is different than trying to translate them into English. The words we use shape our views. And culture is everything – Native "religions" are interwoven with Native cultures, so much so that they are inseparable. It's really more of a spirituality because it is so interwoven, rather than a separate religion.

So it pains me to be the only "official" Native in the room when someone talks about Native spirituality and how they've added it to their own spiritual practices. It's often clear within a couple of sentences that they don't actually understand the source of what they're talking about. Some even try to throw around Native words, borrowed just the way they've borrowed the spiritual concept they're discussing. I'd feel better if they'd just say that they read something, and it resonated with them, so they explored the idea and meditated with it to see how it would fit, rather than claiming an unbroken line, but most can't or won't. It often seems to me, to be a way of appealing to an outside source for authority, rather than claiming their own authority.

One local group tells people about their sweat lodge ceremonies. When I questioned them about their sources, they told me that they learned from another group, and then changed rules to fit their own paradigm...but that their sweats were authentic.

That other group they learned from was a group well known for being a group of "Plastic Shamans" – people who exploit the tradition they claim to be teaching for personal power or ego, often with no legitimate tie to that tradition...and usually for money.

Clearly, we have a different definition of "authentic."

The word shaman is particular to the Evenk and Buryat peoples of Siberia. Their practices are decidedly different than the practices of the tribes of North America. And yet, the same word was used by anthropologists to describe the spiritual leaders of Native Americans. This does a disservice to both the Native Siberians and the Native Americans, all because English didn't have good words to talk about this sort of thing. In either case, these spiritual folks were a part of their community, and the community recognized them for their skills and gifts. Now there are Pagans using that word to describe their own practices with no links to any of the original cultures involved.

Those who practice neo-Pagan shamanism often still work in terms of a vaguely Native American paradigm, with totem animals and vision quests. Over the years there is less overt stealing of material, and more of an attempt to make it unique to the neo-shamanic experience. But it's still packaged as a class, where you learn everything you need to know about being a shaman by reading something that others have written, doing some rituals, and paying your money. By this model anyone can be a shaman if they choose, while in both the Siberian cultures that spawned the term Shaman, and the North American cultures that are copied, this is not a choice one makes – you are chosen by the spirits.

Totems come up often in discussion too. Traditional totems were often something that a clan or band had, not necessarily something an individual had. You might acquire a "spirit animal" on a vision quest – a helper or guide of sorts. Something that might be just for you, or something you might discuss with your elders, but not something the whole world had to know about.

It's hard to know how to respond when someone tells me their totem animal is Wolf (especially since, in addition to knowing how many Tribes approach the idea of totems in the manner I described above, I was taught by one of my earliest Pagan teachers that this isn't the sort of thing you share with people you've just met). It's harder to know how to react when they assure me that the practices they're doing are something they learned in a past life, but they have no ties to the community they're claiming to have been a part of. At the moment it's impossible to challenge their claims of past life experience without seeming to challenge the entire paradigm of reincarnation.

It's harder still to know how I will explain these things to my children – they are growing up straddling both worlds, much as I did, and it still confuses me. I already see how mainstream culture "honors" my culture – fake headdresses, sports teams named for racial slurs, and generally suggesting that we don't exist. How much harder, then, to explain about our Pagan friends who do similar things and say that they are honoring our culture?

One of the most important features of most Native American groups is their focus on the Tribe and the family. There is less focus on owning things, and more focus on sharing the wealth. My Tribe's reservation is among the poorest counties in the United States. Sometimes three or even four generations – 12 people or more – will live in a house or trailer meant for four people rather than leaving family to sleep in a car or on the street. People take care of each other with what they have, just as they always have. When visiting various family members (and it seems to me that everyone on the reservation is related somehow or another – both in the literal blood sense and in the sense that my Tribe has of all creatures being our brothers and sisters), food and drinks are always offered...even when it is clear that the household is barely getting by.

This sense of hospitality is not something I often see from those claiming to be working with Native American rituals. I don't see these people helping the Tribes they feel so strongly connected to. I don't see them raising funds when my people are freezing without enough propane in the winter, and I don't see them stepping up to provide other types of support either. I tend to put my money where my mouth is, by supporting causes that are important to me. How important, then, can Native culture be to these people who are using it and selling it, if they don't give back to the community they take from? [1]

When many Pagans learn that I'm Native American, they assume that's why I'm Pagan. My Native relatives have actually asked me to put a big wall of separation between the two, because of the actions of many plastic shamans. Pagan friends are surprised to learn that I cannot and will not support their belief that when building a sweat lodge in a member's back yard, they don't have to follow the fire codes of the city (true story). They are surprised to learn that I won't partake in their upcoming Beltane event in a tipi that they made themselves (true story). They are surprised that the fact that they have a friend who is a pipe carrier doesn't make me ooh and ahhhh (true story) – I'd rather hear that they have this great friend that they think I'd get along with, who makes great fry bread. The first thing I learn about someone new should almost never be their spiritual title.

But really, it's all because I know who I am. I am Oglala Lakota, and I'm Pagan, and so many other things...but I can't find it in my heart to participate in something that pretends to understand my Lakota ancestors without any contact with them.

---

[1] If you're interested in helping Native Americans, please check any charities on sites such as:

> http://www.guidestar.org/ or
> http:// http://www.charitynavigator.org/

If you have interest in a specific tribe, it's worth contacting the tribe to find out about charities that work with them, and/or what things are most needed.

One of my favorite charities, actually, is a non-affiliated organization named Friends of Pine Ridge Reservation http://www.friendsofpineridgereservation.org/, which is a loose group of people who help agencies on my own reservation. The group is not a non-profit itself, but its members help make sure various agencies get what they need – school supplies for foster kids, books for elementary school libraries, craft supplies for a senior center, propane during the winter to keep people warm, and so on.

Another well-run charity is Adopt a Native Elder, http://www.anelder.org/, a non-profit org that helps Diné (Navajo) elders continue to live according to traditional ways.#

The Quilted Path

Stephanie Rose Bird

While attempting, at times, to ignore race, ethnicity, and the social environment in which I grew up in, it has shaped the way I come to the Pagan Community. I was brought into an eclectic spiritual path through exposure to spiritualism, witchcraft, hoodoo and Santeria at an early age. Eclectic Paganism encourages a spirit of cultural openness, sorely lacking on other paths. Still, out of need for expression of faith that fully embraces inclusivity, I have had to patch together disparate traditions. My journey includes piecing together a craft that encompasses all that I am and wish to be. This is the story of my quilted path into Pagan community.

Against the backdrop of the Civil Rights Movement...

I was born in 1960, an important time during the era of the Civil Rights Movement and an important time to be Black in America. I was three when Dr. Martin Luther King Jr. gave his "I Have a Dream Speech." My grandparents lived on a former slave plantation in Charlotte, Virginia and moved their family to northern New Jersey like many Blacks of those times, to avoid the adversity they endured in the south. My grandfather was biracial and had a very hard way to go where he lived. On the other side of the family, my ancestors were also living on a plantation, on a tobacco farm in Richmond, Virginia. In honor of those Timberlake ancestors I grow bits of tobacco in my garden, hanging it to dry so that I can reflect upon this part of my heritage near the hearth. Thinking of all of them, I also make Kinnickinnick, a peace pipe smoking blend that I use as incense. To find peace there needs to be forgiveness.

It is my daily practice to never forget whose shoulders I stand on...

The racism, the Civil Rights Movement, my beloved family, and growing up surrounded by nature are precious gifts that marked me and the magickal path I walk. While drawn to many elements of the Craft, I couldn't always readily see myself in the Gods and Goddesses or even the language of Wicca or Witchcraft. I could not clearly hear my ancestor's voices coming through on this path that seems quite Western, so I did research, research and then a little more research. Through my studies, I found many commonalities between Earth-based practices worldwide and particularly those of my ancestry which is African, English, Irish, Native American and Iberian. I felt so passionate about what I found that I became a writer in 1999, writing what would become the first of my five published books, "Sticks, Stones, Roots and Bones: Hoodoo, Mojo and Conjuring with Herbs." One of my most recent books, "Light, Bright and Damned near White," is completely devoted to race. It explores bi-racial and tri-racial cultural history in America, in honor of my grandparents and my children.

Constantly, I seek and then see cultural connections...Background is the foreground on which I paint magick...

Many elements of my upbringing shaped my practice and my written work. Moving from a predominately African American community to a rural farming White community was an important, if painful event. Moving to southern New Jersey is where I learned that some people thought my name was Nigger, as this is what my brother and I were repeatedly called. On in the theatre of the little black topped playground, it was Nigger this, Nigger that, Nigger, Nigger, Nigger.

Yet, I still saw and shared the beauty...

South Jersey is also the place where I fell in love with nature, which has become central to my animistic vision and involvement with Paganism and Earth-based Spirituality. The legends and mythology of the Pine Barrens greatly enrich my life and continue to inform my writing. In my first novel, "No Barren Life," my first novel speaks directly to young adults about the healing aspects and options that an eclectic path such as I have chosen, blending Hoodoo and Green Witchcraft with Shamanism, offers a young, abused and confused African American teenager beginning her magickal path. Though it is a work of fiction, "No Barren Life" is set in the very emotionally charged environment in which I grew up—South Jersey's Pine Barrens.

Shaped by a colorful community...

During the late 60s there was electricity in the air. Changes were afoot and the chance for a better life seemed tangible for people in my community. My community, as it were, was a Black enclave on a lake in the woods, first established by the A.M.E. (African Methodist Episcopal) Church. Paradise Lakes is where mostly Blacks lived outside Alloway whereas Whites could live in town or wherever they chose. You wouldn't think there was much segregation in the north, in New Jersey of all places, but it existed. It was brought home by what was called Nigger Lane. This was the place where we were supposedly hung if we "misbehaved" by the still very active Ku Klux Klan. There were also rumors of folks who tried to live in town being fire bombed.

Growing up charmed...

I remember Black History Week which grew into Black History Month, in a bittersweet way. Yes, I was glad that my people were getting their due attention in history class. The bitter part was that everyone would swivel around on their little wooden chairs and turn around to stare at me. I was one of very few African Americans in my class; most of us were place in what was called "Special Class."

My face would grow hot from the curious stares...

It was hard to make friends. I turned instead to nature and the arts. I wrote poetry, painted my environment and most of all danced. Loving ballet as I did, I would practice my pirouettes, spotting from a special tree that called to me. Speaking of which, the water also had its special call. Its movement and ever-changing colors fascinated me, holding my attention for hours. I swam as much as I could during the summers and rowed in our boat. Later, I would learn more of my affinity for the water from my uncle who was a Babalawo and practitioner of Santeria. He recognized I was a child of Yemaya-Ologun.

Having an uncle who was a Babalawo, one Grandmother who was psychic and could read dreams as well as tea leaves, with another grandmother having a reputation as a healer and spiritualist, it is no wonder I chose my path. I come from deeply spiritual people. This makes perfect sense to me, yet it was a very personal attraction and individual choice that lead me in my specific direction. My family has at least one Atheist, and includes Muslims and Christians as well as those into Earth-based Spirituality. Ours is a very eclectic family that can see the divine through many lenses.

My path was forged by creative visioning...

From ballet to North African Belly Dance, Hawaiian, Tahitian, West African and more--it would appear that I dance to the beat of a very different drummer. My family was different. We lived in a unique environment in unusual times and it marked us. I accredit my roots and my individual interpretation of each aspect of them with helping me come to the conclusion that I needed to create my own magical path that respects and honors all that I am...where I came from and where I am going. I practice what I call Conjure Craft, a blend of Hoodoo, shamanism and Green Witchcraft. To illustrate the point, during the month of December I will refresh my ancestor altar, celebrate Yule, Winter Solstice, Christmas and Kwanzaa seamlessly. Each is important; each honors spirit in its way—all will incorporate elements of my heritage.

We are vessels...

Mostly, I am a solitary practitioner yet my written words enable me to reach out to countless others in ways that I may never know. I contribute my time and energy, magickal and mundane, to various communities and causes across the country and specifically in a hands-on way in my very multicultural community. I like volunteering to help with the homeless, the environment and public schools. It is important for Pagans to find creative ways to connect with different communities and to make a difference in the lives of others.

With the majority of my heritage being of tribal people, I seek out my tribe, in whatever form they manifest and together we commune with the divine. Dr. Martin Luther King Jr.'s "I have a Dream Speech" touches me as a Shaman that practices dream work, as much as it does being African American. Hearing King's voice moves me to this day. His words are a call to action to live up to the potential set forth by our ancestors— reaching the potentiality of our highest self and in the process respecting all--regardless of color is an attainable dream. For these reasons and many more, I walk a quilted path and I call it Conjure Craft.

Ashe!

Party of One

Clio Ajana

In the Pagan community, I find myself being the sole person of color quite frequently. Some days I feel like I should have a card: FYI:I am a black, female, lesbian, formerly Christian, formerly Jewish, formerly heterosexual, Pagan High Priestess. Email/Facebook/Cell

Okay. Why the hell would I do this? Why would I leave the familiarity of the black church and a heterosexual norm to change religions twice, followed by a complete change in sexual orientation?

Why would a black girl, raised in middle-class America by Christian church-going parents choose a path that is long, difficult and unusual? The more I found myself in Paganism, the fewer persons of color I saw around me.

It begins with a search for truth, a willingness to step out of the cultural context and to follow an internal compass, rather than the one set by societal norms. The constant search for truth leads to awareness in racial, religious and sexual identity. The determination of what is true and what is right often depends upon those in authority and societal perception of what is permissible and what is forbidden. The desire to learn leads through a path of discovery that ends with an essential truth: the end of the journey lies within the fearlessness of the traveler to keep searching, no matter what. I kept searching until I found my home. My experiences with race and racism actually defined where and how I experienced home in the Pagan community.

I am a former Methodist, a former Jew, a former wanderer filled with experimentation. Now I am a child of earth and starry heaven. I am Hellenic Orthodox. I am a High Priestess in a religion and a group that honors and celebrates all parts of my life: woman, lesbian, writer, clergy, creatrix, traveler, spiritual being.

I begin with the ethos by which I live my life - every day.

I am a human, and I think nothing that is Human is foreign to me.

I am the Universe, and I think nothing in the Universe is foreign to me.

I am responsible for everything I

Say

Feel

Think

Do

For what I do to others; for what others to do me;

And ultimately, what others do to others

Without pride or praise

Blame or shame

Judgment or evaluation

And if it harm none, do as thou Will

By the same mouth that speaks the Word

By the same bone that unites the flesh

Do what thou Will shall be the whole of the Law.

Thou hast no right but to do thy will.

Do that and none other shall say nay.

This is the Law of the strong; this is our Law and the joy of the world.

Love is the law; Love under Will

Thelema.

Agape.

One of the earliest truths that I find on my journey is that race and class define many aspects of my spiritual journey. My search for truth is impacted by racism, classism, sexism, homophobia and religious intolerance, but first and foremost by racism. The religious divisions only demonstrate that bias, be it open or hidden, is present at each step along the way.

The first step to eradicating any intolerance, any of the 'isms" is to acknowledge its presence. The truths I face with this bead fall into the category of calling out the problem by name, when it happens, so that the problem can be corrected.

The second step is to not forget the first step.

Sometimes, I forget the second step.

This bead is a reminder.

When I finally met a group in Minneapolis, Minnesota six years later, I still thought that racism was non-existent in Paganism. These were the alternative folk whose religious practices were unknown to me and to many around me. My only introduction to Paganism came in the most readily available books which concentrated primarily on the Northern European traditions, those of the British Isles and Scandinavia: Druids, British Traditional Groups, and the Asatru. Other traditions, including Greek, Roman, African and Latin American traditions warranted scant mention in comparison to these Northern European giants.

Truth: Free-spirit alternative folk can have their issues as well. Sometimes they are worse than the straitlaced or bigoted members of society.

Truth: What is openly seen can be more easily defeated than what hides beneath a facade of sincerity.

Race in Paganism, as I found when I began in 2004 and in the years since, is biased by tradition. Pagans are divided into solitary practitioners and those who belong to groups (covens, lodges, groves, etc.). Yet in Paganism, in circle, I also felt a sense of 'other'. The British Traditionalists, the Asatru and other predominantly "white" facets of Paganism dominated, while the few blacks I met who were not solitary belonged almost exclusively to an African tradition or to a native tradition, such as Haitian.

Truth: When is racism less about race and more about cultural preservation? If you are wishing to preserve your culture and it is all white, all black, all Asian, all from a certain area, will that make your group racist or simply clearly intentioned?

Truth: Wicca, "as seen on TV", is lily-white, unless it is not.

For over eighteen months, I had maintained a consistent positive engagement with a British Traditional coven which included training classes every other week, rituals, birthday parties, helping coven members move, and cleaning out a few basements. During an average week I spent at least ten hours in active coven participation, in addition to my full-time job and time with non-Pagan friends.

But in a coven, a majority must agree on an initiate's inclusion. I do not know, and will probably never know, the real reason for why things did not progress. Looking back, while I was devoted, I did not "fit" the mold of what the coven probably needed. I found out when I arrived for what was to be my last training session. The normal routine was two hours of non-stop questions and answers.

That evening, I arrived to a room with only three of the seven usual participants: the High Priestess, another male and female coven member. All were Third Degree. The High Priest was absent as well. I should have known.

"Hey, where is everybody?" I asked.

Oh, they won't be here tonight." The High Priestess stood to my right with a cup of cinnamon tea, my favorite.

Not good.

I didn't push. I didn't ask why they weren't there. I didn't know enough to ask why our normal routine was suddenly altered for that evening.

I wish I had.

"Should I start then?"

"Please."

I should have known.

"Tonight's report is on the symbolism of hair," I began, before reading from my notes all of the details I had been able to find in just under four days, since the last full moon circle, on hair.

There was complete silence.

Something is wrong.

And yet, nothing seemed out of the ordinary.

When I finished, all three smiled.

"Very good," The High Priestess said. "You have completed your training."

"Oh. Really?" I remember feeling very surprised. "But what about the next scheduled exercise that you mentioned before?"

The final step before initiation was a series of group building exercises. We had just discussed them a few weeks earlier.

"Well...,"

I wanted to throw up. This was not happening.

The High Priestess briefly explained that the High Priest's schedule was too busy for the foreseeable future to permit the additional exercises.

"After all, the only day he has off is on Sunday and even that is not guaranteed. I can't ask him to make changes. You do understand, don't you?"

So what? If I have to make a sacrifice, why can't he?

I should have been angry. Instead I was numb. I knew and yet I didn't know what was being said. He couldn't make a few hours on Sundays or a few hours on Tuesdays just to see things through? What about commitment? What about the demands this group had made on my time, my life, my religious devotion?

Why couldn't they say something earlier?

"Sure."

"We'll let you know if anything changes."

Boom!

Dumped, after 18 months of consistent, positive engagement.

Later I would realize that the person I was becoming truly did not fit with the coven. I was coming out of my shell, both as a lesbian and as a black Pagan. This meant that I wanted to explore, to do my thing, and this might not work well with this particular group. Was it race? Perhaps not on the surface, but the intimacy of a coven means having folks around whom you truly enjoy and for whom you will sacrifice much if necessary.

While I knew deep down that the High Priestess was the one who decided that I should not be in the coven, it was probably the best thing that happened to me on my journey into Paganism. Just because it is "alternative" does not mean that it is free from "isms". My happiness elsewhere proved that she did me the best favor in the world by releasing me to be where I truly belonged. It hurt because the group could have been more honest.

Experiences like this that remind me of how important it is to maintain honest and open commitment and communication between neophyte or potential initiate and the group. This was not a sudden situation that popped up. The scheduling issue had been known for several months at that point. I can see how many Pagans of Color, who have heard of such experiences or who have had ones worse than mine would run - fast and far away - from so-called mainstream Paganism.

I wondered why a simple call wasn't made: "Hey! It's not working out, but we wish you well!" Or perhaps an inquiry, such as "Do you have any interests other than us?"

Instead, they let me hope.

They let me believe.

They lost my respect.

You are not worthy.

I kept hearing the words over and over, as I kept going to the Hellenic Orthodox group. I told them that it was a technicality, but I knew it was a lie. I felt it was a lie and yet I did not have the truth to tell them.

One issue that entwines with race and Paganism is the reality of group dynamics.

I was no longer an innocent. Commitment in a Pagan group was the slipperiest slope of all: at least I knew where I stood with monotheism. If I signed the dotted line, I could be a Christian, or I could be a Jew. In Paganism, it is not so certain at times. A solitary Pagan of Color might remain so for this very reason. We, who have endured condemnation and mistreatment in many ways, find that there are more obstacles to prove that one is "good enough" for a particular tradition.

Race is the 800 lb elephant in the room: no one speaks about it, but stereotypes mean that if someone's skin color is less likely to be seen at an event or culturally within that tradition, it will be harder for Pagans of Color.

But who gets to say that someone is good enough for a Pagan tradition? For a British Traditional coven, it is the High Priestess, an individual. In other groups, it is a committee. I found a group with a committee approach, where if someone is not a good fit, that person knows up front. In that moment, I was angry, hurt and glad for the experience simultaneously.

On the one hand, the treatment by this one group left me feeling flawed and ready to become a solitary practitioner. I didn't want to trust another Pagan group. Fortunately, I didn't give into those feelings and found a group where I rebuilt my trust in being a part of the Pagan community as an individual. It is in being Pagan that I have safely come out as a lesbian. This would not have happened without the steps of acknowledging the benefits of the Pagan community.

Years Later Truth: I am grateful that I found out sooner than later. I am angry because no one deserves game playing. Honesty and ethical behavior are more than just tenets, they should be the norm in religious groups. Even if this was a one-time slip up, the damage has been done.

Truth: The dirty little secret of the Craft is out: It's all about power. If people gravitate to the Craft to claim or to re-claim individual power, what does that mean if groups get into the mix? When does group power and group dynamics trump the individual's right to religious attainment and freedom?

Truth: It doesn't, except when it does.

Solution: Find a group where that is not the case.

But what about those who are non-white? In 2009, I joined an online forum for African-American Wiccans, if only to find others who were black and who practiced Paganism in some form. The day I joined, someone posted the following question:"Is Wicca just a predominance of white culture? Is there any room for those who are non-white?"

Post after post ignored the question until one day I saw how one woman put it simply:

"Wicca is VERY European, but only because we allow it to be that way. Take a survey of all Pagan civilizations and you will find that most pantheons are Original (Non-white) in Origin. White Wiccans point to Norse, Celtic, Greek and Roman pantheons as if they are the only valid pantheons. For some reason they embrace Egyptian pantheons. I guess they forgot Egyptians were originally melanated people.Not trying to stand on a soapbox, but in order to make this more yours rather than just being a visitor, investigate the dark pantheons as well as the grafted, I apologize, the white pantheons."

This post was the first to make me wonder about the reverse: comments against those who chose to workshop outside of the traditional culture by those of my own background.

Truth: Did being black make me a sell-out since I wasn't following a "dark" pantheon? Was I less of a witch?

Truth: Paganism was just as bad as Christianity. If you weren't "in your box", then you didn't fit.

Truth: Internalized racism, black expectations of black Pagans make being an individual Pagan harder than it needs to be.

I felt insulted at her comments and questioned my own beliefs: did my calling to Kemetic-Hellenic-Numen path, an Egyptian-Greek-Roman path mean that I was a less black, less African-American witch because the pantheons weren't dark enough?

This post only confirmed what I'd seen from those Pagans of Color I had encountered face to face at festivals or in meetings.

There was a running joke:

Why did so few Pagans show up to Pagan gatherings?

A.Why bother? Might as well be solitary.

While I was glad that I joined this group in 2009, I struggled with the idea of what to post online, because I truly believed that the intra-racial push to limit witches of color solely to traditions which reflected melanin content was just as wrong as those who were not of color choosing to restrict members who did not look like them or have the same cultural background as them. It was hard enough to simply find another Pagan of color: you were a minority within a minority. Add being gay to the mix and it became a triple minority.

Truth: It hurts when your choice to choose is challenged by someone who should be cheering for you. Instead you have to fight both sides.

I was relieved to see someone else who stood up for the non-conventional choice a few days later. On the surface, I admired his bravery, because he honored the call of the Asatruar. I did not know where he lived, but I knew in Minnesota I had been warned away from the Asatru, since some of the smaller groups had skinheads as members. He followed the calling of his heart. What struck me were his words:

"I know a lot of folks are coming from the Oppressive anddomineeringreligions like Christianity and Islam; but we don't need to bring our prejudice into our faiths. I think for the most part, people take on this path for the freedom to worship the way they like and not be judge by their peers."

Truth: Race and trust play real roles in the Craft. Pagan on the surface meant white.

Truth: Race was the unspoken interloper in the Pagan community.

The face of modern American "Paganism" appears as the Renaissance Faire or Festival that conjures up images of Medieval England. Tarot booths, psychic fairs and Celtic music play throughout the festival as patrons and workers dress as fairies or in garb more suited to a re-enactment of the character Robin Hood, with or without merry men and Morris Dancers. The "face" of Paganism then rests in Northern European "white" culture.

For the non- white practitioner, there are several options:

1) Gather the books, the Celtic music, join others and fall in with the British Traditionalists or an eclectic variant of some Northern European bent.
2) Follow your cultural or family of origins traditions and practice those or
3) Follow your heart, regardless of where it leads.

Reality check from my first British Traditional Experience: Coven life is social first, religious second.

Truth: I wanted religion first, social life second.

From the Brit Trad folk, I learned that trust was a matter of who was in the group versus those outside the group. The coven was a family more than a religious institution. Despite my stated desire to get away from certain aspects of my earlier Christian life, I loved ritual and the trappings of religion. While I could visit a Ren Faire once or twice a year, I did not want to live there. It was like ingesting a bag of sugared donuts. There was only so much Northern European music, food, dance and worship that I could take.

At one time, I thought that I had to endure this in order to be Pagan. Thankfully, I was wrong. I knew that I was in the right place when race was one of the earlier topics that came up. It was out in the open, which felt refreshing.

One evening after ritual, Geri, one of the priestesses, sat down on Rachel's couch with me. We were shooting the breeze about the ritual focus and cooking.

"I'm so glad you came tonight," Geri said.

"So am I." I paused, "I am still happy with the British Traditionalists, but I really like ritual here. I've never seen a service with Egyptian Gods before, but then, I don't see a lot of anything that is not like, um Ren Faire material."

"Yeah, that's true. Look, we know that Paganism looks white in America. We believe you can and should worship what you want. If you want to be a tree and join the Druids, have at it. But if you are called by our Gods and are up to the challenge, we say come on in - the door is open and we're ready whenever you are."

"Thanks," I smiled. "It's nice to know that you guys are so open. Everything is so public here. Is this normal?"

"For us," Geri grinned. "We love our Gods and we are happy to have anyone here. They are a mix, which helps. Our Egyptian Gods help with spiritual matters, our Greek Gods are great for closeness or higher intellectual matters, and our Roman Gods are very practical. Culturally, the three areas mixed historically as well as in a philosophical and religious sense."

"Really? I didn't know that." I paused. "Is that why you are so open?"

"Well," Gerri added, "Most groups have their balance of open and closed. We just tend to be more open."

Truth: I would remember Geri's comments later, when I would face the silent, yet real face of racism in the Pagan community. It would be one of the reasons that I would claim and maintain Hellenic Orthodox as my true spiritual home.

Unlike other religions found beneath the Pagan umbrella, members of the Hellenic Orthodox faith acknowledge that in addition to generally accepted knowledge of racial injustice in the United States at large, there is racial imbalance in various religious sects and a need to be realistic that race and background matters in choice of religion. In short, race mattered.

Race will always be a difficult subject at best, filled with complexity and complications. Yet, even after seven years, I sometimes forget that racism and Pagan dissemblance can reveal themselves at anytime and in any place.

At a local Paganicon in 2014, I re-discovered how race and being the "sole one" matters. I spoke on eldercare. The reality for most Pagans is that there are few resources for aging, including senior care centers, assisted living facilities, nursing homes or Pagan-specific agencies. Pagans of color are the invisible minority within the hidden religious minority of Pagan traditions. As I wandered the rooms, I saw just one other woman whose melanin shone deep. She was a trader of goods, a local woman whom I'd seen at every Pagan festival in the Twin Cities. We smile at each other. I buy her jewelry and her statues of Aset, Anubis, Sekhmet and Ptah grace my shelves. This is the premiere showcase for Pagan tradition in the Twin Cities, yet the absence of color in the halls makes my skin run cold at times. There is a Kemetic workshop and a ritual, yet I am the sole non-white Pagan who offers a workshop on any tradition.

For a metropolitan area that ranks sixteenth in US population, the reasons why Pagans of Color avoid certain gatherings remain both mysterious and obvious. At Pagan Pride, in September, I know that perhaps three or four solitary Pagans or curious seekers will come out to Minnehaha Park in Minneapolis on the first Saturday to remind themselves that the larger community has something, but perhaps not much for them. At Gay Pride in June, I will see a wide swath of racial and cultural diversity, with Pagans of Color who blend in, but will not come to Pagan Pride.

In a recent conversation with one such woman, she explained why some Pagans of Color, including herself, do not associate with the community at large.

"What is there for me?" she asks. "I am a black and gay. I do not see someone like me there."

Until there is an open realization that race still matters, she and others like her will be a part of two worlds, separate and not equal: the public white face of Paganism known commercially and the invisible minority of traditions which are closed off. We are a community and a world divided due to these problems.

Labels, Assumptions and Paganism

Bethie Jelen Vanderyacht

It began with the Supreme Court's decision on June 25th, 2013 to deem that part of the 1965 Voter's Right Act was unconstitutional, reversing nearly 50 years of social progress in one, quick, senseless act. I was appalled. But why?

One look at me and you might not think "minority." But as they say, you cannot always judge a book by its cover. Extremely fair, ginger-haired, and freckled, you might guess I was Irish or some daughter of the Northern European gene pool. But far from it. Somewhere in the mix of my descendants, two recessive genes came together to give me reddish brown hair. And as for the fair skin? I can only believe the same.

My brother has gray eyes and a brown afro and can tan so dark he makes Coppertone models weep at his beauty. And if you looked at my mother in her youth, you would see olive skin and black hair. My maternal grandmother looked Aztec, her mother was a Dutch lesbian who asked a Mexican Day Laborer building the North-Pacific Railroad to give her and her "best friend" a baby. My maternal grandfather was dark, swarthy, extremely tall and solid; his mother looked Filipina -- centuries of nomadic blood coursing through their veins, giving them an "exotic" flair.

My dad was equally swarthy, but for different reasons, and a wound would be the easiest tell as to why: He keloided when cut. My fraternal grandfather was descended from an African-American plantation slave in addition to the same gypsy blood as my mom's father. My fraternal grandmother was harder to peg, as many stories were made-up over the years to explain her dead-beat dad; but her mother fled the Nazis into Holland during the war, so it is likely there is Judaic lineage there.

So the easiest way to define what I am is that I am a mutt. A mezcla. A mixture of cultures and races. Add to that an impoverished upbringing in downtown Los Angeles, bisexuality, a sexual abuse survivor with PTSD, and the inability to have a child, and my relationship with the label "minority" begins to make more sense. Add-in "non-Christian," Pagan, Heathen, or Gypsy, and I have covered most of the socioeconomic bases. So although I may appear white, and my other labels can easily be hidden from sight (and I do know I have privilege in my life due to the misperceptions that causes) I have still experienced racism, internal racism, prejudice and homophobia. And because of all that, I was appalled by the reversal of the Voter's Right Act.

But what came in the days following the Supreme Court's decision made it even harder to swallow -- on all of my social media feeds, which I had painstakingly made a safe-haven for liberals and Pagans, I saw racism and prejudice rear their ugly heads. At first, I had to walk-away from my social tether -- I needed a breather. I understood where some of my friends were coming from. I am not completely naïve and understand and accept my differences with others. But it was the Pagan community that surprised me. How could these people I love, respect, and look-up-to decide that the desiccation of the VRA was not only acceptable, but long overdue? And how could others very boldly claim that this was not a Pagan issue?

It was from reading all of the blogs, messages, and posts that I formulated the only answer I could: That most of the Pagan community is avoiding the idea of race altogether -- either out of fear (because it is still a dividing factor for some and avoidance keeps us in this false utopian society of Pagans), or out of ignorance (the "I don't see color"über political correctness that frankly shows more ignorance -- and can be even more damaging -- than blatant racism itself).

The idea of the utopian society of Pagans is not a new one. In fact, I freely admit I have contributed to the notion myself. I had long held this idea of a group of progressively-minded social activists who celebrated their diversity as well as their divinity. And although my "Disneyized" Pagan world had already begun to crumble with exposure to anti-Transgender goddess worshippers and neo-Nazi Northern Heathen sects, I still held the belief that at least those people I had surrounded myself with were my Pagan societal ideal. But after the VRA decision, I began to see that I had fooled myself again. That not all Pagans were willing to work toward a common good, or were even willing to acknowledge that something was wrong. That socially and economically, a line had been drawn and those of us on the other side were no longer welcome...and the insult-to-injury was that our Pagan community was looking away, ignoring the fact anything of importance had occurred.

But it should be understood that I have not been completely naive in this notion of a utopian Pagan society. It comes with taking on the Pagan label. That we are a group of people of many different paths that follow -- on some level -- an appreciation of nature and the earth. That by accepting and wearing this Pagan mantle, we come together to be something stronger than we are on our own. That instead of many with little power, we come together as one in strength and work together to protect ourselves from prejudices imbued on our individual religious paths.

For I am even a minority within the Pagan label. I am not Wiccan, nor Gardnerian, nor do I follow Dianic Women's Mysteries. My religion, like my heritage, is diverse. I am of gypsy blood. I am non-Romani, and I identify as Eastern-European Heathen. I convene with the spirits (my people can see and speak with the dead), I believe-in and practice superstitions, I dance and sing as part of my practice, I revere nature and the earth, and I follow old-world style mysticism, practicing the healing magic of my ancestors. If I call myself "Gypsy," I get questions about thievery, selling people and body parts, prophecy via cards/tea/eggs/stones, cannibalism (the myth of Gypsies eating children), etc. But if I call myself Pagan, I am protected by societal confusion over the term. Someone might assume I am Buddhist. Or Druid. Or a Witch. (Ok, so I can't seem to escape the preconception of eating children with that last label.)

But as a Pagan, I do expect that we must also use the label (and the fortitude and protection it lends) for good. I also expect that someone who worships nature in some form must have a respect and love for all living things. And this is where the apathetic and passive reaction by my spiritual community to the VRA decision made me most angry and pessimistic. If we as Pagans do not defend the rights of others, then why would anyone outside our rank-and-file defend our rights?

Furthermore, the people who are being disenfranchised are actually a part of us. Minorities DO exist amongst our echelons. And that leads to the other problem within the Pagan community: The belief that as Pagans we are so incredibly progressive and revolutionary that race and poverty cease to exist. That we transcend cultures, colors, and creeds and that individuals do not show any conditioning from society within our circles. And this belief is folly.

For in denying that the reality of prejudice exists hurts everyone even more. One needs not defend that which does not exist. One need not give thought to issues beneath their transcendental thread. Lazy liberal thought at its finest, the denial of color makes a fight for equality a moot point. And furthermore, it deludes us all into believing we do not suffer from the weaknesses of communal conditioning; that we are not racist, sexist, prejudiced, or privileged. I cannot say I have ever met anyone free from bigotry. I know I have an innate dislike for people of means. And I acknowledge that I am known for locking my car doors as I am driving through a bad neighborhood. And I always get nervous when I am walking alone at night and see a man walking towards me -- because a fragile part of me assumes he is going to assault me because he is male and I am female. These are learned parts of me that may never be unlearned. Some from childhood, or from watching my grandparents, or based on my experiences -- and the tweaked reactions I have from those experiences. But I could never truthfully say that I am above prejudice. That I am free from racism. That I don't see color. Because, frankly, that is such a misled way of thinking that it is a lie to oneself and to the world around us. And dishonesty breeds distrust and hurts us all.

Another aspect that injures our community is the pointed over-correction to cover-up racism and prejudice. Although it is very easy to delete comments from blogs, avoid the race question when Asatru comes up, or deny priests and priestesses an opportunity to present, perform or give reverence at conferences, conventions and festivals due to their personal biases, by removing these things and people from the surface of our community, we still leave behind deeply-seeded xenophobia and animosity. Instead, we should allow their voices to be heard, counter with our own programs, and begin a dialogue -- so that our voices may also be heard and so that we can show that we don't cover-up our flaws, but instead we work together to educate and heal. For if we do not use our combined strength to fight for what is right, to enlighten, and to mend our trauma, what is this community of "Paganism" for?

Derailing the Conversation: Cultural Appropriation in Online Pagan Communities.

Cecily Joy Willowe, M.Div.

The world of social media is becoming the domain of social misfits, outsiders and the traditionally marginalized. This should come as no surprise as the rise of social media created an easy tool for those of us on the outskirts of society to find each other and establish our own revolutionary sanctuary on the interwebs. In the online plane, Black people can take over Twitter with playing "the dozens" and start massive boycotts of products created by racist television chiefs or corrupted jurors, while the rest of Twitter still remains shocked that Black people know how to use computers. Pagans can have their online journals and hangouts without the fear of being pushed out of the "broom closet" too early. They can learn about forms of Paganism that never get much attention from mainstream press. Social Justice Warriors finally have a place where their analysis of privilege and power cannot be silenced. Enough reblogs and now hundreds of people know the basic 101 of feminism, Womanism, anti-racism and so on.

As a hardcore solitary, Black, Womanist Wiccan, I look to the social web when I am in need of spiritual and cultural community. Unlike Pagan groups and events offline, I can disconnect when Pagan ignorance shows its ugly two-faced head. Yet, bigotry and ignorance are still high on social media even among marginalized religious groups. I might be relatively safe on African American Wiccan groups but in spaces dominated by White Pagans, those White imperialism thought patterns will undoubtedly come to surface regardless of how much White Pagans have convinced themselves that they are allies. In fact, in the social media spectrum, White Pagan allies are the forerunner of cultural appropriation.

Online Pagan communities such as Tumblr are full of people who believe they are activists of social change. As marginalized religious folks, White Pagans see themselves as more socially advanced than their Christian counterparts. When they do call out racism in Paganism it is blamed on the new-agers, "Neo Wiccans" or Fluffy bunnies. The lines are constantly being redrawn between the bad White Pagans and the good White allies in discussions of cultural appropriation. In this way, cultural appropriation is talked about in means of how good White Pagans can involve themselves in other cultures in a respectful way. The point is completely missed that cultural appropriation is not about what White people think they should or should not have the rights to or about how they define their Pagan identity. In order for the term cultural appropriation to have any use, it needs to remain about power. Cultural appropriation is about the power to steal, misrepresent, and/or corrupt cultural items from an oppressed cultural group. It is about the history of White colonization and imperialism where White people believe that their god given right to manifest destiny allows them to take over land and steal goods and people for their own personal gain. Cultural appropriation is the same White imperialism thinking being used to justify appropriating cultural goods in the modern age. This is not to suggest that only White people can commit cultural appropriation. People of Color can be guilty of appropriation and cultural theft when they borrow from other oppressed cultures while misrepresenting and demeaning that same culture. A prime example of this cultural appropriation is the group K-pop which profits off the success of hip-hop while committing anti-black actions such as wearing blackface. [2] Although People of Color do not have the same status as their White counterparts they can commit actions that reinforce White supremacy. Regardless of the racial identity of guilty parties, the main benefactor of cultural appropriation remains White dominated culture. Therefore, cultural appropriation conversations must deal with issues of power, privilege and

---

[2] Tracie Egan Morrissey "WTF Is Up With K-Pop and Blackface?! Jezebel (2012) "http://jezebel.com/5889705/omg-wtf-is-up-with-k-pop--blackface (accessed March 14, 2014).

racism in order to be effective. Yet, in discussions of racism within online Pagan communities, the voices of People of Color continue to be silenced.

The over-representation of White voices of authority is not solely a Pagan problem but occurs too often in social justice and multicultural circles. The issues lay in the fact that social justice education is more accessible to people with multiple forms of privilege. Diversity circles may teach better understanding for some but often teaches the privileged new words and how to use them to their advantage. They can now sound enlightened without the hard work of breaking down systems of oppression. Worst still, they can twist the shining terms of social justice to turn themselves into victims and distract from real discussion and activism around oppression. Suddenly, we are talking about Wiccan privilege when we still have yet to really bring to the surface the racism, homophobia, ableism and classism in online and offline Paganism.

For every online discussion about cultural appropriation of Indigenous religions, there are even more about appropriation of Gardnerian Wicca, Norse and another majority White religions. As Kraemer writes in her essay on "Cultural Borrowing/ Cultural Appropriation: A Relationship Model for Respectful Borrowing":

I first encountered the term "Neo Wicca" (used to describe any Wiccan derived tradition that deviates heavily from the work of Gardner and lack initiatory lineage) on British Traditional Wiccan listservs in the early 200s, along with the far more derogatory term "McWicca". Detractors of these Wiccan innovations often point fingers at Silver Ravenwolf, Scott Cunningham, or even Raymond Buckland for watering down of their practices.[3]

Unfortunately, Kraemer gives almost as much energy to the "expressed anger at the appropriation and commodification of "Wicca", from British Traditional Wiccans as she gives to concerns of Native Americans about Pagan appropriation of Indigenous cultures. [4] Internal fighting between Wiccan communities is not comparable to cultural genocide committed

---

[3] Christine Hoff Kraemer, "Cultural Borrowing/ Cultural Appropriation: A relationship Model for Respectful Borrowing", Thorn Magazine, 36.
[4] Ibid.

by White people, including Pagan people, on Indigenous cultures. Still, online Pagan communities are deluded by definitions of cultural appropriation that are divorced from complex oppression analysis. Cultural appropriation is viewed as simply borrowing from cultures and communities that you are not a part of. Privilege is defined not by systemic oppression but instead reframing as "who has the most". For example, instead of having deeper conservations about White, class, cis, heterosexual privileges in Pagan communities, Pagans are coining new terms like Wiccanate Privilege.[5] Wiccanate privilege being the idea that the Wiccan and related Pagans have privilege over other forms of Paganism because they have greater access and notoriety. The irony is that this majority White Pagan has found a clever way to appropriate even the term privilege. For instead of using oppression and privilege to represent that struggles of People of Color, LBTGQ and other victims of systemic abuse, they change the subject to discuss in-group aggression.

When we are talking about how many books Wiccans are selling as opposed to why Black people feel unwelcome in Pagan communities there is a problem. Oppression and privilege is about who can get jobs, who gets arrested, who gets healthcare, who is allowed to practice their religions, etc. It is not about how mean Wiccans are to Non-Wiccan Pagans. Unless Wiccans suddenly became the religious majority and start taking jobs from other Pagans then we have more important issues to discuss in Pagan communities. Another favorite derailing tool of White Pagans is distinguishing cultural appropriation by means of who is initiated and who is not initiated into a religion. In this way, White (particularly middle and upper class) Pagans can ignore the complex issues of race, class, culture and access and simply focus on elitism views of initiation. We forget that many Haitian vodouisants are not officially initiated but White Pagans of a certain class can pay their way to authenticity. As Kenaz Filan states:

---

[5]Heather Greene" An Overview of the PantheaCon Wiccan Privilege Discussion" The Wild Hunt (2014) http://wildhunt.org/2014/02/an-overview-of-the-pantheacon-wiccan-privilege-discussion.html (Accessed March 15, 2015).

Today, many practitioners of Vodou have "come aboveground." Houngans and mambos have Web sites and mailing lists, hold public ceremonies, and offer as much information as they can without violating their initiatory oaths. Unfortunately, many of these houngans and mambos speak disparagingly of "Wicca-Doo" and believe that one can only serve the lwa in the "time-honored traditional way" — meaning, of course, their way. Others will happily take you into the djevo (the initiatory chamber) and teach you their secrets for "one low fee," airfare and lodging not included. A person who is an interested outsider this week can be asogwe (the highest rank in Haitian Vodou) by Sunday, if the check clears. We don't assume that everyone who does a few Yogic stretches is called to join an ashram. We don't believe that everyone who attends Mass should take Holy Orders and join a monastery. And yet many seem to think that the priesthood should be an introduction to Vodou, and not the culmination of years of involvement with the tradition; or they believe that everyone who serves the lwa must do so in a priestly capacity.[6]

These White people who buy their way into Vodou are now seen as authentic because of initiation regardless of whenever that initiation involved acknowledging White privilege. Take, for instance, Mambo Racine, a true initiate of Haitian Vodou who continues to spread anti-Black stereotypes as she writes Facebook posts like this:

> My Haitian membership likewise treats the internationals well. Unlike many Haitian peristyles, they don't mock, or deride, or steal from, or disrespect, the international

---

[6] Kenaz Filan, *The Haitian Vodou Handbook: Protocols for Riding with the Lwa,* (Vermont: Destiny Books, 2007) Location 229 (Kindle Edition)

> participants, instead they have always received the internationals wholeheartedly, taking them into the djevo as sisters and brothers...I have always made sure that things run right, that there is no stealing or other bad behavior, that ceremonies are correct, that the Haitian initiates are on their best behavior, that the drinking water supply is maintained, that each and every detail is correctly discharged so as to provide the international (and Haitian!) members with a safe, positive experience. [7]

Since initiation is viewed as the true path to avoiding cultural appropriation, White Pagans can continue to be ignorant of deeper conversations of racism. White Wiccans can now claim that you are not Wiccan unless you initiated into British Traditional Wicca without discussing that Gardner appropriated many of his ideas of Wicca from groups of color. Such derailing discussions also negate that cultural appropriation is not about protecting White Western religions. This way, we do not have to discuss that initiation and access can often be bought if you have the right access, while Pagans of Color continue to feel unwelcome in covens and Pagan events because they don't have the right look or access card.If your only way of accessing a certain religion or culture is through your pocketbook, you should take a moment think about whether or not your cash is blood money. The reality of communities of color is that they are often impoverished which leads to People of Color selling their cultural goods. This poverty was made possible by White imperialism that robbed cultures and lands of their resources. White Pagans who pay their way into traditions of color are often cashing in on the White history of cultural genocide in order to succeed at their future endeavors of cultural appropriation.

In my own search to incorporate my own culture's symbols into my Pagan practice, I have been met with accusations from White Pagan bloggers that I am appropriating

---

[7] Kenaz Filan, "Why I am Not a Professional White Vodouisant" Kenaz Filan (2012) http://kenazfilan.blogspot.com/2012/02/why-i-am-not-professional-white.html(Accessed March 14, 2014)

African religions because I am not an initiate. What is interesting about such comments is that their ancestors are the reason why I am not initiated into an African religion. In the American landscape of racism and slavery, there existed strict laws against Blacks practicing African based religions. While many communities of color were forced to give up their traditions, White people can now be initiated into the same traditions and become the gatekeepers of our cultures.

Some of the more social justice advanced Pagans bloggers and writers break down cultural appropriation in terms of open and closed religions. On one hand it is refreshing that there are White Pagans who believe that they should not have access to every culture. Furthermore it is true that there are traditions that are not accessible to outsiders and should remain that way. On the other hand, the simplification of cultural appropriation to open or closed religions has leads to the assumptions that religions and People of Color are monolithic. Various religious traditions are thrown into strict categories of open and closed. Buddhism is deemed opened even though there are Asian American Buddhist traditions that are certainly not accessible to cultural outsiders. Even though there are White academics that see themselves as the true voices of Buddhism, White Westerners can claim the title of Buddhists without any realunderstanding of Buddhist philosophy and meditation (outside of meditative spiritual escapism). Even when a religion of color is accessible, it can still be appropriated if the cultural outsider misrepresents, corrupts or belittles that religions or its people. For example, Kraemer writes about the openness of Hinduism and suggests that:

> Some living traditions such as Hinduism, tend to be extremely friendly to non-native seekers and are frequent cross-cultural borrowers themselves; for examples, some Indian Vedantists have cheerfully added Jesus to the list of avatars whom they venerate and have taken an active role in their original cultural context, of course. Since one cannot "appropriate" what is already freely shared, however, the openness of Hindus towards the

> practice of borrowing simplifies the issues for
> Pagan in a way that hostility of many Native
> American complicates it.[8]

It is important that conversations of cultural appropriation be specific about the different cultures involved such as the difference between Hinduism and Native American religions. With that said, Kraemer still commits the error of oversimplifying cultures of color. Hinduism is a vast umbrella term coined by British colonists who lumped various Indian traditions together. Even if some Vedantists are openly sharing their knowledge does not cancel out the Indian Hindus who are tired of White people that claim they are Hindu. There is no agreement among People of Color about cultural sharing yet there a plenty of White Pagan bloggers and writers who seemed to have found the answer.There are no easy answers to moving beyond cultural appropriation. In fact, when we give up the idea of coming up with an easy quick solution we can began the real work of anti-racism.

Conversations in Cultural Exchange

I would be hypocritical if I said that I am absolutely against cultural borrowing; my arm is adorned with an Om tattoo marking myself with the spiritual traditions that brought me the power of meditation, yoga, self-analysis and sacred sounds. My house is filled with both symbols of Wicca, Hinduism, Buddhism, African traditions and even a few Christian saints. African American spiritualties, generally speaking, have always involved syncretizing various religions and practices that are deemed useful for upholding their spiritual growth. It is not uncommon to find New Orleans voodooist, African American Wiccan and African spiritualist altars that include and venerate symbols and deities from several cultures that they have come across. People of Color such as Native Americans, Indians and Black people have been practicing cultural exchanges since our first cross-cultural encounters. Since People of Color are both the prime victims of cultural appropriation and the experts on

---

[8] Kraemer, 38.

cultural appropriation and exchange, it is their voices that are greatly needed in online and offline discussion of racism in Paganism.

In order to turn the conversation around to ideas cultural exchange, the voices of People of Color must be privileged. I am not unaware that even my choices of resources for this essay are White Pagans. The Pagan world is over-saturated with White writers, leaders and authority. Some might argue that this is the case because the overwhelming majority of self- identified American Pagans are middle class Whites. However, this does not mean that People of Color do not exist in Pagan communities. In all likelihood, we would see a rise in People of Color joining Pagan communities and conversations if they felt more welcomed. If they saw their people on the back of books and being invited to present at Pagan events. In the area of discussions of racism, cultural appropriation and cultural exchange there is no question that they should be the center voices. It is up to People of Color and their communities to determine based on their understanding, needs, history and experiences what cultural appropriation looks like, and they should be in charge of avenues for cultural exchange with other groups. From my standpoint, cultural exchange involves activism. It means on focusing on community and the bigger picture over oneself. Asking oneself if my actions and beliefs are benefiting the global community. When we take deities out of context for our own spiritual gain we are climbing for our spiritual achievement on the backs of others. Yet, when we include various cultures, deities, symbols into our practices to order honor the diversity of our world then we are being radical and heading to cultural exchange.

The scary alternative is that White Pagans sink into their whiteness. Scared to call any Brown Gods, they only name White deities and employ practices from White European cultures. While it is wonderful that some Pagans are cautious of misappropriating POC religions, still I find nothing scarier than White people who have convinced themselves that the divine is White. Starhawk presents an excellent example about how to use cultural exchange to benefit one's community. She writes of the importance of honoring diverse set deities for the betterment of her community, especially Children of Color:

> I wish for Florence a world in which she will
> never for a moment see her skin color or the
> texture of her hair as anything but beautiful,
> where every opportunity will be open to her,
> where prejudice, racism and slavery will seem
> as incomprehensible and anarchic as the
> metallurgy tools of a Bronze Age culture. I want
> her to know she is the Goddess, and that the
> Goddess is black, brown, red, yellow, fat, thin,
> old and young.[9]

There is nothing wrong with staying with your own cultures and traditions as long as it is not at the cost of recognizing the various forms of divinity. Cultural appropriation is activated by Western individualism, while in cultural exchange we are stepping into the idea that spirituality is about community and social change.

I am not sure I have the answers for how the Pagan community moves into cultural exchange. Healing racism is beyond simple solutions. To be honest, White culture is so embedded with colonization and greed, it may be impossible for true cultural exchange to occur between Pagans of Color and White Pagans. How do Pagans share equally when White Pagans are endowed with some much societal power? Cultural exchange implies reciprocity. Therefore, the individual Pagan and Pagan communities need to ask themselves what they can give back in return to communities of color. The obvious offering that White Pagans can give is using their power and privilege to challenge racism and support People of Color in and outside of the Pagan world. In online worlds, support means introducing the Pagan community to complex issues of race, class, gender, and other marginalized issues. This can be done in part by your own writing but more importantly inviting People of Color to be guest bloggers or reblog their writing about racism, their culture and their spiritual understanding. In this way, Pagans online learn from, support and promote each other create a healthy online community. Finally, White Pagans must reject the

---

[9] Starhawk, *Webs Of Power: Notes from the Global Uprising* (Canada: New Publishers society, 2002),204.

favoritism and elitism that happens online where a few popular writers become the holy grail of Paganism. Often People of Color are not a part of the popular crowd. They are silenced and attacked easily by popular bloggers if they get out of line. If Pagans of Color are being harassed, allies should not sit on the sideline; instead it is the time to call out your fellow Pagans on their privilege and racism.

In order for the Pagan community to heal from cultural appropriation offline, White Pagans must do more than simply inviting People of Color to the party. Pagans of Color need front row seats at the table, being key presenters at big events and being supported in their writings so that their practices are being represented by the actual inventors. We have enough popular books on ingenious religions written by White people and enough African diasporic practices being taught by White people. If a Pagan wants to learn about someone's culture or tradition they should go to the source. But remember cultural exchange is about advancing your own cultural competency without expecting to be an authority on someone else's cultural goods. Cultural exchange is not simply about how we treated a culture's spirituality; it is more importantly how we treat that culture. If we are to begin the conversation around cultural appropriation and exchange, White Pagans need to come to table ready to support Pagans of Color, our cultures and communities. True support is not easy or come with simple answers. It is educating oneself, learning to listen and knowing when to take a backseat and doing activism for People of Color and the global community.

The Black Witch

Mathew Taylor

Eighteen years. When you make that statement you feel like it is giving strength or credibility to anything that you say. When I speak about eighteen years, I'm talking about the amount of time it has taken for me to see representation of people of color in the Pagan community. I was born into the Pagan community when I was sixteen years old. My mother was a southern Baptist woman and she raised me and loved me unconditionally. Her strong Christian faith was present in our home but never forced in our home, and I am forever thankful to her for that.

When I was sixteen I had multiple things happen in my life that forever would define me as a human being. One of the most impacting was that I came out as bisexual because I felt it was the safe way out. In my family the term gay was not talked about or even really thought about. I remember there always being talks about cousins of mine whom they would call "Funny" or "Sweet" and when they would be with their partners—their partners were always called their "special friends". With this as my atmosphere growing up it was pretty hard to even approach the idea that at the time I was in fact gay and didn't believe in God. Thinking about it now I don't think that there was a loss of a belief in God but more of a disbelief in the God that had been shown to me. Each lie that you told or naughty deed you did, even if it was the first time, meant you were going to Hell. Although claiming that I was bisexual was a path that I felt was safe, my spirit called for a path that wasn't going to be as safe to walk.

As a child I remember my mother would spend countless weekends and family gatherings talking to us kids about how things had been for her and her siblings growing up. She would recount stories of the spirits that visited her and the connections she felt to our ancestors that had transitioned before her time. She always had that longing for our Native American roots. She would tell stories about her youth walking on the reservation and listening to the stories that her grandparents would tell. She told us about the language and how she remembered speaking it, but as she got older she lost it. My mother was strong in her faith but she wanted to share with us this path that she had been on and the experiences that she had.

She may not have known it then but she inspired me to go back to those roots. She inspired me to seek out a religion rooted in nature that would embrace me, and all of my quirks.

When I was eleven years old, like her, I had my first experience of the spirit realm. I remember that night so vividly, we had been living at the 10th Street house and I was just getting to that age when religion really started to peak my interest. It was late one night and I had fallen asleep in our living room during a movie; I was deep in sleep and the house was quiet. I had rolled over in my sleep and had begun to readjust myself when I felt a cold hand touch my thigh. I jumped and woke up fully, right away, and I looked around the room. There was no one there physically, and I remember my mother was asleep on the couch. I got up and tried to wake her but she wouldn't wake up, and the room had this chill. I got back into the pallet on the ground and bundled up tight in the blanket. I closed my eyes tight and prayed for protection from whoever my guardian angels were. After a while that feeling of fear and cold went away, and I went back to sleep.

After that night I could not stop thinking about the stories my mom would tell. Maybe there was truth in all those stories of ghosts and witches and other things occult. . I think that night was the turning point for me and ultimately it was actually the Goddess stepping in and letting me know that I was ready to start my journey. From that moment on I started going to local libraries and reading all that I could find about the supernatural, and about other religions. It wasn't until I was well into my high school years that I found Wicca. I didn't even know what Wicca was. At first it was this buzzword that I remembered hearing around the schoolyard. Some of the Goth kids were rumored to be witches, or wikkeds, or something like that. At that time I went to Waldenbooks and found books about witchcraft and Paganism. I came across the famous Silver Ravenwolf's "Teen Witch" and later Ray Buckland's "Complete Book of Witchcraft."I enjoyed reading those works and still have them in my library today, but I also noticed something about those books that I still am missing. Those books were written by people that were not a complete representation of who I was and who I am.

For me those books were and are a good source for learning about the Craft but they did not represent me, a child of the public assistance system. To me these books put out there that you did need certain tools to make your magick work. I enjoyed Silver's book because it did not put an emphasis on the need of a tool per se, but she did make you aware of the tools that were out there. Mr. Buckland also talked about tools but made me feel like I needed to have those tools to be a better witch in the Craft.

As my years have passed, and I have grown more into the Pagan path, I have found that there are many different groups that identify with me, but there is still an underlying privilege that seems to exist. It is not as apparent in small circles, but in larger ones, it can be disheartening to join in groups and not know the current New Age artist because their music doesn't speak to you. I can't tell you how many times I have walked into a ritual and heard some random Tibetan monks playing or gone into a New Age store and there is Enya playing on the radio. I, at this moment in my life, do not identify with her. I am not saying that there is not a place for her and I mean the music charts show that there is definitely a place for her — but not in my life currently. I want to know when there will be the representation of the New Age shop that is not afraid to play Tupac because he may be an artist that people use to meditate. That sixteen year old in me wants to have music that applies to me in my Craft.

It doesn't stop there, though. I want to be able to walk into a Pagan circle and not have it assumed that because I am of African American descent that I practice Voodoo or Santeria. I want to be able to walk in to any group and proclaim or discuss my faith based on my terms and not on other people's assumptions. This perception of my magick was very prevalent recently when I went to Pantheacon 2014. This was my first year going to the Conference and it felt good to be there among my fellow Pagans but I was disheartened when I had interactions with a few of the conference goers and their first questions were about which Afro-Cuban path I followed. I want to say now that

I am not a practitioner of Voodoo and no matter how much people want it to be true that is not me.

I've often wondered if whether or not this perception comes from the recent influx in media from shows such as "Charmed" or "American Horror Story: Coven" where there are either small roles of witches that seem to have either a limited power or an association of Black witches being Voodoo queens. I remember reading the blogs and thinking about how great of a step it was to see Angela Bassett and Gabourey Sidibe representing our Black culture of Pagans but then again they were both put into that Voodoo box. I also remember reading the comments about Gabourey acting too black or placing too much emphasis on her role with Kathy Bates and how they kept bringing up the race issue. I think that the race issue is going to be there whether we want it or not. I think that race is going to be an issue as long as we pretend it is not one and are not fully represented in the Pagan community.

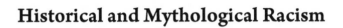

Historical and Mythological Racism

At Least Two Memnons: Anti-Racism Versus Tokenism in the Ancient World and Modern Polytheist Reconstructionism

P. Sufenas Virius Lupus

In its most nuanced definitions, racism is understood as a systematic, institutional ranking of different ethnicities which construe some of them (usually those of white European origins) as inherently superior to others (including all people of color, whether of Asian, African, Native North, Central, and South American, Aboriginal Australian or Pacific Islander descent). All of the effects of discrimination, privilege, and inequality follow from such cultural constructions. The reality of racism has been especially apparent from the 16th century onwards, with the conquest, colonization, and forced conversion of the Americas and the socioeconomic dependence upon the African slave trade and chattel slavery in the Americas. Indeed, racism, as well as second-class status for people of color, and even actual and *de facto* slavery, is still a reality which is alive and well across the world, including North America. There has been, however, an ongoing debate about the existence of racism as we understand it on an institutional and systematic level in premodern societies, including those of the classical Mediterranean world.[10] While racial or ethnic differences have been observed and commented upon throughout written human history, it is another question

---

[10]Among the positive interpretations include: Frank M. Snowden, Jr., *Blacks in Antiquity: Ethiopians in the Greco-Roman Experience* (Cambridge, MA: The Belknap Press of Harvard University Press, 1970). More negative interpretations include: Benjamin Isaac, *The Invention of Racism in Classical Antiquity* (Princeton, NJ: Princeton University Press, 2004). An attempt at a balanced approach is that of Erich S. Gruen, *Rethinking the Other in Antiquity* (Princeton, NJ: Princeton University Press, 2011). A useful sourcebook on these matters is Rebecca F. Kennedy, C. Sydnor Roy and Max L. Gouldman (eds./trans.), *Race and Ethnicity in the Classical World: An Anthology of Primary Sources in Translation* (Indianapolis, IN: Hackett Publishing Company, Inc., 2013).

entirely whether those differences implied an inherent superiority for some races and an inferiority for others.

This uncertainty as to whether noting ethnic differences as opposed to being outright racist might be particularly acute in the ancient and late antique Mediterranean worlds. A Roman might admire the ancient civilization of Egypt and its people yet find some of their cultural practices disgusting (e.g. kneading dough with their feet rather than their hands), appreciate the high culture of Greece but likewise bear its people some ambivalence, view the Jewish god as both mysterious and powerful, but the Jewish people as strange (for being monotheists), superstitious, and prone to rebellion, and think that Gauls, Thracians, Germans, and Britons are all barbarous beyond any capacity for sympathy. The racism which existed, often, and which was most visible and problematic in late antiquity was often inter-ethnic racism within Europe, from our viewpoint, but to suggest that there was any kind of united "European-ness" amongst Romans, Gauls, Greeks, Thracians, Germans, and others would have been considered ridiculous at the time.

Whatever resentments might have existed between different European ethnicities, there was at least some mutual respect of (most) religious traditions between the various polytheistic populations living under the Empire as well as on its fringes. The matter of racism in antiquity is a question involving whether or not it is possible to be positively multicultural without likewise being accepting of racial and ethnic equality across the board. This, at least, seems to have been the reality for people in late antiquity under the Roman Empire.

Modern cultures in North America, as well as modern cultures more widely, are certainly a plurality rather than a unity, but whether these cultures are a salad bowl or a melting pot, and which (if either) of these models is preferable, is another question altogether. In such situations, religions tend to change to become more universally accessible and less local in their focus,[11] and syncretism becomes the norm rather than the

---

[11] Jonathan Z. Smith, "Here, There, and Anywhere," in Scott Noegel, Joel Walker, and Brannon Wheeler (eds.), *Prayer, Magic, and the Stars in the Ancient and Late Antique World* (University Park: The Pennsylvania State University Press, 2003), pp. 21-36.

exception.[12] The religio-cultural matrix of the late antique Mediterranean world is an appealing one for many modern polytheists, not only because of the inherent attractiveness of the panoply of the deities of Greece, Rome, Egypt, the Near East, Gaul, Britain, and other localities, but because the promiscuous religious syncretism of the time speaks of a profound respect for other religions and their deities, and a great interest in multiculturalism.

But, it is possible that this situation could be interpreted in other ways. Does it speak, rather than of multiculturalism and respect, of an unbridled level of cultural appropriation and a climate of imperial domination and colonization, and all of the entitlement that goes along with such situations? Individual pieces of evidence—almost all of which, in and of themselves, present the viewpoints of an economic and socio-politico-religious elite—can be marshaled to support either viewpoint. It, thus, seems likely that the reality on the ground for individual people in the past would have varied as widely as it does for people today, and for every exemplary case of acceptance and embracing of multiculturalism which exists, there are also cases in which discrimination, condemnation, and other things we would associate with racism were in operation as well. Surely, though, not every theological idea from a given set of cultures which might have members that espouse racism is inherently and automatically tainted with it (in most cases), and thus there can be models from the ancient and late antique worlds which might be useful to consider for modern polytheists.

And yet, there is a tendency to counter accusations of racism, or even of the less-overtly-offensive but still real and noteworthy phenomenon of non-inclusiveness, with particular types of statements. "We're not racists: we've got Latinos in our group!" "I'm not a racist: I initiated an African-American just last year!" These are textbook cases of what is known as tokenism,

---

[12] Though, one could argue that syncretism has always been the norm, at every stage of every religion, with the exception of the Abrahamic creedal monotheistic religions—but even these have had periods in which they have been open to syncretism, and they often begin as a "reformed" earlier tradition. For more on syncretism, see P. Sufenas Virius Lupus, "Super-Syncretism: Creating Connection and Preserving Diversity," in *A Serpent Path Primer* (The Red Lotus Library, 2012), pp. 1-59.

the inclusion of people who are often deprived of privilege in some respect or another (although ethnic differences are the most prominent examples) that are then held up as examples proving the apparent contrary of the stated accusations. Tokenism is something that often well-meaning but uninformed or naïve people who wish to be multicultural (as well as being inclusive in other ways) might engage in unknowingly. In groups where the majority is still white, the limited number of people of color in a group might seem that much more visible simply as a matter of course; but how can more people of color be welcomed and made to feel safe and respected without engaging in the excesses of tokenism?

This is a problem that I have been very aware of for many years with the Ekklesía Antínoou. Earlier Antinoan groups I helped to co-found included several Latinos as the other principal figures and co-founders, such that I was the only one of the original three who was not Latino. I was also the only one who wasn't "purely gay," "purely male/a man" (or, in fact, at all of that gender, even in its wide variations), but was also the only one not living in the United States at the time, and was also the only one who had an advanced post-secondary education—all of these being varying levels and types of relative privilege or its lack. Yet, the majority of the group that eventually formed was white gay males over the age of 40. The Ekklesía Antínoou was founded after a schism in June of 2007, and I have been successful in making the newer group more open to and inclusive of women, bisexuals and trans*/gender-variant and other types of queer people, and to various other people from less privileged demographics, and yet in the realm of race and ethnicity, the group is still mainly white. Among the initiated Luperca/e/i of the group, there has been one half-Native American male, one African-American male, a Latina woman, and one genderqueer individual of Mexican heritage; the African-American male is also an "Assistes" in the Antinoan Mysteries, and an additional Puerto Rican-American woman and a Native American woman have likewise assisted with the

Mysteries, but no people of color have been initiated at this point.[13]

While what we are offering is certainly a niche-within-a-niche as far as modern Pagan groups are concerned (a reconstructionist polytheist syncretist group that is also queer and focused on a particular deified mortal!), the lack of active people of color within our group is something that has troubled me for many years now. What are we doing wrong? How can we convey the message that we are inclusive and accepting to a greater extent than we have done previously? Or, perhaps more importantly: what can we offer people of color that springs from our own authentic spiritual roots, but which will appeal to them? And if there is nothing to offer (and it would be good to know that, certainly!), how can that be changed, if it can be at all? Desires and intentions toward being multicultural and inclusive in our membership are certainly positive, but the proof is in the pudding in terms of who actually shows up, and why they do. While there may simply not be a huge number of people of color who want to be a part of a tradition like ours, which is certainly possible, likewise, if there is something that the group or I personally am doing wrong, I'd like to find out so that it can be addressed.

As someone who is heavily invested in the ancient world's polytheistic heritage, I often look to the past to see if there might be answers waiting there that have not been considered previously. In this effort, I find two figures that existed in the ancient and late antique worlds might be able to assist in this regard,[14] and both of them are named Memnon. The first Memnon was an Ethiopian[15] demigod and hero who fought on

---

[13] Another Latina woman has inquired about the process of initiation, but we have not been able to make it happen yet.

[14] By this, I mean not only studying their examples phenomenologically and thinking about what they might tell us about the ancient world and the modern world, and becoming familiar with them from the extant evidence, but also engaging with them directly through cultus and other devotional activities. As a polytheist, the reality of these individuals as divine beings (specifically, as heroes, if not as a minor deity in the case of the original Memnon) must constantly be kept in mind when engaging with them, and any other hero, deity, ancestor, land spirit, deified abstraction, egregore, pop cultural entity, or other variety of divine being which can (and does!) exist.

[15] The notion of "Ethiopia" was notoriously confused for the Greeks and Romans, and often interchanged with the term "Nubian," which could designate anyone

the Trojan side in the renowned epic cycle of ancient Greece, who eventually became divinized because of his valor and his divine heritage after being killed by Achilleus. The second Memnon was the *trophimos* ("foster-son") of the famed consul, sophist, and philanthropist of Marathon, Herodes Attikos. This second Memnon lived in the mid-second century CE, and was likewise heroized after his untimely death as a late teenager. The second Memnon has been an active part of our cultus in the Ekklesía Antínoou for a number of years now; the first, however, has not been, and perhaps this should change in the near future.[16] A fuller examination of both Memnons, and what can be understood about the classical world from their reception in it, would be useful at this stage.

Although the first Memnon is the subject of a series of recent books by Brother G (a.k.a. Gregory L. Walker),[17] his

---

who lived from the latitude of the first cataract of the Nile in upper (southern) Egypt, all the way further south through the modern territories of the Sudan and Ethiopia itself. These were considered Nilotic cultures, but were also seen as distinct from Egypt itself, which is how the Egyptians themselves also viewed the situation. Though it is important to realize that Egypt is *just as African* as any other people or country from the African continent, at the same time the distinctiveness of each of the cultures in Africa need not entail the racism of some modern Egyptians against being considered "black" (i.e. African). At the same time, some attempts to re-Africanize the Egyptians are less successful than others on various grounds; see Robert Bauval and Thomas Brophy, *Imhotep the African: Architect of the Cosmos* (San Francisco: Disinformation/Red Wheel/Weiser, 2013), and my review of it, "Eyes on the Stars: A Review of *Imhotep the African*" at Patheos.com: http://www.patheos.com/Pagan/Eyes-On-Stars-Sufenas-Virius-Lupus-12-23-2013.html.

[16] By the time of publication, the first hero feast of Memnon the Son of Eos and Tithonos will have been celebrated by the Ekklesía Antínoou on April 20th, 2014, a date determined during the course of the writing of this essay through the mention of Memnon by Ovid in his *Fasti* on that date, which was then re-confirmed via divination. See Sir James George Frazer (ed./trans.), *Ovid's Fasti* (Cambridge: Harvard University Press, 1931), pp. 240-243 (4.713-720). I stumbled upon this resource as a result of following an oddly obsessive and insistent prompt to look in my library for Michael Routery's book, *From the Prow of Myth* (San Francisco: Vindos Press, 2013), which contains the poem "Balbilla to Sabina at Memnon" on p. 73, and the following lines:

> *...But on the morrow*
> *as the fecund waters lap the sere shore,*
> *the giant Ethiope, shattered son*
> *of Eos and once champion of Troy,...*

[17] Brother G (Gregory L. Walker), *Shades of Memnon: The African Hero of the Trojan War and the Keys to Ancient World Civilization, Book One* (Chicago: Seker Nefer

cultural currency for modern people is far less than it was in the past. Memnon is first mentioned in Hesiod's *Theogony*, lines 984-985, in the midst of a listing of the demigods born between deities and mortals who went on to become renowned heroes: "To Tithonos Eos bore bronze-geared Memnon, / king of the Ethiopians, and also lord Emathion."[18] The Homeric *Odyssey* also mentions Memnon briefly but favorably in book 11 when Odysseus, in the context of the *nekyia* episode in Book 11 — in which he relates his interaction with Achilleus in Hades to King Alkinous and his court — discusses the beauty of the hero Eurypylus: "He in truth was the handsomest man I saw, next to noble Memnon."[19] The love of Eos for Tithonos is described at greater length in the Homeric Hymn to Aphrodite,[20] but no mention is made of Memnon as the offspring from it. Memnon's fatal battle with Achilleus at Troy is the subject of the lost Greek epic cycle poem known as the *Aethiopis*, likely by Arctinus of Miletus and written in the late 7th century BCE, and titled after the Ethiopian origin of Memnon himself.[21] Herodotus also mentions Memnon in several places, and identifies various statues in Asia Minor with him, as well as the city of Susa.[22] Though Memnon was on occasion associated with various Asian locations and peoples (as his father Tithonos, the brother of the Trojan king Priam, would have been Phrygian and thus considered Asian),[23] his later appearances prefer to give him an African association.[24] In Virgil's *Aeneid*, his armor is mentioned

Press, 1999); *Shades of Memnon, Book II: Ra Force Rising* (Chicago: Seker Nefer Press, 2000); *Shades of Memnon, Book III: African Atlantis Unbound* (Chicago: Seker Nefer Press, 2005).

[18] Apostolos N. Athanassakis (ed./trans.), *Hesiod: Theogony, Works and Days, Shield* (Baltimore, MD: The Johns Hopkins University Press, 1983), p. 37.

[19] A. T. Murray (trans.), *Homer, Odyssey, Books 1-12*, revised by George E. Dimock (Cambridge, MA: Harvard University Press, 2002), pp. 438-439 line 522.

[20] Apostolos N. Athanassakis (ed./trans.), *The Homeric Hymns* (Baltimore, MD: The Johns Hopkins University Press, 1976), pp. 53-54 lines 218-238.

[21] For a concise synopsis of the contents of this poem, known from a summary by a second-century CE writer known as "Proclus" (most likely not the more famous neoplatonist and theurge), see M. L. West, "'Iliad' and 'Aethiopis,'" *The Classical Quarterly* 53.1 (May, 2003), pp. 1-14 at 1-2.

[22] Robin Waterfield (trans.), *Herodotus, The Histories* (Oxford: Oxford University Press, 1998), pp. 134-135 (2.106), 323 (5.53-54), 457 (7.151).

[23] Snowden pp. 151-153.

[24] Gruen, p. 200. In light of the example about to be discussed, however, it is interesting that he is mentioned twice in the medieval Irish *Imtheachta Aeniasa*,

in particular, thus showing that the "armor of Memnon" was somewhat a proverbial phrase;[25] not unlike Achilleus, Memnon was said to have had armor forged by Hephaistos. In Ovid's *Metamorphoses*, Aurora (the Roman counterpart to Eos) asks Jupiter (Zeus) to give him some posthumous honor, which he allows when he transforms the smoke from Memnon's funeral pyre into the birds that are later known as Memnonides, and Aurora's tears for her slain son are the morning dew.[26] According to Pausanias in the later second century, these birds go to Memnon's grave once a year to honor his memory.[27] This summary of his minor appearances in ancient literature is far from exhaustive.

The longest still-extant literary treatment of Memnon is his battle and death in Quintus of Smyrna's *The Fall of Troy*, often known as the *Posthomerica*. The life of the author and thus the date of this work is uncertain at best, and ranges from anywhere during the Second Sophistic (the mid-second century CE) to the mid-fourth century CE; this matter might have implications for what will be discussed subsequently. As it is currently known, the events in *The Fall of Troy* correspond to what would have been in the lost *Aethiopis*. Memnon arrives at Troy with an army beyond counting in its number of soldiers, and is heralded to be the savior of Troy by Priam, and he is favored by Zeus in the battle, who instructs all the other gods not to interfere with the battle to come. Memnon kills Antilochos, the son of Nestor, who is especially beloved of Achilleus, and the two join battle despite a prophecy by Thetis that Achilleus will die soon after if he fights the Ethiopian hero. In the battle, Zeus favors both warriors, and gives them endurance and enlarges their sizes so

the Irish version of Virgil's *Aeneid*, and in his first mention, he is said to have been the "dark" (*dub*)-skinned king of Persia; George Calder (ed./trans.), *Imtheachta Aeniasa, The Irish Aeneid*, Irish Texts Society Volume 6 (London and Dublin: Irish Texts Society, 1995), pp. 16-17 lines 234.

[25] H. Rushton Fairclough (ed./trans.), *Virgil, Volume I: Eclogues, Georgics, Aeneid I-VI* (Cambridge, MA: Harvard University Press, 1935), 274-275 line 489.

[26] Frank Justus Miller (ed./trans.), *Ovid, Metamorphoses, Books IX-XV*, revised by G. P. Goold (Cambridge, MA: Harvard University Press, 1984), pp. 268-273 lines 576-622.

[27] Gregory Nagy, *The Best of the Achaeans: Concepts of the Hero in Archaic Greek Poetry* (Baltimore and London: The Johns Hopkins University Press, 1981), pp. 207-208.

that everyone can witness them battle together. In the end, Memnon is defeated by Achilleus, and Memnon's army mostly scatters, though his Ethiopian attendants at his funeral become the birds who continuously honor him by removing the dust from his tomb.[28] The gods collect Memnon's blood and make it cause the River Paphlagoneion from Mt. Ida to flow red once a year in remembrance of the hero's death-day.[29] While the text is unclear on the exact divine honors the gods bestow on Memnon after Eos implores Zeus for this favor, the wider tradition agrees that he was made divine in some sense (whether as a hero or a god is not entirely clear), and that Eos transported him back to Ethiopia, which is a common place for the gods to visit to receive their sacrifices directly,[30] and thus his return to his homeland is a favorable afterlife equal to any other Greek hero known to tradition.

Perhaps most amusingly, however, from the viewpoint of a discussion of race and modern Paganism, is the fact that Memnon also makes an interesting but brief appearance in medieval literature in the thirteenth-century Icelandic *Prose Edda* of Snorri Sturluson, in the prologue, section III:

> One king among them was called Múnón or Mennón; and he was wedded to the daughter of the High King Priam, her who was called Tróán; they had a child named Trór, whom we call Thor. He was fostered in Thrace by a certain war-duke called Lóríkus; but when he was ten winters old he took unto him the weapons of his father. He was as goodly to look upon, when he

---

[28] According to Arrian of Nikomedia in the second century CE, a similar group of birds showers the temple of Achilleus on the Black Sea's isle of Leuke—Achilleus' traditional resting-place—and cleans it with seawater with their wings; Alain Silberman, *Arrien Périple du Pont-Euxin* (Paris: Les Belles Lettres, 1995), pp. 18-20; translated in P. Sufenas Virius Lupus, *Devotio Antinoo: The Doctor's Notes, Volume One* (The Red Lotus Library, 2011), p. 383.

[29] Arthur S. Way (trans.), *Quintus Smyrnaeus, The Fall of Troy* (Cambridge, MA: Harvard University Press, 1913), pp. 100-115.

[30] Nagy, pp. 205-208; Jonathan S. Burgess, *The Death and Afterlife of Achilles* (Baltimore, MD: The Johns Hopkins University Press, 2009).

came among other men, as the ivory that is inlaid in oak; his hair was fairer than gold.[31]

This is fascinating from a variety of perspectives, amongst them that the Thracian roots of an ultimately African-in-ancestry figure is painted of the Norse deity Thor. The racialist Pagans who often look to the Norse deities for spiritual support of their white supremacist views, and who also often hold the works of Snorri as an unquestionable and almost biblical piece of lore, seem to be ignorant of Snorri's euhemerizing tendencies here, and his placement of Thor as an ultimately half-Phrygian, half-Ethiopian person, golden hair or no.

The second Memnon, who will be referred to henceforth as Memnon Topádein ("the Little Topaz," his nickname in the two inscriptions to him which survive),[32] is, in certain respects, easier to deal with in terms of the variety and nature of the sources relating to him than the first, though the most essential sources (which were likely only oral anyway) have been lost just as the *Aethiopis* has.[33] Most of what we have about him is conjecture based on his other two foster-brothers, Polydeukion and Achilles,[34] though two mentions of him in literature do exist, and two inscriptions as well as a statue head that likely depicts him do survive. Philostratus' *Lives of the Sophists*, written in the early third century CE, contains the following passage:

> ...his foster-sons Achilles, Polydeukes, and Memnon...he mourned them as though they had been his own children, since they were highly honourable youths, noble-minded and

---

[31] Arthur Gilchrist Brodeur (trans.), *The Prose Edda by Snorri Sturluson* (New York: The American-Scandinavian Foundation, 1916), p. 6.

[32] Jennifer Tobin, *Herodes Attikos and the City of Athens: Patronage and Conflict under the Antonines* (Amsterdam: J. C. Gieben, 1997), p. 97; P. Sufenas Virius Lupus, *A Garland for Polydeukion* (The Red Lotus Library, 2012), p. 22.

[33] It is possible that more has been written about Memnon as a hero for cultic purposes during the last four years than had ever been written in the ancient world: see Lupus, *Garland*; he also has an important role to play in the birth of the Tetrad++ Group—see Lupus, *A Garland for Polydeukion* (The Red Lotus Library, 2012).

[34] For simplicity's sake, I have tended to distinguish the *trophimos* of Herodes Attikos, "Achilles," using the familiar English transliteration of his name, whereas I use "Achilleus" when referring to the Greek hero.

fond of study, a credit to their upbringing in his house. Accordingly, he put up statues of them hunting, having hunted, and about to hunt, some in his shrubberies, others in the fields, others by springs or in the shade of plane trees, not hidden away, but inscribed with execrations on any one who should pull down or move them. Nor would he have exalted them thus, had he not known them to be worthy of his praises. And when the Quintilii during their proconsulship of Greece censured him for putting up the statues of these youths on the grounds that they were an extravagance, he retorted, "What business is it of yours if I amuse myself with my poor marbles?"[35]

Another work by Philostratus, *The Life of Apollonius of Tyana*, also has the following strange digression at one point:

And they were about to halt in the neighboring village, which is hardly distant a single stade from the eminence occupied by the sages, when they saw a youth run up to them, the blackest Indian they ever saw; and between his eyebrows was a crescent-shaped spot which shone slightly. But I learn that at a later time the same feature was remarked in the case of Menon, the nursling of Herod the Sophist, who was an Ethiop; it showed while he was a youth, but as he grew up to man's estate its splendor waned and finally disappeared with his youth.[36]

"Herod" in the translation here is most certainly Herodes Attikos, and thus "Menon" seems to be a mistake for

---

[35]Wilmer Cave Wright (ed./trans.), *Philostratus, Lives of Sophists; Eunapius, Lives of Philosophers* (Cambridge, MA: Harvard University Press, 1921), pp. 164-167 (2.558-559).
[36] F. C. Conybeare (trans.), *Philostratus, Life of Apollonius of Tyana, The Epistles of Apollonius and the Treatise of Eusebius*, Two Volumes (Cambridge, MA: Harvard University Press, 1912), Volume 1, pp. 250-251 (3.11).

"Memnon." This Taliesin-like quality[37] in the young Memnon might account for his association with Artemis (to be discussed below), given that she has lunar connections. But, this also tells us that he did grow up to be older than his other foster-brothers, who likely died between the ages of twelve and fifteen.

The two inscriptions which survive dedicated to him call him "Memnon Topádein," and one of them adds "beloved of Artemis" (*Artémidos phílos*) — thus, in addition to perhaps alluding to his crescent-shaped radiant forehead, likely indicating his skill at hunting[38] — followed by a curse inscription which Herodes often put on his public monuments to dissuade would-be vandals from damaging or moving his monuments, just as the passage from Philostratus indicates.

It is very likely that Memnon, and his two other *trophimoi* brothers Polydeukion and Achilles, were among the "alphabet boys" that Herodes Attikos adopted with the thought that his learning-disabled (possibly dyslexic) son Attikos Bradua could learn his alphabet if he was able to memorize all of the names of his friends, each of whose names began with one of the letters of the Greek alphabet.[39] Given that both Memnon and Achilles were likely among these various adopted children, Homeric names for many of the other "alphabet boys" no longer known to us seems likely as well. As a rich adoptive father who loved Memnon, and who was a renowned teacher and an innovator in dealing with learning disability in his child, it seems that a modern parallel (perhaps not entirely pleasing to some) would be that Herodes Attikos was both Mr. Drummond from *Diff'rent Strokes* and Jim Henson from *Sesame Street*! And like the latter, the world presented by the "alphabet boys" of Herodes Attikos and his genetic children seems to have been ethnically diverse and respectfully multicultural.

Interestingly, there is a further connection between the two Memnons, apart from the second one being named after the first. There was a pair of statues of the Egyptian pharaoh Amenhotep III (the Greeks called him Amenophis), the father of the heretic

---

[37] Taliesin, the famous Welsh poet, has a name which means "radiant-brow."

[38] Though, the favor of Artemis also often ends badly for young heroes who are good hunters and dedicated to her, such as Hippolytus in Greek tradition, and Virbius in Roman.

[39] Lupus, *Garland*, pp. 11-12.

king Akhenaten, which stood near Thebes in Egypt. These were identified with the original hero Memnon, and were referred to as the Colossoi of Memnon. A miraculous "singing" occurred with one of the statues at dawn, which was a hum likely created by water expansion, but in Greek thought, it was a kind of response of the divinely heroic child to his mother Eos, the Goddess of dawn's daily arrival. At some point during the Severan dynasty (late second-early third century CE), by imperial order, the statue was "repaired" and no longer sang, which made tourism to it drop off considerably. This site became a tourist attraction for Greeks and Romans, and over the years, many people came there and carved their names on the legs of the statue.[40] Among the people to do this was the Emperor Hadrian, who had his visit in November of 130 CE immortalized on the stones by several poetic inscriptions by the poetess Julia Balbilla.[41]Herodes Attikos was a friend, admirer, and imitator of Hadrian, and likely would have had this imperial visit in mind when he named Memnon Topádein.

Philostratus (who, recall, is the only currently extant source who wrote of Memnon Topádein) also wrote of the Colossoi of Memnon as being representative of the Ethiopian hero in both the *Heroikos* and the *Life of Apollonius of Tyana*, whose philosopher and wonder-worker subject was said to have visited the statues, and he mentions Memnon's shrine in the Nubian/Ethiopian city of Meroe as well. However, Philostratus likewise states that the Ethiopian king Memnon—who lived for five generations among the long-lived Ethiopians, but was considered a youth by them when he died—was not the Memnon who killed Antilochos at Troy, but the latter Memnon was instead an unknown who was then slain by Achilleus and his head was burned on Antilochos' pyre.[42] The source for this differentiation between the Ethiopian Memnon and the Trojan slayer of Antilochos, in Philostratus' *Heroikos*, is the hero Protesilaos, the first to die at Troy, whose hero cultus and ongoing engagement with his devotees is the subject of most of

---

[40]André Bernand and Étienne Bernand (eds.), *Les Inscriptions Grecques et Latines du Colosse de Memnon* (Paris: Institut Francais d'Archéologie Orientale, 1960).
[41] Lupus, *Devotio*, pp. 342-346.
[42] Conybeare, Vol. 2, pp. 12-17 (6.4).

the text.[43]

But further, Lukian of Samosata, the late second-century CE satirist, who was a critic of the cultus of Antinous as well as that of Herodes Attikos' heroized wife, Appia Annia Regilla, and his foster-son Polydeukion, may likewise have alluded to the deification of Antinous and the heroization of Polydeukion, Achilles, and Memnon Topádein in his work *Philopseudes*, the "Lover of Lies." In the final tale of this collection, in which a frame-tale of the rich but sickly Eucrates talks with various friends about the magicians they know of or have met, Eucrates himself talks about his teacher in magic, Pancrates, who he met at the Colossoi of Memnon. This "Pancrates" (which means "All-Powerful") is described as an Egyptian magician and initiate of the Mysteries of Isis, and Eucrates goes on to narrate a tale which is the first literary appearance of the "Sorcerer's Apprentice" story so familiar from Disney's *Fantasia*: Eucrates as an eager but uninformed dabbler in magic and mysteries loses control of a household object gathering water, and then chops it up, but each of the pieces then becomes a double of the original object, and the water-gathering continues until the house is flooded and Pancrates arrives at the last moment to say the magic words which will stop the animated objects. There was a person known to history as Pancrates or Pachrates of Heliopolis, who was associated with the Emperor Hadrian, and was an Egyptian priest, magician, and poet, who wrote a poem involving Antinous, and likewise gave a spell to the Emperor which now exists in the *Greek Magical Papyri*. It seems almost certain that Pancrates/Pachrates was in Egypt when the Emperor Hadrian lost Antinous to his death by drowning, and likely helped with his deification, and perhaps then accompanied the Emperor on his trip to the Colossoi of Memnon the following month. Hadrian was known to have been interested in mystery traditions, magic, philosophy, and astrology. Herodes Attikos was known as a great sophist, and was likewise the hierophant of the Eleusinian Mysteries and also exhibits interests in the Orphic Mysteries, but whether or not he was involved in magic

---

[43]Jennifer K. Berenson Maclean and Ellen Bradshaw Aitken (eds./trans.), *Flavius Philostratus, Heroikos* (Atlanta: Society of Biblical Literature, 2001), pp. 82-83 (26.16-18).

is uncertain.[44] He did most certainly base his heroic cultus for Polydeukion, Memnon, and Achilles on the divine and heroic cultus of Antinous, however. Egyptian magic in the hands of an eager but ignorant would-be magician becomes uncontrolled, and its results only replicate and threaten to destroy everything: the rich dabbler Eucrates in Lukian's tale is likely a reference to both the Emperor Hadrian himself, and to Herodes Attikos, and their animate household object that splinters but then replicates itself is the cultus of both Antinous and the *trophimoi*, Polydeukion, Achilles, and Memnon Topádein.[45] And it all began when Eucrates met Pancrates at the Colossoi of Memnon son of Eos and Tithonos.

Snowden argues, using the example of Memnon Topádein, that there was a very positive view of Ethiopians by the Greeks and Romans of late antiquity.[46] Gruen's treatment is far briefer, but agrees with Snowden's.[47] What intrigues me, though, is the possibility that Hadrian's visit to the Colossoi of Memnon, Herodes Attikos' naming of his *trophimos* Memnon Topádein, and then his heroization, might be reflective of a larger "Memnon-mania" in the early and later second century CE, which may in turn have resulted in Quintus of Smyrna's treatment of him in *The Fall of Troy*. Ovid's account of the Memnonides birds occurs in the late first century BCE; Hadrian's visit was in 130 CE; Arrian of Nikomedia's account of the birds at Leuke for Achilleus' tomb-cleaning was written in the 130s CE; it is likely that Memnon Topádein lived from c. 145 CE to around 160-165 CE, and his hero cultus would have followed it immediately after; Pausanias' account of the Memnonides birds, as well as of the Colossoi of Memnon, occurs in the later second century CE; and Philostratus' writings on the Colossoi and on the Memnons of Ethiopia and of Troy occur in the early third century CE, before the statue itself stopped singing after its "repair." Quintus of Smyrna's account, all of which might draw in various ways on what is mentioned here, in addition to the *Aethiopis*, could have been written at any point during the

---

[44] For the Greeks, though, an interest in mystery traditions and an interest in magic were almost synonymous.

[45] Lupus, *Garland*, pp. 131-137; *Serpent Path*, pp. 72-74.

[46] Snowden, pp. 20, 187-188.

[47] Gruen, p. 211.

Second Sophistic (when Herodes Attikos lived) through to the later fourth century CE. Perhaps an earlier date is likely, therefore, and may have reflected the vogue of both Memnon's cults.

So, was this "Memnon-mania" a singular phenomenon, one select example of an African "local boy done good" and considered a hero, or were the various manifestations of Memnon—as a Trojan and/or Ethiopian hero as well as a more recent heroized mortal youth—something more reflective of the possibility that anyone could be up for consideration as divine, or as a hero? In other words, are the Memnons an example of tokenism in the ancient and late antique worlds, or are they an example of multiculturalism and the plurality of interest and respect observed amongst the more literate and elite persons in various Mediterranean cultures? Did young African boys in the Greek-speaking Eastern Roman Empire, like Memnon Topádein himself, feel included as a result of the heroic figure of his famous name, and was the original Memnon's cultus and recognition a sign that even for the "dead white men" themselves that are so over-emphasized in Western education and culture now (and for the past several centuries), their heritage and their sense of respect extended to a much wider realm of possibilities than it has generally done for us? These are questions that are likely to produce a number of possible answers depending on one's own view of the evidence, which is entirely dependent upon one's socio-cultural preconceptions that were formed long before this evidence would have come to one's attention.

For my own part, these two main Memnons represent something even more important in my sense of spirituality and my ongoing religious devotional practice. For a few years now, I've been feeling a call toward several deities from what the Greeks and Romans (and many modern historians as well) would consider the Nubian cultures (whether these are Meroitic, Kushite, Napatan, or otherwise), in particular Apedemak[48] and

---

[48] Louis V. Zabkar, *Apedemak, Lion God of Meroe: A Study in Egyptian-Meroitic Syncretism* (Warminster: Aris & Phillips Ltd., 1975).

Mandoulis.[49] I have felt that there is a connection between these deities and Memnon Topádein, and making the connection between them and the original hero Memnon, it seems, might be a prudent move forward in terms of pursuing this. These two gods were revered in Egypt at various periods, and other originally Nubian gods (like Bes) also enjoyed an Egyptian cultus; it is very possible to re-engage with them on Egyptian reconstructionist terms, but it feels somewhat dishonest, or at very least incomplete, to do so knowing that their origins were in a distinct and different culture. I know of few (if any) modern polytheists or Pagans who revere the Nubian gods, nor am I aware of any modern traditions that are involved in Meroitic reconstruction or have lineages traced directly to those ancient cultures. Even if there were such groups, would it be possible to approach them respectfully without being just as guilty of cultural appropriation as the ancient Egyptians, Greeks, and Romans (if, indeed, that is how one views their syncretistic tendencies)? While respectful cultural borrowing is certainly possible,[50] if there is no one living and practicing to borrow directly from, that is an entirely different situation altogether.

Not unlike Protesilaos in Philostratus' *Heroikos*, the original hero Memnon himself might be able to reveal some of these connections, and help to establish contact with the sundered traditions of Meroitic polytheism, and to make introductions to Apedemak and his wife Amesemi, Mandoulis and Mehit, Dedwen and Arensnuphis and Sebiumeker. Many years ago, I had a dream of Antinous in which he appeared in a form never before attested in ancient or modern cultus, but which I was told ahead of time was most definitely him, though I might not recognize him immediately: as a beautiful, bald, black African man. Given that Antinous is known to have particularly full and luxurious hair, that baldness was the aspect of him which was most surprising to me; that he could appear

---

[49] Arthur Darby Nock, "A Vision of Mandulis Aion," in *Nock, Essays on Religion and the Ancient World*, ed. Zeph Stewart, Two Volumes (Oxford: Oxford University Press, 1986), Vol. 1, pp. 357-400.

[50] Indeed, I have done this with the Shinto practice of *Misogi-Shuho* in the Ekklesía Antínoou's ritual known as the Inundation, which I developed after participating in this purification ritual, and many others, at the Tsubaki Grand Shrine of America, and adopting some Shinto *kami* and practices into my daily and yearly devotional activities: see Lupus, *Devotio*, pp. 66-70.

with an African face and skin was not much of a surprise at all. Perhaps this was not "only Antinous," but instead was a form of him which had joined with one of the Meroitic deities, or perhaps even the hero Memnon himself. As Antinous is a deity who owed his deification to the Nile River, and was considered both a hero and a god in various locations (including in his homeland in Asia Minor), and has further connections to Achilleus, it seems that the hero Memnon, coming from the lands closer to the source of the Nile, lamented by a river in Asia Minor, and served by birds at his tomb similar to those who served Achilleus' temple, there is a great deal more in common between the two than may at first seem apparent to those looking at them strictly based on their ethnicities.

Memnon connected, for the Egyptians, Greeks, and Romans, and for later peoples as well, the cultures of Asia Minor and Ethiopia, the cities of Meroe and Susa, the cultures of Egypt, Persia, Thrace, and even Iceland, the polytheistic syncretisms of the Mediterranean world and even the first inklings of monotheism with Amenhotep/Amenophis III's son Akhenaten; there is no reason that these various Memnons cannot connect modern polytheists, and in particular Antinoans like myself, to these ancient African traditions. And, most importantly for the wider questions of this anthology, I hope that this contact on the divine level with the heroes and deities of Africa might create the divine precedent for a continued reaching out of our group to include, rather than to appropriate the traditions of or tokenize the members of, various people of color.

Marketing "Rad Trad": The Growing Co-influence Between Paganism and the New Right

Amy Hale

This chapter examines the ways in which a variety of allied and intersecting right-wing groups are marketing to Pagan and esoteric communities. Most of the groups in question are driven by the philosophical underpinnings of the European New Right and despite a general coherence of ideology, the political aims of these groups vary greatly and range from regionalists, identitarians and radical ecologists to radical cultural separatists and White supremacists. The uncertain political and economic climate of the early 21st century has coincided with attempts to further crystallize modern Pagan religious identities, which has created an atmosphere in which Pagans can be perhaps more receptive to the ideas of the New Right, many of which, almost ironically, compliment the movements' flowering in the counterculture of the 1960s.

The implications for this convergence can be seen in the increasingly overt radicalization of New Right inspired groups concerned with issues such as immigration and radical environmentalism as they fuse with the longer standing White nationalist movements. It could be argued that the New Right constitutes a more approachable, palatable and intellectually present form of White nationalism, which has a far wider appeal than the Christian Identity, Neo-Nazi skinheads which are popularly (and incorrectly) envisioned as forming the bulk of White nationalists. Here I explore the various intersections of New Right thought with contemporary frameworks of both Pagan and esoteric communities, ultimately examining the impact of one upon the other.

By way of a slight demarcation, despite the historical connection that contemporary Western style Paganism has with the Fin de Siècle esoteric/occult revival and the roots of modern

Paganism within the Hermetic traditions, there is nevertheless sometimes a cultural separation between people who self define as esotericists and Pagans today. A number of esotericists participate in broader Pagan culture and recognize their historical and cultural affinity, but it is more accurate to consider these groups as interconnected, overlapping and related, rather than lumping them together in one single group. Some of the ways in which the New Right and its offshoots are being marketed will appeal more to Pagans, and some more to the esoteric community (although the producers market to both groups simultaneously), and because of the overlap, I will be addressing both and will make distinctions when necessary.

What is the History of the New Right?

The New Right is grounded in philosophical principles primarily developed from Traditionalism. Traditionalism is a movement which emerged in the early 20th century and which is frequently associated with a group of European esoteric philosophers including René Guénon (1886-1951) and Julius Evola (1898-1974). Salient features of this movement include a critique of modernity, and a belief in a return to a "Traditional" society based on Perennial, universal spiritual principles which once guided the development and governing of ancient civilizations, and which were passed down through initiatory traditions. According to Traditionalists, the roots of this "Tradition" can be seen in some latter day faith systems, most notably those of the East, in Hinduism or Islam or in Orthodox Christianity. Traditionalists critique modern society as deeply degraded, chaotic, and corrupt, and argue that only through a return to traditional social structures, values, and belief systems can the world be redeemed and returned to the state of divine order.

Traditionalism, however, has a number of different iterations. The philosophies of Guénon and Evola, for instance, diverge in terms of their political applications. Guénon has been much more influential in the development of modern Islam, while Evola has provided many of the intellectual seeds for the European New Right and other more overtly fascist subcultures probably as a result of his relationship to Historical Fascism in Italy and Nazi ideologues in Germany. Guénon focused ultimately on the redemptive position of Catholicism for Europe and personally embraced Islam, while Evola's work promotes a much older point of reconstruction for European culture, which would obviously be more influential for the Pagans supporting the European New Right, particularly those influenced by Alain de Benoist.

Much of the European New Right of the late 20th and 21st century has taken its theoretical and strategic direction from the work of Alain de Benoist and the French *Nouvelle Droite*, which emerged in the late 1960s as a response to the European Right's apparent decay and lack of effectiveness in the face of left wing protest[i]. De Benoist has drawn from strategies and ideologies of both the Right and the Left to promote a vision of European regeneration based on antimodernism and Evolan Traditionalist beliefs about culture and society. The New Right ideal is one of radical regionalism where homogeneous cultural groupings reflect elitist "natural" Indo European social stratification and order. Tamir Bar-On notes that the New Right has a list of negations shared with Historical Fascism, among them, anti-modernism, anti-capitalism, anti-immigration, anti-materialism, anti-egalitarianism and anti-Americanism[51].

An important rhetorical feature of the New Right is the way in which its intellectual base argues against multiculturalism and egalitarianism with recourse to discourses of diversity. Proponents of the New Right maintain that cultural separation increases diversity, as do "natural" hierarchies. In this way the New Right rhetorically distinguishes itself from the racism and anti Semitism associated with Historical Fascism, while still providing the intellectual justification for White nationalism. The focus on ethnoregionalism also distinguishes the New Right from right-wing organizations such as the British National Front, which are more concerned with protecting the cultural integrity of the nation.

The primary characteristics of New Right thought and discourse include:

---

[51] Bar-On "Fascism to the Nouvelle Droite: The Dream of pan European Empire" in *Journal of Contemporary European Studies* (2008) 16(3) p. 331.

*The belief in a perennial, universal traditional society and religion
* The belief in a Golden Age to which we have the ability to return
* A dislike of capitalism
* A critique of the modern condition
* A distrust of rational thought
* Small, culturally homogeneous political units.
* A belief in the restoration of "natural" social hierarchies and cultural or racial division
* A belief in virile, masculine leadership.
* Advocating the divine right of kings and theocracy
* Authoritarianism
* A dislike of multiculturalism

Primarily, the New Right is concerned with leveling a critique against the liberalism of the West, characterized by individuality, materialism, progress and Enlightenment, rationalist ideals. The intellectuals of the New Right believe that ethnically homogeneous grounded communities, organized around natural hierarchies will restore meaning and connectedness to Europe, and European diaspora communities.

Is the New Right Fascist?

There is a great deal of scholarly debate about what constitutes fascism both historically and in the modern sense. It is most certainly a loaded term which evokes emotional and defensive responses, and which is, frequently, popularly used by both the Right and the Left as a general term of condemnation and abuse. The discourse surrounding the term, therefore, makes it difficult to historically and theoretically situate the policies and practices of the New Right and its offshoots because there is a strong desire in general to distance the movement from historical fascism. In fact, there is continuing and heated debate regarding the relationship of Evola, Traditionalism and the New Right to Fascism, particularly Historical Fascism, which is defined as Italian Fascism (and which sometimes includes German Nazism) of the 1930s and 40s. Historian of fascism Roger Griffin and Tamir Bar-On both make very cogent arguments that Evola, de

Benoist and the philosophies of the New Right absolutely reflect the key ideological underpinnings of fascism and that they also promote a fascist agenda[52]. However, proponents of the New Right in Europe and elsewhere reject any association with fascism, particularly with centralized or authoritarian beliefs and racism (although this is quite a debated topic as well). Many of these emergent, fascist, "third positionist" (self ascribed neither Right nor Left) ideals are not reminiscent of and do not reflect what people popularly conceive of as fascist in that they do not universally include an anti Semitic element or a racial supremacist element. Rather the elitism is couched in terms of "natural" spiritual development, which is reproduced at a local or tribal level through hierarchical structures similar to sacred kingship. In fact, the rhetorical emphasis on maintaining cultural diversity initially appears very Leftist, and hardly fascist at all. Cultural diversity is to be promoted and cherished, as long as racial purity is maintained[53]. This, of course, is the perfect rhetorical breeding ground for sophisticated identitarian politics, which are centered on maintaining and promoting homogenous cultural identities.

In many ways, however, it can be argued that the New Right, in its more radicalized manifestations, closely conforms to historical fascism to at least the same degree as many of its post WWII counterparts. Robert Paxton defines fascism as:

> A form of political behavior marked by obsessive preoccupation with community decline, humiliation or victimhood, and by compensatory cults of unity, energy and purity, in which a mass-based party of committed nationalist militants, working with uneasy but effective collaboration with traditional elites, abandons democratic liberties, and pursues with redemptive violence, and without ethical or

---

[52] Michael O'Meara "New Culture New Right" (Bloomington:1st Books 2004) p. 17.

[53] See "National Anarchist Movement No. 5: Racial Separatism September 18, 2010" for a coherent articulation of diversity in a New Right context. http://www.national-anarchist.net/2010/09/part-5-racial-separatism.html

legal restraints, goals of internal cleansing, and external expansion[54].

The expansionist aims of most New Right proponents is quite arguable. Most attain to small scale separate territories, however, there is no doubt that the more radicalized elements of the New Right, such as those associated with ecofascism and the White nationalism segments conform to this definition. Certainly the contemporary Eurasian movement which derives its philosophical impetus from the New Right is expansionist in nature, and also promotes a policy of legislating cultural "hygiene" to preserve the homogeneity of the Russian population[55].

How is the New Right "Pagan"?

There are three aspects of the New Right which are effective in marketing to Pagans and esotericists: first, are the underlying shared intellectual frameworks and social concerns which will be covered in more detail below. Second, is that generally Pagans and esotericists consider themselves to be culturally and socially marginal and are frequently seeking outlets for unconventional social agency, which the activism of the New Right can potentially provide[56]. Third, the New Right is a movement which uses "Paganism" as a way to distinguish its values and trajectory from the perceived Judeo-Christian value system which is believed to underpin contemporary liberal society. Radical Traditionalism is a term adopted by Pagans to characterize a uniquely Pagan approach to the New Right. It employs the "Pagan" rhetoric of Evola and de Benoist to attract Pagans invested in "antimodernist" aesthetics and so called "Traditional" lifestyles. However, the "Paganism" of de Benoist and Evola is less about the worship of culture based deities than it is about replicating hierarchical social structures. While de Benoist's philosophies are explicitly Pagan in orientation and he

---

[54] Robert Paxton *The Anatomy of Fascism* 2004, 218
[55] Anton Shekhovtsov "Aleksandr Dugin's Neo-Eurasianism: the New Right *a La Russe*" *Religion Compass* Vol 3 (4) 2009, p. 707
[56] Sabina Magliocco "Witching Culture" (Philadelphia: University of Pennsylvania Press 2004) 185-204.

encourages polities to emerge around culture based deities[57], de Benoist, like Evola before him, believes that the Pagan world view of pre-Christian Europe was essentially hierarchical, theocratic and nondemocratic. In fact, de Benoist characterizes the ideal revival of Paganism as not literal, as not engaging in acts of devotion or worship of the ancient Gods, but in a resacralization of the world and as a replication and reclamation of the values of ancient peoples, and importantly the structures of their consciousness[58]. In fact, New Right theorist Tomislav Sunic is rather derisive of the notion of an actualized Paganism, arguing that revived Paganism would detract from serious discourse[59].

The interest here is in what New Right theorists believe to be deep structural features of the Indo European culture and psyche. De Benoist uses the trifunctional social theories of Georges Dumézil to support his positions of a natural European hierarchy separated into three castes, the priest, the warrior and the cultivator[60]. Therefore, the "diversity" of European cultures is basically surface level and expressed through colorful "folk" traditions. On a deeper level, the Dumézelian Indo European hierarchical society is actually perceived as reflective of an unchanging, eternal divine order. The return to this state will result in a smoothly functioning society low on internal conflict. Pagan leader Stephen Flowers has thus championed the academic field of Indo European studies as a way of further understanding and promoting the underlying natural social order of Europeans and their descendents[61]. For the esoteric practitioner who may not be as attracted to folkish Pagan aesthetics or cultural religiosity, the attraction to the New Right becomes more rooted in the potential participation in an elite

---

[57] Alain deBenoist "On Being a Pagan." (Atlanta: Ultra Press 2004).

[58] Alain de Benoist "Comment Peut-on Etre Païen?"trans Irmin Benoist (Paris: Albin Michel 1981).

[59] Tomaslav Sunic Introduction to Alain de Benoist "Monotheism vs. Polytheism" in *Chronicles: A Magazine of American Culture),* April 1996

[60] Alain de Benoist, "Priests, Warriors, and Cultivators: An Interview with Georges Dumézil," *Tyr: Myth, Culture, Tradition,*1 (Atlanta: Ultra, 2002), 41-50. First published in 1978 in *Figaro Dimanche.*

[61] Stephen Flowers and Michael Moynihan "Wisdom of the Wolf Age: A Conversation with Dr. Stephen Flowers" in *New Dawn* March 21, 2003

priestly class, entry to which is gained by initiation and which holds the key to transmission of the Perennial wisdom.

Nevertheless, the New Right philosophically provides a powerful argument for those who are practicing Pagans, and importantly can be interpreted as providing a culturally, socially and politically legitimate space for Pagan religions. As such, the New Right has been marketed specifically by and for Pagans in a religious context under the phrase "Radical Traditionalism", primarily to Heathens (Pagans with a specific interest in Germanic and Scandinavian traditions), but also to Reconstructionists and Pagans with a strong generalized interest in folk traditions, radical environmentalism, and antimodernism. In fact, the term "Radical Traditionalist" appears to have been coined specifically in this framework by John Michell in the 1970s[62], and has been promoted by a loose network of Evola and New Right supporters working to establish the New Right within Paganism and other groups in the United States and elsewhere. While the right-wing leanings of some Heathen groups are well known, Radical Traditionalism is an attempt to widen the ideology beyond Heathens to other Pagans. In the American context, publisher and musician Michael Moynihan, who published John Michell's 2005 *Confessions of a Radical Traditionalist*, along with Joshua Buckley have been key figures in promoting the use of the term "Radical Traditionalist" to an emerging right-wing Pagan market. The term Radical Traditionalism seems to be gaining currency outside of strictly Pagan circles, as it has been adopted by some to express a more general Eurocentric and White Nationalist Paleoconservative (as distinct from Neoconservative in the US)[63]. In fact, internet searches of "Radical Traditionalism" very frequently reveal a wider application by White Nationalist activists[64].

---

[62] Paul Screeton "John Michell: From Atlantis to Avalon." (England:Alternative Albion Press 2010), p. 89.

[63] See www.alternativeright.com

[64] It may also be worth noting that the Southern Poverty Law Center has reported on the business partnership between ULTRA Publisher of TYR Joshua Buckley and prominent Atlanta based White supremacist and activist Sam Dickson, noting Buckley's past involvement with American Neo-Nazis. SPLC Intelligence Report, Fall 2006 "How Sam Dickson Got Rich" http://www.splcenter.org/get-informed/intelligence-report/browse-all-issues/2006/fall/how-sam-dickson-got-rich?page=0,2

Moynihan and Buckley also have worked closely with figures such as Germanic Pagan Stephen Flowers (who also writes as Edred Thorsson), who has also been a promoter and publisher of de Benoist's work under Runa Raven Press, and who has openly expressed the importance of promoting the New Right among Pagans in the United States[65]. This conglomeration's primary modes of outreach are through publishing and music producing, focusing primarily on metal and neofolk. Moynihan and Buckley employ what de Benoist and other strategists within the New Right and other fascisms refer to as metapolitics. They argue that they are engaging in "apolitical" cultural activity which is working to change perceptions in order to shift the nature of society from the ground up. It is not a call to arms, but a call to intellectual engagement. Rooted in Evola's notion of *apoleiteia*, proponents activities exist at what they believe is a higher level of discourse which rises above base political action, what Anton Shekhovtsov refers to as a "hearts and minds strategy" of modern fascism[66]. New Right metapolitical activities are designed to expand avenues of dialogue and to alter the cultural discourse through the dissemination of ideas, but many metapolitical activists deny any direct political involvement. Roger Griffin notes that this tactic allows the New Right to keep from being ideologically pigeonholed, but mostly, they are taking pains to not be overtly affiliated with the more overtly revolutionary factions of right-wing culture[67].

Part of the metapolitical program involves creating markets and spaces for the production and dissemination of New Right ideas. The cultural vision here is all encompassing, involving the production of books on both theory, tactics and lifestyle, music, spirituality and even fashion. For Pagans and those involved in esoteric subcultures, metapolitical approaches create a variety of cultural spaces which can present attractive

---

[65] See Stephen Flowers introductions to de Benoist's *On Being a Pagan* and Flowers' introduction to Alain de Benoist and Charles Champetier *Manifesto for a European Renaissance* (Texas:Runa Raven Press 2010)
[66] Anton Shekhovtsov *"Apoliteic* Music: Neo-Folk, Martial Industrial and 'Metapolitical Fascism'" in *Patterns of Prejudice* volume 33, issue 5 (December 2009) pp. 431-457.
[67] Griffin 2000.

"lifestyle options" without claiming to be promoting any direct political affiliation.

The initial metapolitical thrust has been in the republishing and translation of the works of Julius Evola and Alain de Benoist, and making them available to an English reading audience. Evola has been a primary influence and he penned a number of well considered works on occult themes, including Tantra, yoga and the Holy Grail in addition to his political writings. Evola's revolutionary framework includes a spiritual essentialization of race and gender, the celebration of the solar male as divine leader and a dedication to a martial society, where the struggle for dominance continually proves the fitness of the group. For Pagans and esotericists, the appeal of Evola is his focus on the spirituality of Tradition, and the rejection of the perceived shallow materialism of modern capitalism. The return to a traditional order guided by the spiritual principles he outlines, patriarchy, caste, honor and discipline, will lead to the return of the spiritually ascended world order that was enjoyed in ancient times, before the rise of modern decadence. Evola's vision is one of eternal, unchanging truth and ultimate stability. Promoting his esoteric material and placing it alongside other esoteric publications becomes a gateway to his more challenging political material. Esoteric publishers Inner Traditions started reprinting Evola's work in translation in the 1990s. They printed Evola's *Men Among the Ruins* in 2002 with a forward by scholar of esotericism Joscelyn Godwin and Moynihan's Dominion Press also later published a special hardback edition of this text. New Right esoteric publisher Arktos has made publishing Evola's works in English translation a priority, in addition to publishing English translations of other New Right activists such as de Benoist, Guillaume Faye and extreme environmentalist Pentti Linkola.

Many introductions to Evola, however, can also be found through the many right leaning esoteric and Pagan journals which have emerged since 2000, and which seem to have skyrocketed in production since 2010. Many of these journals represent entryist tactics and provide an easy introduction to Evola and other New Right theorists for an esoterically minded audience. Moynihan and Buckley's slick journal TYR was first published in 2002 and featured a mix of articles on Germanic mythology, Evola, de Benoist, Linkola, and interviews with neofolk musicians. Since then a number of New Right inspired esoteric and Pagan journals and magazines have appeared which combine political rhetoric with much less threatening "folkish" material.

Troy Southgate, a well known British New Right activist, has argued for the use of entryist tactics on his Nationalist Anarchist website[68]. As the publisher behind Black Front Press, he has delivered a number of anthologies devoted to the work of prominent esoteric figures such as Aleister Crowley, and also a journal devoted to esoteric thought and culture *Helios: A Journal of Metaphysical and Occult Studies*. Additionally, the press has published editions related to the work of fascist leaning literary figures such as Ezra Pound and T.S. Eliot. Southgate has claimed that these are "neutral" publications with no political agenda, and that he attempts to get a variety of contributors, although this strategy of widening the contributor base naturally helps to legitimize the overall publication. Ultimately, the goal is to market these books and journals to the esoterically minded reader interested in these topics, and then include essays which more clearly represent a political perspective. The wider catalogue of Black Front, is not surprisingly, a bit more pointed, including works on Hitler, National Anarchism, and a compendium on the work of British New Right activist Jonathan Bowden. Other entryest tactics employed by the activists of the New Right have included wider participation in Pagan and esoteric events, through purchasing merchandise space, putting forward speakers and musical acts.

The musical subgenre of Neofolk, which emerged in the 1980s, is another avenue of metapolitical engagement for the New Right, one which is hotly debated and which also has a significant Pagan and esoteric fanbase[69]. Neofolk can be characterized as broadly related to industrial and various forms of heavy metal music, sometimes incorporating elements of

---

[68] Troy Southgate "the Case for National Anarchist Entryism" *National Anarchist Movement* September 18, 2010. http://www.national-anarchist.net/2010/09/case-for-national-anarchist-entryism-by.html

[69] See Stéphane François trans. Ariel Godwin "The Euro-Pagan Scene: Between Paganism and Radical Right" in *Journal for the Study of Radicalism* (Vol 1 no 2 2008) pp. 35-54.

traditional European folk music. Thematically the lyrics address European historical glory and heroism as well as themes from Germanic culture, Julius Evola and the occult. Neofolk can be quite martial, and bands frequently reference fascist aesthetics in their appearance through wearing uniforms and camouflage. Shekhovtsov argues that Neofolk, while steeped in the aesthetics and values of fascism is not actually part of any organized political effort, although this assessment is highly debatable[70]. There is no doubt that neofolk appeals to and is being marketed as the soundtrack to the right-wing Pagan movement, and that it is nearly impossible to separate metapolitical activities from organized political outcomes. Even when these cultural activists may not be actively affiliated with political organizations or candidates, they are directly informing and influencing movements and generating more activists. Most publishers and distributors marketing books to this market also distribute Neofolk titles and in the case of Moynihan and British nationalist Troy Southgate produce and promote the bands and distribute them along with New Right publications. Neofolk has served to legitimize the New Right among Pagans and to provide an emotional and immersive connection with these ideals, as well as creating communities for recruitment and dissemination of information.

Some New Right activists are more explicitly political, however, and being inspired by the martiality of Evola, are outright promoting revolution. Publishers Arktos and Counter Currents both feature publications devoted to survivalist techniques and fictionalized accounts of revolution in the United States and support podcasts, conferences and activist networking initiatives. Counter-Currents publishing, which is explicitly New Right and White Nationalist in orientation is not as specifically targeted to the Pagan and esoteric communities as is Arktos. However they clearly serve and market to Pagans and feature Pagan material such as TYR and publish Pagan writers such as Collin Cleary in addition to publishing the works of Savitri Devi, which are classified as Esoteric Nazism. The editors at Counter-Currents are actively promoting both metapolitical and more revolutionary solutions. In 2010 they published

---

[70] Shekhovtsov *Apoliteic* Music p. 431.

Michael O'Meara's *Toward the White Republic*, which explicitly fuses the ideals of the New Right with White nationalism, and calls for more direct revolutionary action. In general, Pagans and esotericists have been very active in the promoting and disseminating the ideas of the New Right. While these New Right activists may be attempting to promote these ideas among Pagans, it is also important to recognize that Pagan and esoteric New Right activists and publications are also becoming influential within the wider arena of Paleoconservative and White Nationalist activity, perhaps providing a Perennialist spiritual sensibility which reinforces and supports essentialist blood and soil ideologies.

Common Frameworks

In addition to the idea that the New Right is fashioning itself as a broadly Pagan movement, or at least a movement where Paganism is accepted and seen as a legitimate critique of the system, there are a number of ideological frameworks within contemporary Paganism which make it very compatible with many New Right philosophies. Interestingly, a number of these cultural foci initially emerged from the relationship between Paganism and the counterculture of the left in the 1960s. Perhaps most important of these are an interest in the preservation of folk traditions, antimodernism, neo tribalism, and environmental preservation. Within the articulated philosophies of the New Right, all of these features work together to produce an idealized vision of separate isolated ethnically pure polities, working in close relationship with the land, embracing folk traditions, and promoting handicraft over industrial labor.

Modern Paganism and esoteric culture has been variously characterized as a response to modernity, which both engages with and resists modernity simultaneously. For many Pagans, part of their radical response to societal and cultural pressures, is an embrace of antimodernism, tradition, and the notion of an imagined past[71]. In fact, the stance is not actually antimodern, but alternatively modern. Contemporary Pagan religions are absolutely a modern phenomenon, yet most rely on some sort of

---

[71] Magliocco 2004, p. 8.

connection with an imagined past, frequently situated in pre Christian European tradition. Nearly all Paganisms today, despite the creativity of many of their rituals and celebrations, draw upon the idea of traditions from a pre Christian past as part of their origin myth. Even esotericists who may or may not identify culturally as Pagans, generally believe in the inherent traditionality of their practices and beliefs, frequently situating them in the pre Christian Western Hermetic tradition. The two features here which resonate with the ideologies of the New Right, include the importance of tradition as a culturally guiding framework, and the inherent challenge to the notion of progress. While many Pagans may actually accept the notion of progress, and while many Pagan rituals are extremely modern and creative, in general the aesthetics and mythic origins of their religions privilege a religiously conservative framework and often structurally hearken back to an imagined tribalism. While Bar On argues that the New Right itself is not antimodern, but alternatively modern, there is no doubt that the branding and marketing of the New Right to Pagans is predicated on antimodern aesthetics and the return to an imagined Pre Christian, Pagan Golden Age[72].

Additionally, for many Pagans, tradition itself is authoritative and confers legitimacy on practices, which to many outsiders might appear irrational. Appeals to genetic models of cultural transmission, initiation, and continuity thus provide arguments for the existence of Paganism within a diverse religious society. A primary key to this shared discourse is that there is the tendency to locate authenticity in essentialist ideas about culture and cultural transmission. People who believe that culture and tradition are transmitted genetically and are inherently linked to place are more likely to find the ideas of the New Right acceptable. Furthermore, the idea that there is a sacred link between people and place can inspire fixed ideas about the relationship between people and territory.

It is almost ironic that this wider conversation about cultural preservation and a desire to not appropriate have created the conditions for the New Right to be successful among

---

[72] Tamir Bar-On "The French New Right's Quest for Alternative Modernity" in *Fascism: The Journal of Comparative Fascist Studies*. Volume 1, 2012, pp. 18-52.

Pagans. Particularly in the United States where Pagans and practitioners of New Age religions have been accused of appropriating symbolism and practices from Native American traditions, Pagans have become especially sensitive to these complaints and wish to practice their religion with a sense of cultural integrity. In short, Pagans do not want to be seen to be stealing traditions that "do not belong to them." As a result, Pagans feel as though they need to be able to legitimately claim ownership to the traditions they practice, which has led to an increase in ethnic reconstruction Paganism within the United States, as people try to become involved with traditions they feel they can legitimately claim as their own. The models for this type of practice tend to be heavily culturally bounded, using a genetic model of cultural transmission, one anthropologists recognize to be greatly flawed and incorrect, but which is a defining feature of New Right ethnopolitics. What tends to be missing in this, however, is the explicit discussion of power dynamics and commercialization that underpins the discourses of cultural theft.

Another place of common ground between Pagans and New Right activists is the value placed on environmentalism and communion with nature. The degree to which environmentalism is part of the discourse and identity forming strategies of the various esoteric but nonspecifically Pagan identified communities has not yet been determined, but many definitions of Paganism include the idea that Paganisms are to be defined as earth based spiritualities, with a special reverence for nature, and the understanding that divinity is inherent in nature[73]. For many Pagans, natural preservation, the privileging of the rural and the emphasis on conducting religious ceremonies in non-urban environments, directly demonstrates the human relationship and care for the earth as a living sacred system, and a desire to work in harmony with the planet rather than destroy it[74].

---

[73]Graham Harvey *Contemporary Paganism*. (New York: New York University Press 1997) p.1.

[74] Bron Taylor's *Dark Green Religion: Nature Spirituality and the Planetary Future* (Berkeley and Los Angeles: University of Caliifornia Press 2010) provides a wide ranging discussion of sacred environmentalism, including the position of Paganism.

Additionally, there is a tendency for Pagans to become involved with environmental activism, which is another historical connection between Paganism and the countercultural movements of the late 1960s. This is also perceived to be a value which distinguishes modern Paganism from particularly Christian traditions which are frequently believed by Pagans to hold values which are exploitative of nature. In fact, the pamphlet "What is Contemporary Paganism" found on the Cherry Hill Pagan Seminary Website, states that indigenous religions and pre Christian religions can provide a "more authentic relationship" to nature and the divine[75].

The New Right generally embraces and promotes a form of radical environmentalism and environmental preservation that is consistent with their views of anti modernity, anti capitalism and anti industrialism. In short, this is a part of their wider endorsement of "natural" organically defined ecosystems which are preserved and maintained free from outside intrusion. Finnish radical environmentalist Pentti Linkola, who has been translated into English by esoteric New Right publishers Arktos, represents the type of radical environmentalist thinking which is being promoted to Pagans by the New Right through such venues as TYR. Linkola believes that the current condition of the environment is going to lead to an apocalyptic state which requires drastic measures to reverse, such as a total dictatorship, eugenics and genocide. Linkola also argues that all technological advances must cease and that humans should revert to only small tool household agricultural production. People will only be allowed to travel short distances and immigration will not be allowed under any circumstances[76]. "Unabomber" Ted Kaczynski's antitechnological ideas are also promoted to Pagans and esotericists by New Right publishers, as are the environmental writings of Savitri Devi[77]. The strategy here for the New Right is to appeal both to the wider Pagan interest in ecoactivism, and also to acknowledge a common theoretical framework of the deep connection of people to their environment. In fact, this perceived relationship between people

---

[75] Cherry Hill Seminary http://www.cherryhillseminary.org/wp-content/uploads/2012/01/WhatIsTrifold.pdf
[76] Pentti Linkola *Can Life Prevail?* (Arktos Media, 2009)
[77] See the catalogues of both Arktos.com and Counter-Currents.com

and land, wrapped in the discourses of both cultural and environmental preservation, then become the justification for radical ethnic separatist politics and anti-immigration platforms.

Why Now?

It would appear that in the past five years the New Right has been steadily advancing its efforts to impact Pagan and esoteric communities. Obviously, there are quite practical reasons why this may be occurring, primarily the fact that communication technologies and publishing are making it much easier for activists to circulate their ideas. As a result, in the years between 2010 and 2012, there has been an increase in the number of journals, magazines and podcasts which are devoted to promoting the New Right. Overall, the world economic crisis and the instability within the European Union in particular has also had an impact in making more space for the ideas of the New Right.

There has also been wider cultural activity within contemporary Paganism seeking to improve the public profile of Paganism as a legitimate form of religious expression. To that end, there has been an increase in interest in developing Pagan institutions, and also in encouraging wider inclusion of Pagans in public debates about religiosity and freedom of religious practice. In the past five years, within the Pagan community, certainly in the United States, there has been an expansion of high profile interfaith activities, the promotion of Pagan seminaries, and greater attempts at wider Pagan outreach within institutions such as prisons and the military. Within the UK, Pagans have been working more closely with bodies such as English Heritage on management of Pagan sites. There is also an ongoing discussion concerning proper burial of Pagan remains by archaeological researchers, on the grounds that they are considered to be the ancestors of modern Pagans.

A rather inevitable consequence of establishing more socially acceptable images for Paganism and greater cultural inclusion, has necessitated tighter definitions of what Pagan religion is and also what it is not. Frequently definitions of Paganism include a belief in the imminence of deity, pantheism or polytheism and the sacrality of nature[78]. Cherry Hill Pagan Seminary refers to nature, ritual, lack of scripture, embodied revelation and an interest in ancient and indigenous religious traditions as being key features of modern Pagan practice, a set of descriptions which at times comes close to a "noble savage" paradigm. Many Pagans activists and leaders use comparisons with established indigenous religious traditions as touchstones to help make Paganism more understandable, and also more acceptable. Additionally, there has been a recent movement in the United States to establish modern Paganism as a surviving European indigenous tradition, thereby conferring upon it the legitimacy of established discourses of oppression and colonization[79].

In this process, a number of debates have emerged, as some groups are now trying to promote some branches of Paganism as more legitimately Pagan than others. For the most part, some Reconstructionist Pagans and Traditional Witches (who are not Wiccan), those who aim for some sort of accuracy in their reconstruction of European pre Christian religion, are trying to claim they are more authentically Pagan and that they possess some form of continuity and connection with historical pre Christian European populations. Wicca in particular is being reframed within this discourse as inauthentic and spurious in comparison. Paganism is thus being recast not as the child of the occult revival of the 19th century rooted in Hermeticism and literacy, but as a series of indigenously rooted religious traditions. This emphasis on continuity, cultural integrity, ethnicity, and tradition is further increasing the potential for building relationships with the European New Right, which sees continuity and tradition as its ideological core.

The New Right is often billed as an intellectual, theoretically informed alternative to the Neoconservatives (in the US) and also the European nationalist parties which are

---

[78] Alta Mira Press Pagan Studies series draws on these features, as does Cherry Hill Seminary. See the pamphlet "what is Contemporary Paganism" at http://www.cherryhillseminary.org/wp-content/uploads/2012/01/WhatIsTrifold.pdf

[79] Sabina Magliocco and Lee Gilmore "Pagans at the Parliament: Interfaith Dialogue between Neo-Pagan and Indigenous Communities." Paper delivered at the American Academy of Religions Annual Meeting, November 2011, San Francisco CA.

perceived as promoting a crass racist agenda. The New Right also presents a critique of materialist values and promises an enriched, spiritually enlightened future based on timeless essential principles, which in times of great uncertainty must seem attractively comforting. For Pagans and esotericists, the ideals of the New Right can potentially resonate with an attraction to an imagined past of simplicity, folk aesthetics, tradition and premodern social orders. As Pagans continue to define their place in the modern world, however, an increasing desire for legitimacy through tradition based authenticity, may prove to be even more challenging. Perhaps increased internal conversations within both Pagan and esoteric communities around the way in which legitimacy and authenticity is constructed will produce a more critical paradigm which is less reliant on tradition and transmission as being ultimately authoritative. This will at least provide a more broadly analytical framework for assessing the assertions and platforms of the New Right when they are encountered.

#

The White Goddess: Racism in the Classics and Whitewashing on the Altar

Brandy Williams

White Athena

She stands proudly at the center of my hearth altar, Athena Polias, wearing her crown and holding her shield, the little goddess Nike in her hand. The cast resin statue gleams like marble, alabaster, bone; like Leukothea, she is a White Goddess.

But why does she look that way? Why is she white?

Don't make a big deal out of it. The resin is white, that's all.

Other unpainted statues on my altar have color – pink, brown, black. Why not Athena?

Athena is a Greek goddess for heaven's sake. Greeks are…white.

Hmmm. Are Greeks white? That question will get you a range of responses on the internet. Pale northern Europeans may look down on their tanned southern neighbors. When Greeks first came to America they were marked as "strange" – think of the phrase "It's all Greek to me" – and faced political, economic and cultural discrimination. There was an immigration quota, some communities were hounded out of town, other communities were typed non-white and targeted for harassment.

But for the purposes of the construction of racial hierarchy and imperialist privilege, Greeks are quintessentially white. For those purposes too it is essential that Athena comes to my altar in the palest possible aspect. It was exactly to challenge that privilege that Martin Bernal called Athena "black."

Wait, how can Athena be black?

Black Athena

Bernal was not a classicist, but a scholar of politics and Near Eastern history. In 1987 at the age of 50 he published the first volume of his most controversial work. He spent the rest of his life defending it.

The full title of the book was *Black Athena: The Afroasiatic Roots of Classical Civilization*. Later he added a subtitle, *The Fabrication of Ancient Greece*. He had been struck, he said, by the fact that archaeologists made discoveries that classicists discounted. What was going on here? It seemed to him that there was something wrong with the basic assumptions of the academic study of ancient Greek civilization. Specifically, classicists denied Egyptian and Phoenician influences on the development of Greek culture, and any evidence supporting those influences was censored. It seemed suspiciously important for classicists that Greece had been settled by Indo-Europeans, that Caucasians were responsible for the philosophical and political innovations at the foundation of modern civilization.

He called this the Aryan Model. Against this he placed the Ancient Model, the evidence of the ancients themselves who credited Egyptian and Phoenician influences on Greek culture. The word Aryan, he said, carries anti-Semitic and racist meaning.

Classical scholars were not pleased to be typed as racist. The outcry was immediate and virulent. Because he was an outsider, not a classicist, his work could be attacked on the basis of his scholarship.

Mary Lefkowitz titled her rebuttal *Not Out of Africa*, with the subtitle *How Afrocentrism Became an Excuse to Teach Myth as History*. Lefkowitz describes the reasons she decided to write the book; when a graduate student accused her of concealing the true origins of Socrates because the student had learned in Afro-American studies that Socrates was black, Lefkowitz was offended that a student would think that classicists deliberately concealed truth. Socrates was Greek; so was Cleopatra; Egypt did not contribute to Greek civilization. Yes, the Greeks pointed to Egypt as a source of some of their learning, but contemporary scholarship into Egyptian culture refutes this. Insisting that Greek ideas had Egyptian origins might offer a boost to African-American self-esteem but it is just a story. It is not history.

African Egypt

There was no denying that Egypt had a magnificent culture. It was however possible to deny that that culture was African. The world of classical scholarship was still not reconciled to the idea that the ancient Egyptians were *black*. Scientific racism categorized only Africans south of the Saharan desert (in sub-Saharan Africa) as "true Negroid" peoples. Those peoples north of the Sahara, specifically the Egyptian people who built those magnificent monuments, were mixed with "Caucasoid" and Arabic elements. Egyptian culture was one of the cultures in the Mediterranean basin. They weren't white exactly, more like tan, but they weren't black either.

Cheikh Ante Diop challenged this construct. As a native of Senegal educated in Paris he wrote largely in French, but the English translation of his 1974 work *The African Origin of Civilization: Myth or Reality* brought his work to wide attention. He noted that the Egyptians called their land Kemet, the black land, and referred to themselves as the inhabitants of this land. They recognized themselves as relatives of the Sudanese, inhabitants of ancient Nubia, Kush and Meroe. It was only when European scholarship began to recognize the achievements of the ancient Egyptians that they detected the light color of the ancient Egyptian skin.

Diop left an extensive body of work. Along with Maulana Karenga and Molefi Kete Asante, he reshaped the discussion of Africa, Egypt, and race. These names are widely respected in African studies but hardly known outside of them. It is also noteworthy that even though Diop wrote decades before Bernal, his work did not force classicists to re-assess their viewpoint.

In the years since Bernal's work upended the classical academy, scholarship has quietly moved in his direction and is more likely to take the testimony of ancient Greek and Roman writers seriously. In his book *TheEgyptian Hermes: A Historical Approach to the Late Pagan Mind*, Garth Fowden traces the Egyptian foundations of the Greek Hermetica. Gregory Shaw discusses the impact of Egyptian thought on the philosophy of Iamblichus in *Theurgy and the Soul*, and Clarke et. al trace Egyptian mythological images in Iamblichus' *De Mysteriis*.

Peter Kingsley goes a step further. He challenges the concept of the "Oriental Mirage" which historians use to discount the testimony of ancient writers. The mirage, he argues, is the academic attempt to create a wall around classical Greek and Roman culture, denying influences from Egypt and from India.

East and West

Wait, did you say India? East is east and west is west, right? I always heard there was a trade of goods but not ideas between East and West.

Kingsley points out that the ancient biographies of Pythagoras recorded that he travelled to India to learn. The Neo-Pythagorean philosopher Plotinus joined the army attacking Persia to try to make it to India to learn for himself. There were Buddhist temples in Alexandria. The second century B.C.E. edicts of Ashoka list Greek rulers who had been introduced to Buddhism, including Alexander, whose army marched all the way to India.

So where do we get the idea that there is some kind of wall between East and West – that there is a meaningful distinction at all?

It was Rudyard Kipling who coined the phrase in the poem "The Ballad of East and West" in 1899. It tells the story of an encounter between an Arab chief and a British officer which ends in friendship. It concludes:

> Oh, East is East and West is West, and never the twain
> shall meet,
> Till Earth and Sky stand presently at God's great
> Judgment Seat;
> But there is neither East nor West, Border, nor Breed, nor
> Birth,
> When two strong men stand face to face, though they
> come from the ends of the earth!

That macho reconciliation at the end of the poem is sometimes cited as proof that Kipling did not mean to disparage the Arab in the poem. However, Kipling was an apologist for British imperialism. The attitude of the British elite toward the rest of the world is nowhere more clearly articulated than in his poem "The White Man's Burden" published in the same year. It begins:

> Take up the White Man's burden —
> Send forth the best ye breed —
> Go bind your sons to exile
> To serve your captives' need;
> To wait in heavy harness,
> On fluttered folk and wild —
> Your new-caught, sullen peoples,
> Half-devil and half-child.

The justification for colonialism was to bring the benefits of advanced civilization to the primitive savages, surely a more than even trade for carting away the resources of their lands. Non-Christian peoples were "Half-devil" and required converting to the most advanced religion on earth. They were also "half-child", neither emotionally nor intellectually adult.

Although the heathen could be converted, European psychology held that the child would never grow up. This idea can be seen in the work of Carl Jung. Graham Richards analyzed Jung's work in *Race, Racism and Psychology: Towards a Reflexive History*. Richards argues that for Jung the non-Western psyche was qualitatively different from the Western one. Travelling in Africa and America, Jung fears "going black", being swamped by a primitive mode of consciousness. In his paper "The Racism of Jung," Farhad Dalal noted that Jung explicitly equated black consciousness with white unconsciousness and the adult black with the white child.

Contemporary Pagans know Jung's work because of his studies in alchemy. Jung mapped descriptions of physical alchemical processes onto psychological processes. The process begins with the nigredo, the dark matter, represented in some medieval images by an "Ethiopian", that is, by a black man. This nigredo is the raw material to be transformed into the philosopher's stone. Jung equated the nigredo with the chaotic state of mind, the shadow. He explicitly linked the "primitive" African and Native American people he met on his travels with a "primitive" state of mind, the unconscious, the shadow, and the nigredo.

Pagans also know Jung for his theory of archetypes, characters in the collective unconscious. Jung proposed that the archetype had a dual nature, it exists both in the psyche and in the world at large. Jung's articulation of the concept developed over his lifetime, culminating in the theory of archetypes as universal psycho-physical patterns manifesting in specific human cultures.

Pagans sometimes use "archetype" as a synonym for gods. The archetype became for Pagans a kind of classification system for gods, leading to formulations like "archetypes of deity" and "moon goddess archetypes". However the Pagan world is engaged in re-assessing the value of Jung's work. Some contemporary polytheists argue that the gods are real and that Jung's formulations psychologize and trivialize the universal forces. As we conduct this assessment it is also important to take into account the fundamental flaws in the theory of archetypes itself, especially the racism built into the system.

Many Pagans encounter Jung's work through the lens of Joseph Campbell, who engaged in extensive folkloric comparisons to arrive at the "monomyth", the basic human story, described in *The Hero with a Thousand Faces*. In this story, the journey of the hero, a young man hears the call to adventure and walks a road of trials, conquering tasks either alone or with allies, and finally receives a boon which he brings back to the world. Campbell identified seven archetypes which fill out the characters of the journey: the hero himself, his mentor, the threshold guardian, the herald, the shapeshifter, the trickster and the shadow.

The hero's journey includes women as love interest or one of the challenges, "temptress", but never as the main character. In *Pathways to Bliss* Campbell made this exclusion explicit, stating that all great mythologies are from the male viewpoint, and only fairy tales, told by women to children, capture women's stories.

Noting the sexism in Campbell's work, is it also racist? We have already seen that Jung equated "dark" peoples with the shadow and Campbell included the shadow archetype in his list. Are there other examples of racism in his work?

Not so much in his public work, but in the private comments which surfaced after his death. His colleague Brendan Gill spoke directly to Campbell's personal opinions in "The Faces of Joseph Campbell". New York Review of Books writer Richard Bernstein followed with "After Death, a Writer is

Accused of Anti-Semitism," in which he reported on interviews he conducted with Campbell's peers. While Campbell's friend and biographer Bill Moyers defended him staunchly, other colleagues stepped forward to describe his anti-Semitism and his dismay that black students had been admitted to Sarah Lawrence College where he taught. One professor described him as "cryptofascist" but added that his work should be judged in the context of his mythological studies of the Greeks, Hindus, and Celts.

We would expect a student of comparative mythology to create work which honored diversity, but even if Campbell had read every myth in the world, can a man who is privately bigoted create publicly useful work? Nisi Shawl provided a great rule of thumb in "Appropriate Cultural Appropriation". Writers can enter into other cultures as guests invited to share, as tourists drawn by beauty, or as invaders, taking without respect. Simply reading or incorporating mythological elements is not sufficient to ensure that the elements are honored appropriately. There is enough doubt about Campbell's attitudes to call for a critical re-assessment of his techniques.

White Isis

Like Jung and Campbell, Robert Graves mined Greek, Roman, Celtic and Egyptian culture in search of the muse who inspired poetry. He was familiar with the work of Sir James Frazier in *The Golden Bough* exploring the various myths of the sacrificed god. Graves detected a goddess in relationship to this god. He mapped her three aspects (Maiden, Mother and Crone) to the phases of the moon, and documented his search for her *The White Goddess, A Historical Grammar of Poetic Myth*. First published in 1948 and reprinted in paperback in 1960, the paean of praise to the Goddess hit at just the right time and clearly answered a deep need in the newly developing women's spirituality and Pagan communities.

Although his work answered a need for cultural explorations centered on a goddess, Graves did not set out to create theology; he was searching for a divine force in women that he could tap for poetic inspiration. Graves famously collaborated with Laura Riding; after she left him, numerous other women served as his personal inspiration.

Any unified theory of deity will elide difference. In the case of Graves, his goddess of the moon incorporated every other deity, whatever her genuine aspect. The Kemetic/Egyptian goddess Isis, great of magic, wearing the solar disc, regulating the courses of the sun and the moon, became, as for Plutarch, simply a goddess of the moon. This goddess of the moon is the female force which inspires men to write poetry. For Graves, the White Goddess dwells in the women around him and he sees Her in their faces.

Toward the end of his life Graves began to work with a Black Goddess as well. He saw this goddess as a secret source of wisdom. Comparing the poet's suffering to the trials of the dying/reborn god, he said in an interview with Leslie Norris that the reward for surviving a series of affairs with the white goddess was to find the black one.

Black Isis

Jung, Campbell and Graves inherited the mindset of empire that Kipling created. While today we do not talk about the "white man's burden" or colonized peoples as "half-demon and half-child", this formulation continues to structure cultural relationships. Wherever we fall on the spectrum of privilege we are all affected by this. It is incumbent on those of us who reconstruct the Pagan religions of the ancient world by using academic material to be alert for racism and anti-Semitism in that material.

Knowing what we know today, that Egyptian/Kemetic culture deeply influenced the Greeks who credited them with great wisdom, that Egypt is not separate from Africa but rooted in African geography and culture, that attempts to define these as Caucasian are clear examples of racist colonialism, it becomes embarrassing to describe the Great Goddess as *white*. It is equally embarrassing to read Graves' discussion of the Black Goddess as a hidden source of wisdom.

European culture assigns oppositional values to the colors white and black.

White	Black
Light	Dark
Conscious	Unconscious
Advanced	Primitive
Adult	Child
Life	Death

These are far from cultural universals; the ancient Egyptians called the black soil which nourished the crops the color of life, and treated the red of the desert as the color of chaos and death.

When genetic heritage is associated with these colors people get labelled too. In the twenty-first century it is both inappropriate and inaccurate to continue to push these cultural values into the future.

Contemporary statues of the neter, the Kemetic deities, come in several colors. Some are bronze or are painted to look like bronze. Some bear white faces even when their costumes are painted in bright colors; others are black. This reflects the varied clientele that purchase these statues. Contemporary European and European-Americans, Pagan or not, like seeing deity with European features. Students of African history create a demand for deity with African features.

As the Pagan and magical communities open up to the discussion of race and the impact of colonialism on our lives, we need look no farther than our own altars for a starting point. Swapping out a few statues won't immediately redress the wrongs of the past, but the ebony statue of Isis standing next to alabaster Athena reminds me of my obligation to question, challenge, and acknowledge.

Works Cited

Bernal, Martin (1987, 2004). Black Athena: Afro-Asiatic Roots of Classical Civilization: The Fabrication of Ancient Greece, 1785-1985 Vol. 1. London: Free Association Books.

Bernstein, Richard (1989). "After Death, a Writer Is Accused of Anti-Semitism." New York Review of Books. Web site: http://www.nytimes.com/1989/11/06/arts/after-death-a-writer-is-accused-of-anti-semitism.html.

Campbell, Joseph (1968). *The Hero with a Thousand Faces.* Princeton: Princeton University Press.

Campbell, Joseph (2008). Pathways to Bliss: Mythology and Personal Transformation. Accessible Publishing Systems PTY, Ltd.

Clarke, Emma, Dillon, John M., Hershbell, Jackson P. (2003). *Iamblichus On The Mysteries.* Atlanta: Society of Biblical Literature.

Dalal, Farhad (1988). "The *Racism of Jung*", Race and Class 19(3).

Diop, Cheik Anta (1974). *The African Origin of Civilization: Myth or Reality.* Chicago: Chicago Review Press.

Gill, Brendan (1989). "The Faces of Joseph Campbell." New York Review of Books. Web site: http://www.nybooks.com/articles/archives/1989/sep/28/the-faces-of-joseph-campbell/

Graves, Robert (1966).*The White Goddess: a Historical Grammar of Poetic Myth.* Farrar, Straus and Giroux.

Isaac, Benjamin (2004). *The Invention of Racism in Classical Antiquity.* Princeton: Princeton University Press.

Kingsley, Peter (2009). "Paths of the Ancient Sages: A Pythagorean History." Rosicrucian Digest, No. 1. Web site: http://www.peterkingsley.net/cw3/Admin/images/Kin gsleyPaths.pdf.

Lefkowitz, Mary R (1997). *Not Out of Africa: How Afrocentrism Became an Excuse to Teach Myth As History.* London: Free Association Books.

Norris, Leslie (1970). "Where the crakeberries grow - Robert Graves gives an account of himself to Leslie Norris". The Listener, 28 May 1970. Web site: http://net.lib.byu.edu/english/wwi/influence/graves.ht ml

Shaw, Gregory (2010). *Theurgy and the Soul, the Neo-Platonism of Iamblichus.* University Park, PA: Pennsylvania State University Press.

Shawl, Nisi (2004). "Appropriate Cultural Appropriation". The Internet Review of Science Fiction. Web site: http://www.irosf.com/q/zine/article/10087.

A King Concealed:
White Privilege in Thelema

Zack Anderson

White privilege and race play an often-ignored but important role in American Thelema. In an institutional context, several factors directly and indirectly create obstacles for non-white people attempting to access these spiritual communities. These obstacles arise from not only the history and current manifestations of systematic, institutional racial discrimination, but from the privileged perspective of Crowley and the majority of white Thelemites. Thelemites should examine their interpretations, practices, and communities in this light, to eliminate the many barriers to participation.

OK, real quick: Thelema is a religion/philosophy/viewpoint developed by the notorious English poet, mountaineer, mystic magician Aleister Crowley. The point is pretty simple: Do what thou wilt shall be the whole of the Law. Love is the law, love under will. Ordo Templi Orientis describes itself as a fraternal organization. It incorporates E.G.C., Ecclesia Gnostica Catholica, a religious organization. O.T.O. and E.G.C exist to promulgate Thelema, were shaped by the work of Aleister Crowley and are Thelemic. Want to learn more? Google it.

When one of the editors of this volume on racism in magical communities asked me to contribute a piece on racism in Crowley's work, I said I had already been thinking about a sociological analysis of how white privilege in the macro culture reinforces racism/elitism in Crowleyanity. I would love to see such an analysis. I was tempted to apologize for the lack of academic rigor, but the editor put it succinctly: "We don't need a sociological survey to start confronting racism, we need to speak our experience." I am not a Sociologist by training but I dabbled in college. Not enough to do the subject any real justice in an academic sense, but my experiences in Thelemic theory and practice have helped me see that all paradoxes must be reconciled if an aspirant is to transcend logic and gain true understanding. Everyone has their crutch, I suppose, for I have such hope that Thelema will be the vehicle that gives spiritual purpose and direction to the international proletarian revolution, yet I have had so much heartache because so many of my white brothers cannot or will not see how this is either not possible, necessary, desirable, or not even in their sphere of consciousness.

"In this country, American means white. Everybody else has to hyphenate." Toni Morrison.

In the grand ol' United States of America, it's all about who you are, and who you aren't. What I am is a White U.S. Euro-American colonial descendent of invaders and squatters, occupying stolen indigenous land, consuming indigenous resources, and taking advantage of a social, economic, and political system that was set up to benefit people like me at the expense of everyone else. My ancestors—mainly Spanish, Norwegian, Scots, and German—came here with their slaves and stole this land, committing genocide on an unparalleled scale in human history. I have no Ellis Island story in my family, no early 20th-century immigration to buffer responsibility for participation in these atrocities. I should probably mention that I am not a 'normal' white person. I'm from the hood; my best friends growing up were black, most of my friends are non-white people, the majority of people in our neighborhood and at our schools were black, I listen to black music and watch black movies, my casual and default mode of speech falls far outside "Standard American English" My parents are political activists who instilled in me anti-racist values. I don't consider myself a part of white culture at all, at least in any voluntary way! So I think it was interesting that I ended up joining an order that is so painfully white.

White normativity is problematic when it is the context in which Thelema is promulgated. *Do what thou wilt shall be the whole of the Law*; this is much less of a challenge for someone who has had countless benefits from birth bestowed upon them. I argue that it is much harder for someone to discover and do their True Wills—the sole commandment of Thelema—when they are hindered from before birth by intergenerational poverty, poor nutrition, substandard education, lack of interesting or meaningful employment, and an oppressive police state that singles out non-white people for mass incarceration. These problems are far from just black problems, but as race and socioeconomic status are inseparably intertwined in ameriKKKa, they are not problems that the average white person has to face daily. That's the point that I am trying to make: if O.T.O in the USA, and US-Euro-American settler/invader descendent Thelemites in general, aim to implement the Law of Thelema in any real context, they are going to have to see Thelema from the point of view of those who are expected to take orders. How can someone blind to their own privilege see how the Rights of Man are thwarted when they have never had their rights seriously challenged?

So where do we begin to challenge white Thelemites' perspective? I think that Cat Yronwode has proposed a good first step:

"If Crowley's aeonic dream of a world that embraces Thelemic religion and practice is to ever develop into anything more than a small club, the international O.T.O., like the Mormon church before it, is going to have to work out a strategy to acknowledge and deal openly with the fact that the originator of virtually the entire corpus of Thelemic theoretical, practical, and liturgical text was a racist and that his personal reminiscences and magical lessons contain explicitly racist statements of belief and/or advocate specific forms of racist behaviour."

Oh yeah, that's right, Aleister Crowley himself was a huge bigot. So of course a lot of the discourse around the political interpretation of Thelema has been by right-wingers of various degrees of viciousness; sure, you can interpret the Book of the Law as the ultimate Libertarian wet dream, with such gems as: "We have nothing with the outcast and the unfit: let them die in their misery. For they feel not. Compassion is the vice of kings: stamp down the wretched & the weak: this is the law of the strong: this is our law and the joy of the world."

and:

"Therefore the kings of the earth shall be Kings forever: the slaves shall serve. There is none that shall be cast down or lifted up: all is ever as it was."

Of course, there are Christians who use Bible verses to justify bombing abortion clinics, Muslims who use the Quran to justify stoning adulterers to death, and Jews who use the Torah to justify apartheid in Israel, so we all know that right-wing fascist conservative ideas can be justified by taking pretty much anything out of context. It's not my place to tell people how to interpret the Book of the Law, but I've seen about eight years' worth of white men using it to justify their racist views and political activity.

This is not an exhaustive survey of Aleister Crowley's views on race—not only has it been done already, and I recommend you read it[80], but I honestly don't think I can stomach any more of the nastier details of The Beast's views about and treatment toward people of color. Here's a nice sample from one of his more available editions:

"...we [British] always somehow instinctively think of the Italian as a nigger. We don't call them "dagos" and "wops" as they do in the United States, with the invariable epithet of "dirty"; but we have the same feeling."[81]

I think that the number-one reason there are barely any people of color in the OTO is that people who have blatantly racist views are accepted, and any attempt to properly address the people who spout these views is met as a violation of Pax Templi or slander, unfraternal conduct or some other such garbage.

Luckily, there are plenty of non-white Thelemites to ask about this matter. Wait... are there?

US Grand Lodge doesn't ask for race on their initiation forms, nor do they keep or publish demographic statistics such as race. This paper is limited by my own perspective, and while I certainly have not met the majority of Thelemites in the US or visited a great number of O.T.O. Bodies, I can count the non-white Thelemites I know on one hand. 85 of my friends on Facebook are O.T.O. members, and 4 are non-white. Virtually all the key executive leadership positions, nationally and internationally, are filled by exclusively white (or at least passing white) males. After many years as an extremely active O.T.O.

---

[80] http://www.arcane-archive.org/faqs/crowleyracistfaq.php
[81] Diary of a Drug Fiend" Book I, Chapter 9

member, I know barely any non-white Thelemites. Sure, there are a few, but from everything I saw in seven years, the O.T.O. is almost completely white.

I got into the O.T.O. because my late best friend (who was black) and I got really into conspiracy theories, New World Order, and the Holy Blood, Holy Grail stuff. Rappers like Jay-Z, Prodigy and Tragedy Khadafi all talked about the Illuminati and we were watching old-school Afro-Futurist bootlegs like Sun-Ra's *Space is the Place*. There's a huge interest in the occult in the hip-hop community (like urban, an academic way to say black people). I personally have so many black friends, living and dead, that are or were into the occult or at least really fascinated with conspiracy theories and secret knowledge or Egyptian gods or Afro-futurism, or whatever, that I can't even count. I found a bunch of Crowley books and studied the shit out of them, looked up O.T.O. online, and found a genuine Lodge of the actual O.T.O., right in my hometown! And me with all this Crowley and Qabalah and Tarot and everything else under the sun under my belt? And two willing sponsors and eighty bucks is all I need to be initiated into the same Holy Order that THE BEAST TO MEGA THERION ALEISTER CROWLEY HIMSELF was the Head of? Shit man, sign me up! And I thought it would be a quick jump to sign up all my esoterically-inclined political revolutionary friends from the hood too! Why didn't they? I mean, isn't the Law of Thelema the perfect vehicle for change, for personal transformation and group organization toward the People's Revolution? What sweeter song plays on the ear of any anti-racist human being than "Every man and every woman is a star"? The Centennial edition of Liber AL ends with a colophon about organizing for the fight for freedom! The Fight for Freedom? Dressing up like a Pharaoh with a naked Priestess? Sign us all up, I thought!

So what happened?

No black people that I know wanted to join the O.T.O. This is not stated as a universal, objective fact, but as a personal observation. This is a huge problem if the O.T.O. in the United States is to achieve the goal of creating a new society along Thelemic lines (or any major significance whatsoever). None of my black friends wanted to join the OTO, because they all asked me how many black people were in our local lodge. When I said "well, none that I have met", that was that. Red wine and brie and English poetry and industrial music? The lodge that I was a member of created a very suburban setting, despite our urban warehouse location, and I personally felt that most young black people didn't feel like they were made especially welcome, when they came at all. Either that, or the reception was *too* friendly, and non-white people can tell the difference between a legitimate interest in them as a human and a Thelemite, and the glee of guilty liberal whites to have a potential new token black to legitimize their white hegemony.

There is a reality that white Thelemites need to face. Racism doesn't end at the doors of the temple. Becoming initiated in the mysteries doesn't deconstruct a lifetime of conditioning as a beneficiary of a racist system. I think that the O.T.O. is organized as an intentional culture—there are multiple documents that explicitly lay this out, such as *Liber CI* and *Liber CXCIV*—but we bring in all the baggage of our underlying cultures with us when we come into the door, including white privilege.

The O.T.O. has its rules and regulations, but Crowley left a very skeletal system for us to monkey around with and fill in the gaps. Naturally, a lot of these gaps are going to be filled in by people who exist in the context of their place and time in history, and when this context is the context of invasion, colonization, genocide, slavery, war, greed, pollution, and ongoing structural institutionalized racism in every facet of amerikan life, we are going to get a lot of subliminal, covert racism in the mix. What do we expect to happen when black people make contact with the O.T.O., seemingly so full of progressive ideas, and the system is exposed to be just as white-dominated as the rest of our society? From the outside, the O.T.O. looks like just another power structure, set up by white people, in which success depends on following white patterns of speech, dress, and life? When you are forced to spend your entire life struggling to please white Hierophants—teachers, judges, bosses—why pay monthly dues for just another white boss to have to dance for? Thelema has so much to offer to all people, especially the oppressed peoples of this world, but the O.T.O. has very little to offer those who still struggle to break free from the chains of oppression.

Peggy Macintosh wrote: "In my class and place, I did not see myself as a racist because I was taught to recognize racism only in individual acts of meanness by members of my group, never in invisible systems conferring unsought racial dominance on my group from birth."[82]

I think a lot of white Thelemites would benefit greatly from looking at how, even though they themselves might find racism abhorrent, they still personally benefit from a racist system, both in the O.T.O. context, and in the real world. That is the MEAT of what I am getting at, and what really sucks is that it has to come from my perspective, a white perspective, and maybe I am more advanced in my contempt and disdain for the honky cultural steamroller of homogeneity, genocide, lukewarm slavery and all the rest of the amerikan dream bullshit, but goddamn, I know so few black Thelemites that I can't even present you with one lousy direct quote from a single non-white Thelemite. I can tell you one thing though, from my own perspective, and that is that when I challenged racism (or fascism) in the Thelemic community, I was made unwelcome.

Maybe that's the bare root of the O.T.O.'s problem right there: many O.T.O. members can probably count all their black friends—make a list of all the black people they know, and it would not be the longest list in most cases. Yes, there are exceptions, but from my experience, most white Thelemites are living in the bubble of white privilege, at least to some extent.

White Privilege is simple: the undeniable facts of amerikan HIStory are that this nation was founded by genocide, conquest, and slavery. The entire land area of the United States was stolen from indigenous peoples by my ancestors who destroyed countless ways of life, cultures, languages, histories, economies, social structures, and religious practices. Asymmetric warfare, scalping, smallpox, concentration camps, death marches, rape and mutilation and murder. Our ancestors also kidnapped millions of people from Africa, destroying their ways of life in just the same fashion, and brought them here to work as slaves, to build this Great Nation for free, streets and bridges and buildings for the white man to set up his institutions and governments in.

---

[82] https://www.isr.umich.edu/home/diversity/resources/white-privilege.pdf

In his Slate article "Why Do White People Think Mitt Romney Should Be President?", Tom Scocca observed, "White people don't like to believe that they practice identity politics. The defining part of being white in America is the assumption that, as a white person, you are a regular, individual human being. Other demographic groups set themselves apart, to pursue their distinctive identities and interests and agendas. Whiteness, to white people, is the American default."[83]

The history of ameriKKKa as a racist empire built on slavery and genocide is a matter of record, but what does this have to do with occultism, Thelema, Aleister Crowley, or the current incarnation of Ordo Templi Orientis in the United States?

The simple answer is: context. Our history shapes the present, and the present day social, economic, political, and (in our case) religious institutions have been set up to systematically perpetuate a racist, white supremacist ideology. Which means that the white man set up the system to give himself every advantage, primarily by denying non-whites access to the same housing, education, economic opportunities, civil rights, fair and impartial judiciary, and social status that we, as White Americans enjoy. I recommend the seminal article on White Privilege, called "Unpacking the Invisible Knapsack" by Peggy Macintosh. The author presents a very long list of societal benefits that white people take for granted, such as:

"I can if I wish arrange to be in the company of people of my race most of the time.

When I am told about our national heritage or about "civilization," I am shown that people of my color made it what it is.

I can do well in a challenging situation without being called a credit to my race.

I am never asked to speak for all the people of my racial group.

I can remain oblivious of the language and customs of persons of color who constitute the world's majority without feeling in my culture any penalty for such oblivion.

[83]http://www.slate.com/articles/news_and_politics/scocca/2012/11/mitt_romney_white_vote_parsing_the_narrow_tribal_appeal_of_the_republican.html

I can be pretty sure that if I ask to talk to the "person in charge", I will be facing a person of my race.

If I have low credibility as a leader I can be sure that my race is not the problem.

I can easily find academic courses and institutions which give attention only to people of my race.

I can expect figurative language and imagery in all of the arts to testify to experiences of my race."

Let's look at White Privilege in an O.T.O. context:

I can expect to meet a number of Thelemites of my race.

Members of my race are well-represented in Thelema, both historically and presently. Aleister Crowley was a white Englishman. His 3 successor heads of O.T.O. have all been white.

I can reasonably expect the local officers, my initiators, and clergy to be mostly white.

My interest in Thelema will not be considered unduly unusual for a member of my race.

If I wished, I could practice Thelema exclusively with members of my own race without difficulty.

I can act inappropriately at an O.T.O. event and my actions will not reflect on my race.

I can expect my subculture to be represented in O.T.O.

I am never looked upon as the White Thelemite in the group

I am not asked by my brethren for advice on how to attract new initiates from my racial group.

I will probably not be personally offended by Aleister Crowley's characterization of my racial group.

My tastes in clothing, music, &c. will not be attributed to my race.

Any scrutiny toward my ability to maintain financial obligations (i.e.: monthly/yearly dues, initiation fees, wine & roses, feast food and candles) will not be based on my race.

Racism in societal, educational, governmental, and religious institutions does not negatively impact my ability to Find and Do my True Will! This is arguably the most important privilege that white Thelemites possess—the deck is not stacked against us to begin with—we are free to Eat Pray Love and the biggest obstacle is saving up vacation time at work. We are not hampered by substandard education from resource-starved inner-city schools, we do not have to overcome bigoted barriers to meaningful and fulfilling employment, we are not forced into survival mode by a culture that is hostile to us from childhood so that "Do what thou wilt" isn't even a possibility. The American Dream is actually very Thelemic — but only if you're white.

This is the tip of the iceberg. I am pretty sure that any Thelemite reading this can probably name at least a few more privileges that White people enjoy without even realizing it.

Upon joining the O.T.O., I had to deal with being called 'ghetto' and being subject to extra scrutiny because of my cultural and social connections within the black community. When my best friend was brutally murdered a few years later, I found a local Thelemic community wholly unprepared and unable to provide any meaningful support, because the experience was so far from the realms of the "normal" that I actually began to feel like I was in the wrong for "bringing in" such bummers as murder and racist police indifference. The insensitive comments alone should have led to my resignation, but I really *believed* in the mission of the O.T.O.!

I had to deal with being ridiculed for my subcultural clothing choices. I would get hassled for saggy baggy jeans while the freakiest Goth gear was accepted without comment, usually enthusiastically. I was told I-don't-know-how-many times to pull my pants up! Me, a grown Man and Brother, being told to hike up my pants like I was a schoolboy! I am not wasting space to explain why sagging pants should fall under Man has the right to dress as he Will — a quote from Liber OZ, Crowley's Declaration of the Rights of Man.

Quick note on Islamophobia: There's a fine line between the expected and encouraged general disdain for Abrahamic religion, especially the fundamentalist varieties, that you would naturally expect in a group with the O.T.O.'s Aeonic view of religious validity and rightful spiritual succession, and blatant band-wagoning on Post-9/11 Islamophobia. I've heard some vicious rants and blatant bigotry against leveled unfairly against Muslims. My hometown is host to several very large Muslim immigrant communities. We should be establishing an ecumenical dialogue to better facilitate social reform along mutually beneficial lines, not putting ourselves on a pedestal and vilifying our neighbors because of the actions of fundamentalists. In fact, I have witnessed a woman in hijab leave a Gnostic Mass before it even began because she felt a palpable unwelcoming presence in the room; a heartbreaking loss, she didn't even get to see the Priestess embody the Divine Feminine and show the other side of the veil, so to speak.

This is an example of the Hate Stare in action. John Howard Griffin, the intrepid author of *Black Like Me*, experienced something in his weeks undercover as a black man in the South that astounded him, sickened him, and made him realize something that most white people never will—that most white people have a visible adverse reaction upon the sight of a non-white person. He called it the Hate Stare. I am not saying that all, most, the majority, or even a sizable minority of Thelemites give non-white guests the hate stare—but it only takes one person to alienate.

We talk about how our series of magical rites progressively conditions a person to become a more efficient Thelemite, more able to find and do our True Wills, but I question if we really change that much when the initiator is white, the assistants are white, the candidates are white, and—come to think of it—sometimes everyone in the room might just be white. We dress in our interpretation of ancient cultures, we pluck and choose the cool stuff from every sacred creed and faith in the name of syncretism, mangle divine names and promulgate false etymologies, and we eat our way across the Mediterranean. How could we be racist? Our exalted status does not permit us to allow the possibility of any non-Thelemite as an equal, much less those scary black people we see on the drive to our rented warehouse lodge spaces in gentrified hipster urban enclaves.

The high cost of O.T.O. is also a barrier to non-white participation (of course, not all non-white people are poor and not all white people can afford it either). This is not a specific critique of the cost itself—I was there for years, it costs a lot to run a lodge—but I spent about $1000 a year on O.T.O., including dues, fees, local dues, donations, costumes, wine, feasts, incense, candles, roses, and temple improvements. That is a LOT of money for oppressed people. Speaking of dollars, if I had a dollar for every time some Thelemite took offense because I implied they were racist, I would never had had to come out of pocket for a single bottle of wine or missed a monthly dues payment!

My O.T.O. career is marked with several 'incidents' that all stemmed from mycompletely unfraternal intolerance for intolerance! I guess Peace, Tolerance, Truth is the O.T.O.'s motto on their frontispiece but not on their minds, because I every time some white person made some abominably racist or classist remark and I told them what the fuck I actually thought of them, I was always told that I was being unfraternal, intolerant of others' views, and disrupting Pax Templi.

Do you, the reader, know that Latin phrase? It means "Peace in the Temple", and was supposed to allow even combatants in war the chance to worship in peace: "Public enemies of the country of any Brother shall be treated as such while in the field, and slain or captured as the officer of the Brother may command. But within the precincts of the Lodge all such divisions are to be forgotten absolutely; and as children of One Father the enemies of the hour before and the hour after are to dwell in peace, amity, and fraternity."

I argue that confronting racism in the O.T.O. is a necessary part of Pax Templi, but I guess the leadership must not feel that way. It took me eight years and a liberal arts degree to figure out that there was no Pax Templi, because overt racism and white supremacy is not challenged in the O.T.O. Nothing really is, and while there have been whole mini-movements (mostly online but including vanity press and local disruptions) that challenge what they perceive as the complacency of the O.T.O. in X, Y, Z... the point is that those critics usually tend to be the libertarian white upper-class socially-introverted egocentric fascist crowds. Hey, there's one I got in trouble for, calling someone a fascist who publicly aligned with a fascist political party! Or calling someone racist for making a derogatory remark about Martin Luther King Jr on a podcast released on his federal holiday! Or when I cussed out two Republicans who laughed in my face when I described the treatment of Indigenous peoples during their genocide here in our hometown (not two miles from one of their homes, no less)! See the pattern? White people don't like to be called racist, because they can't even see the many ways in which the deck is stacked for them, or the many ways in which they are socialized to think and act within a system that seems totally normal.

Macintosh wrote: "It is an open question whether we will choose to use unearned advantage, and whether we will use any of our arbitrarily awarded power to try to reconstruct power systems on a broader base."

If American Thelemites are ever going to have a chance to reconstruct our power systems, we are going to have to come to terms with Thelema's race problem, because like America's race problem, it won't just go away by ignoring it. We have to leap headfirst into the Abyss, certain that the power of Thelema as a revolutionary force for freedom will propel us past the gulf of ignorance, superstition, and tyranny that is Whiteness in America.

Ancestor Work and Anti-Racism

Rhiannon Theurer

As a white American living on occupied land, I have had the luxury of taking my race for granted, not having to think about my whiteness because it is the cultural default. I was taught as a child that racism was bad, and that I should not perpetuate discrimination and hate. Being anti-racist was part of a general set of values around fairness and equality, but I was never taught exactly how racism affected me personally.

As an adult I took on the project of understanding my own whiteness, moving beyond the idea of seeing my own marginalized identities and instead examining unearned powers bestowed upon me. I read books by people of color and white allies and reflected upon these stories, recognizing them as gifts given in the face of much pain. I learned to sit quietly, especially when I didn't understand what was being said, and recognized that my impulse to immediately contest experiences and to feel alienated by how the information was presented was itself a reflection of my privileges.

I still believe in the values of fairness and equality that I was taught as a child. But being an anti-racist activist solely for the benefit of others has an air of self-congratulatory paternalism. We are all implicated in systems of oppression, and it is only by examining what is at stake for each of us – both privileges and loss -- that we can build a new world.

I have often heard laments about "not having any culture" from fellow whites, particularly from progressives who feel alienated from the American capitalist overculture. I remember one friend years ago wishing she was from Europe, and another friend rightly pointed out that we were in the South, with all its astonishing cultural richness. I nodded uneasily, grateful for the acknowledgment of local culture, yet uncomfortable since we were all white and so much of what makes the South "the South" is rooted in its unacknowledged black culture. Moreover, it did not address the root cause of my friend's pain: What is my culture? I have heard complaints and wistful laments that people of color get to have, well, "color" – however denigrated and derided that color is -- while white is blankness, blandness, a monochromatic stillness.

Yet for those of us who are white, our ancestors did not arrive on these shores as "white." They may or may not have had the cultural status of whiteness when they arrived (since race is an ever-changing social construct, not a biological reality), but they were English, Irish, Italian, Latvian. But to successfully assimilate and become "American," they had to give up languages, customs, cuisines and other markers of their home cultures. For their descendants today, it is by looking to our ancestors and what they gave up that we can truly begin to understand the cost of white supremacy in our own lives.

I did not understand this cost until I built an ancestor shrine. It is a simple affair, a wooden box with three shelves, lined with pictures and a few mementoes. Every morning I make my coffee and go and greet the ancestors, both the few I have pictures of, and all the many others whose faces I do not know. The picture of my mother's mother's mother greets me. It is from later in her life, and she stands small yet strong, looking every inch the archetypal wise woman. I am compelled by her picture above all others, and as I look at her I wonder what she would think of her great-granddaughter half a world away, trying to reach out across the barriers of time, distance, language, and American and Soviet imperialism to connect with her. I keenly feel how much has been lost between us. It has been easier to find factual information on my paternal line[84], as they have been in the United States for longer than my maternal line, yet in some ways that makes them even more remote. There is no living memory of the language or customs they brought with them. Every day as I stand in front of my ancestors, I am reminded of what has been lost.

---

[84]Genealogical work itself lends itself to an examination of all kinds of privilege, both in the content and existence of records. Who are there official records on, and what is the quantity and quality of those records? Can you read the language the records are in? If your ancestors are listed in sources like the US Census records, you may be able to learn literacy, education level, occupations, whether or not your ancestors owned or rented their homes.

I recognize my privilege in knowing even the most general information about my ancestors; I know that is not the case for everyone. But whether you know your ancestors or not, they are still waiting for us and have lessons to teach. In the center of my ancestral altar is an empty space. For a long time I felt the need to put something there, yet nothing seemed quite right. It is only in writing this essay that I realize why: we need to hold a space for the unknown ancestors, those hidden from us by time, trauma, and other disavowals and dislocations. For some of us, that is all we have. But at some point, all of our ancestors are unknown; at some point, all of our ancestors are the same. The space in the center of my altar reminds me of this mystery, and invites space for those who have been lost to be remembered.

Ancestor work can encompass not only those ancestors of blood, but of affinity as well. Whites seeking to dismantle white supremacy and racism will face criticism, and may not have family members or peers who will support this work. But there have always been people who have fought for equality, including whites who fought racism. Reflect on the lives of John Brown, the fervent abolitionist who attempted to overthrow slavery by armed insurrection; Helen Keller, who in addition to being a disability rights activist was an ardent socialist and vocal opponent of segregation; Viola Liuzzo, the civil rights worker who died in support of what she described as "everyone's fight"; Peter Norman, the Olympian who never backed down from his support of John Carlos and Tommie Smith's Black Power protest, even at the cost of his own career and legacy. Meditate on those Polish mercenaries who, sent to Haiti to suppress the Revolution, instead chose to fight alongside the Haitians. Light a candle for the factory workers in Northern England who recognized their common cause with enslaved Africans and so agitated for abolition. These histories have also been suppressed in the furtherance of a racist agenda; it makes our work so much easier when we know others have begun the path.

Some questions you may ask as you dig deeper into your own ancestral work to support anti-racism are: Do you have the privilege of knowing anything about your ancestors, and what historical forces have shaped your access to that information? Are there ancestral lines you or your family emphasize or downplay? What are your feelings about the groups you are descended from? When have you felt closer or more distant to different parts of your heritage? Are your ancestral cultures represented in the overculture? If so, how? Who are the ancestors of the land, both human and not human, where you live? If they are no longer here, why is that? What are their stories and how can you honor them as well?

A few words of caution: cultural change and exchange are not inherently negative processes and are perhaps inevitable. That our ancestors adapted to new lands and experiences is a sign of strength, resiliency, and creativity, such as Chinese cooks in Mississippi making stir fries of turnip greens and salt pork. Much richness is to be found on these cultural edges. But cultural exchange becomes more problematic, however, when one group has economic and military power over another. When people are implicitly or explicitly told they must give up their cultural practices to access what they need to live, that is a process of colonization.

I also want to emphasize that the effects of white supremacy fall on a continuum. I have no doubt that my Irish ancestors faced discrimination when they arrived in the United States, on top of centuries of being the laboratory for British imperialism. Even more recently, my Polish grandparents endured concentration camps and enforced labor because the Nazi regime considered our people "subhuman." This suffering is real and needs to be acknowledged. However, I also need to acknowledge that my ancestors were able to find refuge in this land because it had been forcibly taken from indigenous people; I do not suffer housing or employment discrimination on the basis of my ethnic heritage; I can easily find images of culturally sanctioned beauty that resemble me; no police officer would be pulling me over for "driving while Irish/German/Polish." The sufferings of my ancestors can give me a window into imaging the experience of those currently more of a target of white supremacy, but it does not make my experience equivalent to those groups.

Honoring our ancestors restores the complexity and diversity lost under the blanket of "whiteness." By reclaiming all the parts of our pasts, we become more powerful and more of who we are. We cannot recreate the past; I am not Polish, Irish, or German. But I am Polish-Irish-German American, and that is fertile ground to begin playing in. Let us join together in our uniqueness, honor all the ancestors, and create a more beautiful and just future for our descendants.

Racism, Heathenry, and Frith

Ryan Smith

In September 2013 there was a virtual explosion of activity, discussion, and debate on the question of racism in Paganism. These recent kicked off on August 19th when the blog *Who Makes the Nazis* published a piece on Stella Natura, a rock festival attended and endorsed by a number of racist and neo-Nazi acts. This article was circulated on social media by a number of different Pagan bloggers. This was followed by a four part series by the Circle Ansuz collective on the beliefs, ideas, and associations of Stephen McNallen and the Asatru Folk Assembly (AFA). A Wild Hunt Community Notes update on August 20th reported on the Circle Ansuz piece.

Next Piparskeggr Skald, a prominent AFA member, posted a blog entry titled, "A short note on my associations" at *Witches & Pagans* which began with, "I am a man who freely admits that I am most comfortable with folks who resemble me most strongly". Morpheus Ravenna, another blogger on *Witches & Pagans*, swiftly responded with the excellent rebuttal "Whose Ancestors". Due the controversy which erupted over these entries the Piparskeggr piece was deleted in its entirety. Morpheus Ravenna said of her post "It was subsequently deleted by the site's editor, Anne Newkirk Niven, specifically in order to censor its content, because she objected to my calling the AFA a racist organization." John Beckett added his voice to the debate on Patheos, joining Ravenna and other anti-racist Pagan voices in their condemnation of racist and racialist ideology in Paganism. On Wednesday, September 11th Sam Warren joined in, neatly summarizing the fallacies and falsehoods of racialist practice at *Witches & Pagans* while providing the only online record of Piparskeggr's words.

The handling of this, in particular Witches & Pagans' decision to censor Morpheus Ravenna and destroy the record of Piparskeggr's racist statements, is unfortunately par for the course in the Pagan and Heathen communities. As is often the case in the Heathen community whenever the issues of racism, racialist affiliations, or fascist sympathies come up, the first response from those in positions of authority is nearly always, "Don't break the frith!" Regardless of whatever vile, morally repugnant, or outright false claims are being made what is most important is not causing a scene. The wider Pagan community shares a similar discomfort with rocking the boat for fear that if we cause too much trouble we'll capsize our collective ship. What this line of reasoning fails to consider is whether keeping an even keel is a good idea when someone has hijacked the helm and is setting course for destruction.

Thankfully this attitude is no longer the only norm as the outcry has demonstrated. Unfortunately the outcry is the exception to the rule. For every Pagan who has spoken out on this issue there are many more Heathen leaders, teachers, and authors who have remained silent for fear of breaking frith. This in spite of the fact that most in the Heathen community have been exposed to at least one hair-raisingly racist story about Stephen McNallen and the AFA. A personal friend of mine reported being asked by AFA officers NOT to use their Hispanic last name in their email handle on AFA discussion lists because it would cause problems. Another Heathen related the time they were informed by an AFA group in no uncertain terms they could not guarantee their safety if they chose to attend an AFA blot solely because of the color of their skin. When AFA members were seen attending a white supremacist conference Stephen McNallen rose to their defense. McNallen's post on the AFA blog "Wotan v. Tezcatlipoca: The Spiritual War for California and the Southwest" argues that the return of the goddess Tonatzin among Chicanos will result in the subordination of European-Americans to Mexican-Americans unless the European settlers engage in cultural resistance.

These stories are not unique; if anything they're distressingly common. It's not as if there is any great mystery on the subject as to how McNallen feels or what his organization stands for. The only thing recent discussion and blog posts have done is put it all together. Among the allegations and examples given by Circle Ansuz the only ones which surprised me were his paling around with Afrikaner death squads, and the rumors of a coup in Forn Sidr, the Aesir and Vanir faith community in

Denmark, purging those who did not agree with AFA-style politics. Sadly these latest charges Circle Ansuz has put forward, far from being an unusual exception, are directly in line with many of the other ugly facts which have been swarming around McNallen and his cohorts for years.

Considering these recent actions I feel binding ourselves to some illusory peace, which the AFA clearly has no intention of respecting, is foolish in the extreme. Our community is growing and becoming increasingly visible. As one example of this we have a recent survey by Indiana University of Pennsylvania which pegs "Wicca" as the fifth largest and fastest growing religion in the United States. Now, granted, many Pagans do not identify as Wiccans, and, it is likely the survey lumped Pagans under the Wiccan umbrella. Whatever they meant by the term, it is notable that "Wiccans" are more numerous than Buddhists in America.

The result of this growing popularity is that it is very likely Heathenry will be coming under the scrutiny of mainstream society within the next decade. In popular culture things Viking-related, ranging from the recent *Thor* movies to the History Channel's series on the Vikings, are already making themselves more visible to the public. It is only a matter of time before the mainstream starts asking serious, probing questions about our ideas, practices, and the makeup of our community. The moment they see our community not only has a large, vocal racist tendency but that the rest of the community treating it like an invisible two ton gorilla, it is highly unlikely broader society is going to draw any distinctions between the racialists and everyone else. If you don't believe me just hop on over to any Pagan group out there and ask if people think Heathens are all racists; you'll be picking your jaw up off the floor after the first flood of comments subsides and that's coming from a community that knows us better than society at large does.

To this issue the racialists and their apologists, defenders, and enablers inevitably cry, "You're a hypocrite! How can you call for tolerance on one hand while denouncing Folkish practice on the other! You're the real racist here, not us!"

Of course these screams and protests miss the point completely. In making this argument they imply those who take a tolerant position MUST accept all viewpoints regardless of the actions, consequences, and implications of those positions. By arguing those opposed to racist and racialist practice are the real bigots they are twisting the meaning of two important words into something completely different from what they mean.

As a point of fact here is the definition of tolerance as per dictionary.com:

> 1. a fair, objective, and permissive attitude toward those whose opinions, practices, race, religion, nationality,etc., differ from one's own; freedom from bigotry.
>
> 2. a fair,objective, and permissive attitude toward opinions and practices that differ from one's own.
>
> 3. interestinand concern for ideas, opinions, practices, etc., foreignto one's own; a liberal, undogmatic viewpoint.

And here is the definition of bigotry:

> plural bigotries.
>
> 1. stubbornand complete intolerance of any creed, belief, or opinionthatdiffers from one's own.
>
> 2. the actions,beliefs,prejudices, etc., of a bigot.

Having consulted this very simple, easy to verify definition it is clear that claiming any individual who does not meet the appropriate blood descent criteria may not practice Heathenry fits squarely under the heading of bigotry. Furthermore, there is nothing in the definition of tolerance which suggests the tolerant must tolerate those who actively work to force their prejudices on others.

Racialists argue that racist, ethnocentric determinations for spirituality are not racist because there's plenty of other cultures that do it. They are often quick to cite Judaism and Native American practice as two prominent examples. From here they claim those opposed to racism are being hypocritical whitepeople are denounced for doing what non-white people can do with impunity.

This is, yet again, a gross distortion of the facts. Citing Judaism and Native American practice as justification does not hold water. In the case of Native Americans the blood quotient system was not an organic development of the myriad of cultures which fall under that broad umbrella but was imposed by the Bureau of Indian Affairs as one tool of many used to break the last vestiges of resistance following their near-extermination and confinement to reservations. Judaism, similarly, accepts converts in even the most Orthodox of branches.

While it is true that both Native American and Jewish communities have practices based on specific descent, what the racialists completely miss is that this descent is not based on ethnicity. Native American and Judaic practices have very specific rules for this. In Judaism one is considered part of the community and is accepted into the faith without question if at least one of their parents is also Jewish. It doesn't matter where the parent is from, what color their skin is, or which Jewish tradition they come from - if one parent is Jewish then their child has the right to make the same claim. Native American practices vary wildly from tribe to tribe but what they all have in common is a specific, quantifiable claim, such as requiring a specific level of verified descent from the tribe in question. Even in the case of the Scottish clans, an example from my heritage, the only requirements for being a member of a clan is proving descent from Scotland and having a surname which is part of a recognized clan. In contrast, the Asatru Folk Assembly and other prominent Folkish advocates have no set standard, consistent measurement, or other uniform approach for determining the "correct" amount of Germanic descent to participate.

On a deeper level the problem of racialism and racism in our community isn't just an issue of the lack of justification for the proponents' claims or the shame society as a whole will heap on Heathenry and Paganism when they really start paying attention. Racism, prejudice, and bigotry in many ways are head-first at odds with the core of Heathen ethical practice. As Heathens we are encouraged by the Eddas to boldly face obstacles, struggle, and challenges to our communities, seek out knowledge and experiences so we may grow as individuals and as a community, and live every moment knowing our honor is the sum of our speech and actions.

Those who wallow in shallow, artificial prejudices do so in defiance of these virtues. By fearing others based on superficial differences they forsake their courage, living the life of the craven coward quivering in fear of their fellow human beings. In shutting themselves off from vast swaths of the world they atrophy their minds letting ignorance, myopia, and dogma reign. Above all else their speech and actions propagating their brand of hatred shames their own honor, and by calling themselves Heathens it brings unwarranted shame on the whole of the Folk.

It is long past time for the Heathen community to stand up to these honorless cowards. They have made it plain they see it as a holy mission to drag as many as they can into their fold. The purge in the Denmark group shows no matter what noises they and their apologists make for frith and community they will not respect the boundaries set by others. Standing up to them will not be easy, quick, or painless by any stretch of the imagination. Many fear what may come of a genuine struggle to redeem the honor of our Folk, seeing the price as too high.

Yet in spite of these understandable reservations, events have made it clear the price of doing nothing is far steeper than the price of doing something. It is time we heed the example of the wisdom of the lore, all of our ancestors, and of the Holy Powers and take necessary action. As is eloquently stated in the Sayings of the High One:

> The sluggard believes he shall live forever,
> If the fight he faces not;
> But age shall not grant him the gift of peace,
> Though spears may spare his life.

Havamal 16

Beyond the Pale:
Lifting IK and Inventing Identity

Pegi Eyers

After years of dwelling in the margins of the dominant society, the First Nation Elders, leaders and academics of Turtle Island are finally coming forth to tell modern spiritual seekers that *"everyone needs to get back to their own Indigenous Knowledge (IK)."*[85] This simple statement has massive ramifications, and exposes years of systemic racism and white privilege that has led to the cultural appropriation of native spirituality on a colossal scale. First Nations have endured genocide, displacement, colonial oppression and assimilation for centuries, and the least we can do, as the descendants of the Settler Society (or those more recently arrived to Turtle Island) is to listen deeply to this directive coming from Indian Country, and all that it implies.

---

[85] The mandate to recover one's authentic indigenous roots is being reinforced by elders, indigenous activists, scholars and visionaries all over Turtle Island. Highly-esteemed mentor, wisdom keeper and Professor James Dumont (Anishnaabe) is telling us that *"everyone needs to get back to their own IK."* (James Dumont, "Introductory Remarks," *Traditional Elders Conference*, Trent University, Peterborough, Ontario, 2011) Chief Arvol Looking Horse (Lakota/Dakota/Nakota), Keeper of the Sacred White Buffalo Calf Pipe stated in 2012 that *"the effort to protect Mother Earth is all of humanity's responsibility, not just aboriginal people. Every human being has Ancestors in their lineage that understood their umbilical cord to the Earth, and to always protect and thank Her. Therefore, all humanity has to re-connect to the Indigenous Roots of their own lineage - to heal their connection and responsibility to Mother Earth."* ("Letter from Chief Arvol Looking Horse in Solidarity with Idle No More," http://ndnnews.com/2012/12/this-is-about-mother-earth-statement-from-chief-arvol-looking-horse) Simon Brascoupe (Anishinabeg/Haudenausanee) in his 1998 essay "Aboriginal Peoples' Vision of the Future: Interweaving Traditional Knowledge and New Technologies" tells us that *"the world will have to change its basic value system to save the planet. This is not to say that westerners should become like aboriginal peoples. But Western society needs to learn from indigenous peoples about respecting and living harmoniously with Mother Earth, and return to their own religious and spiritual teachings, their own ancient systems of knowledge, and the customs and practices that respect Mother Earth."* David Long and Olive Patricia Dickason (editors), *Visions of the Heart: Canadian Aboriginal Issues*, Thomson-Nelson, 1998.

The challenge today is to turn back or move forward to more sustainable eco-ethics, and to take on the work of decolonizing our hearts, minds and opulent lifestyles. We need to re-enchant and rebalance the world with a massive injection of holistic principles promoting biophilia, personal and planetary healing, rewilding, peace-making, social justice, earth-connected sustainability and peaceful co-existence. This resurgence is happening in all sectors of society, and the Pagan Community is also doing a wonderful job at bending the curve.[86] But what is often missing in these practices are the spiritual expressions that would arise from a strong, grounded connection to the land itself, from the recovery of our own ancestral traditions, and from "*getting back to our own IK.*"

Too often, statements of eco-consciousness that are present in Pagan ventures and projects are token injections of some aspect of blended philosophy (i.e. Lakota or Hopi), lifted from an earth-connected culture worlds away from the place and natural landscape where one is actually living. These fantasies and fabrications follow the lead of the countless native-identified spiritual practitioners and authors who have been offering their appropriated versions of "tribal wisdom" since the rise of the 1960's counterculture. The phenomenon known as "pan-Indianism," whereby different traditions are blended together to create so-called knowledge systems and cultures that never existed in the first place, has had tragic consequences for sovereign First Nations. In the New Age and Neo-Pagan community, brand-new spiritual practices and ceremonies have been created by borrowing aspects of vision quests, healing modalities and purification rituals from First Nations as diverse as the Lakota, Navajo and Cree. This artificial combining of cultural elements reinforces false ideologies and romanticized stereotypes, and does nothing to strengthen actual First Nation communities and their recovery of nationhood, ancestral lands or cultural traditions. You can see the evidence of pan-Indianism

---

[86] According to Paul Hawken in *Blessed Unrest: How the Largest Social Movement in History Is Restoring Grace, Justice and Beauty to the World* (Penguin, 2007), there are over two million organizations working toward ecological sustainability and social justice on the planet (with this number rising exponentially). "*The 'largest social movement in history' stems from a commitment to act for the sake of all life on earth, and having the vision, courage and solidarity to do so.*"

everywhere, in publishing, fashion, trends and movements, and in the marketing of so-called "First Nations" products. The authentic voices and indigenous knowledge (IK) of First Nations peoples have become lost in this hodgepodge and *"Indians who are trying to find their way back to the old ways become hopelessly lost in the morass of consumerist spirituality."*[87]Unfortunately today, most people's knowledge of First Nations is erroneous information and distorted stereotypes based on some element of synthetic pan-Indianism.

Across the Pagan spectrum, elements of cultural and spiritual property that have been lifted from Turtle Island First Nations are found in rituals for creating sacred space, four directions petitioning, smudging, talking stick circles, drumming, "featherwork," vision quests, sweat lodge recreations, sacred fire gatherings, initiation rites, and the delights of indigenous material culture such as wardrobe, jewellery and decor. These days I wince whenever I see a Pagan offering newly-created teachings such as "sweet medicine,""native medicine-ways,""great spirit mandalas" or "sacred shields" and I cannot believe the audacity of a so-called "Twyla Dancing Raven" or "Susan Moon Feather" who is visibly disconnected from any real ancestral lineage or membership with a First Nations cultural group. These homogenous quasi-native practices and statements are looking more and more ridiculous, when:

> a) one is practicing Turtle Island IK without holding themselves accountable to their own local First Nations communities,
> b) one has the infinite beauty of their own ancestral traditions (IK) to access,
> c) one is not connecting to the highest truth of their self, their own cultural group and their Ancestors,
> d) one is not exhibiting a genuine desire to do the hard work that is required to develop authentic ancestral and neo-indigenous practices, to involve oneself in genuine cultural expressions and

---

[87]. Andrea Smith, "For All Those Who Were Indian in a Former Life," *Cultural Survival Quarterly*, 1994.

stewardship of nature, to join the circle of all life grounded in the truth of one's being.

It is true that human ingenuity can cross social boundaries to create new cultural blends and aesthetic combinations, and stories, iconographies, technologies and articles of commerce have been traded and shared throughout history. Cultural exchange is a good thing and knowledge is endlessly shifting and changing, but when looked at closely, fragments of knowledge have been constantly taken from sacred Turtle Island IK systems without any ethical consideration whatsoever. Like precious jewels on a string, the elements of an IK system are built up over millennia, and the sacred keystones and heart of that specific worldview are connected to every other component. Like a house of cards, pieces and parts cannot be taken out and used without serious harm or collapse being done to the whole system. IK theft happens with the manipulation and simulation of clothing, objects, story, ritual, image, song or ceremony by a non-native person which culminates in a newly-packaged identity, enriching the public self these "shamanic practitioners" offer to paying clients.

Any kind of identity theft from Turtle Island First Nations perpetuates the white supremacist colonial agenda which moves first to seize the land, then the resources, and finally, specific elements of the indigenous cultural identity that have already been subjected to ethnic cleansing and genocide. Cultural appropriation is an act of **domination**, and identity theft disempowers people of colour and takes away their dignity. They no longer have their own autonomy or control over how they are represented in the public domain, which is a fundamental right for all human beings. When non-native academics, scholars, writers, New Age and Neo-Pagan practitioners (those with the advantage and power) appropriate, write and teach about the cultural and spiritual traditions of indigenous societies, they are in fact dominating the original indigenous knowledge. Their versions of IK become the valid narratives, fabrications that are sold back to the white majority and even to indigenous peoples themselves. The white privilege of cultural appropriation undermines the efforts of indigenous groups to preserve their own specific IK, and 168 Nations around the world have acknowledged these rights by signing the *United Nations Declaration on the Rights of Indigenous Peoples.*[88] A major victory for the many indigenous people who took part in drafting this monumental declaration, September 13, 2007 marks the day when the United Nations and its member states, in collaboration with indigenous societies worldwide, began the process of reconciling the painful legacy of colonization and moving forward guided by the standards of international human rights.

From Grey Owl to Mary Summer Rain to Little Grandmother,[89] playing around with one's personal identity is clearly an indulgence of the white leisure class, a privilege for those whose ownculture is*"not under siege or in danger of annihilation."*[90] The reality is that First Nations communities and their allies are shocked, horrified and insulted by any adoption of native identity in any sphere of popular culture or spiritual life. There are absolutely no conditions that make it acceptable for a non-native person to assume a native identity and become a "cultural ambassador" of First Nations IK to other white people. Also, we need not doubt for a moment that every pseudo-Shaman is an object of ridicule and derision by First Nations peoples. If you do not believe this to be true, then I would suggest following the work of indigenous activists and organizations[91] that monitor cultural appropriation, such as *NAFPS/New Age Frauds and Plastic Shamans, F.A.I.R. Media (For*

---

[88] You can view or download the full Declaration adopted by the General Assembly on Thursday, September 13, 2007 at the *United Nations Permanent Forum on Indigenous Issues* website
(http://undesadspd.org/IndigenousPeoples.aspx).

[89] Jamake Highwater, Evelyn Eaton, Sedonia Cahill, Dhyani Ywahoo, Carlos Castaneda, Osheana Fast Wolf, Shequish Ohoho, Robert "Ghostwolf" Franzone, Wolf Moondance, Mary Summer Rain, Brooke Medicine Eagle, Jamie Sams, Lynn Andrews, Harley "Swift Deer" Reagan, White Eagle Medicine Woman (Rachel Holzwarth and her giant "medicine drum"), Little Grandmother (Kiesha Crowther) and James Arthur Ray have all been exposed as frauds by First Nations community.

[90] Facebook comment, *F.A.I.R. Media (For Accurate Indigenous Representation)*, 2013.

[91]*NAFPS/New Age Frauds and Plastic Shamans* (www.newagefraud.org), *F.A.I.R. Media (For Accurate Indigenous Representation)* on Facebook (www.facebook.com/realIndigenous), and *Native Appropriations* (http://nativeappropriations.blogspot.ca).

Accurate Indigenous Representation) on Facebook or *Native Appropriations* for a couple of days. And it is a good idea before using **any** indigenous element in your project, spirituality or marketing to find out what First Nations people actually think about it.

The popular practice of assuming the title of "Shaman" to describe one's quasi-native practice is now so widespread that it is impossible to send it back to the Pandora's box, or misguided inclusivity from which it came. First coming to light in the 1914 reports of American ethnologists, the origins of the term "shaman" describe the specific practices of the Tungusian and Samoyedic tribes of eastern Siberia, and it could be argued that only practitioners from those indigenous societies have the entitlement to use it. "NeoShaman," "Urban Shaman" or even "Post-Urban Shaman" may be a better choice, as it at least honestly indicates that the shamanism being practiced is a modern hybrid, created from disparate and pan-Indian elements of traditional IK. To deal with this problem of nomenclature, when we go back to our ancestral lines and specific IK (or combination thereof), we can find words that replicate the various roles and responsibilities of a "shaman" in our own original pre-colonial culture. Ban-Filid (Irish Seer), Ban-Draoi (Irish Druidess), Ingheaw Andagha (Irish Priestess and "daughter of fire"), Gallicenae (Gaulish Priestess), Senae (Priestess of Brittany and guardian of the sacred cauldron), Seiðkona (Old Norse), Drabarni (Romany Gypsy), Curandero (Spain), Enaree (ancient Scythian Amazon Priestess), Celtic Priestess, Anglo Druidess or Waeccan Green Seer are all examples of acceptable alternatives. It has also been my observation that individuals in Anishnaabe or Haudenosaunee community respond with perplexity or cognitive dissonance when "shaman" is mentioned in the conversation, as the term is not part of their traditional language or worldview.

"Shaman is NOT a North American Indian word......shaman is a word created and stitched together by European anthropologists, a Euro-colonial code word for spiritual and cultural appropriation."[92]

"Native people do NOT use the label 'Shaman.'"[93]

---

[92]N. Jostein Hetland, *When White People Go Bad*, Facebook comment, 2013.

[93] Introduction, *NAFPS/New Age Frauds and Plastic Shamans*, undated(www.newagefraud.org).

As "exotic" as these self-created novice "shamans" are, paradoxically they fulfill (for a price) the yearning arising from non-native people today for a simpler life, a connection to nature and community, and a return to earth-based Pagan values. In actuality, the contemporary yearning for IK and ecological civilization is a healthy, valuable consciousness that will hopefully culminate in the "tipping point" necessary to halt the destructive practices of Eurocentric Empire, and lead to the healing of ourselves and the planet. Keeping in mind however, that the first European settlers were transplanted in massive population movements and diasporas to Turtle Island, we who are their descendants still need to practice the ancestral knowledge that is authentic to us.

Who Gave You Permission?

As much as contemporary Pagans try to deny it, those in the Wicca, Neo-Pagan and Goddess Spirituality communities who are descended from the original Settler Society do not exist outside of the rubric of white dominance. We have been entitled through white privilege to imitate, assume or borrow the spiritual traditions of any culture, without asking if those people would approve or give us permission for that enjoyment, and our personal growth comes at their expense. White privilege bestows on us total access, and to all appearances we have been thriving on a cultural and spiritual banquet of multi-ethnic practices, symbols, objects and belief systems, unrestrained in their exotic diversity and extravagance. One wonders if our dilettante attraction to the "other" and our indulgence at the spiritual feast can ever completely ring true, satisfy us, or fill the void, as evidenced by the diverse and endless outpouring of self-help practitioners, ideologies, books, courses, workshops, conferences, oracles and tools. The unrestrained consumption of diversified spiritual products made possible by New Age capitalism has taken away our critical thinking process and our ability to focus, which is the only way one can master a specific cultural or spiritual practice. Contemporary Pagans are part of the generation that has been told we can "have it all," and for the first time in human history via travel, the internet and other resources, we have full access to the indigenous knowledge of any culture we choose, including our own. Then why must we take bits and pieces from the IK traditions of Turtle Island, when we have our own ancestral belief systems,[94] sacred objects and ceremonies that are bursting with earth-connected wisdom, beauty and power?

The popularity of the New Age and Neo-Pagan canon and the successful marketing of tribal ideologies and "shamanic training" products to white spiritual seekers, has created a devious moebius loop linking superficial pan-Indianism with the newly-emerging themes of earth-connected spirituality. Until one deliberately acquires some knowledge regarding the specific history and traditions of First Nations communities (hopefully the communities in one's own backyard), the conflation of native identity with homogenous stereotypes and inaccuracies will persist. It is so much easier to believe in the romantic notion of a generous all-knowing quasi-native medicine woman or "shaman" than to delve into the xenophobic challenges and racist persecutions faced by actual contemporary First Nations communities, who continue to suffer the fall-out from cultural genocide. Critical thinking has not been paramount to spiritual seekers as they take a cruise through the spiritual supermarket, and our obliviousness to the specific histories and traditions of indigenous cultures has long been the hallmark of white privilege. Modern spiritual seekers are completely oblivious to the monumental work that is required within indigenous communities to heal themselves, and recover and restore their sovereignty and traditional IK. And as for "getting over it" and

---

[94] If you are still practicing the earth-connected spiritual traditions of your ancestors, kudosto you! However, if like the vast majority of diasporians transferred to the Americas you have been separated from your ancestral EIK, the challenge is to reclaim your own specific heritage and legacy, such as Sinnsreachd (Irish and Scottish Polytheistic Folk Religion), Scottish Paganism, Welsh Reconstructionism, Gaelic Polytheism, Celtic Reconstructionist Paganism (CR), CR Druidry, the Faery Faith, Kemeticism (reconstructionist or eclectic Ancient Egyptian religion), Hellenismos (Hellenic Polytheistic Reconstructionism), Religio Romana (Roman Paganism), Modern Norse or Germanic Paganism, Heathenry, Ásatrú or Forn Siðr (for example). If your EIK has been lost to the mists of time, the renaissance of eclectic belief systems such as Pagan, NeoPagan, Druidry, Wicca, the Avalon Tradition and Goddess Spirituality is good news indeed, and contemporary nature-based spiritualities such as Pantheism, Animism and Ecomysticism hold elements of both ancient and modern practice.

moving on, Winona LaDuke says *"you cannot get over it if you are still in the same circumstance as a consequence of what happened a hundred years ago!"*[95]

Many spiritual practitioners and members of the Pagan community are surprised to learn that what they have been doing is a form of cultural appropriation. Without being told otherwise, they have assumed that fabricating a tribal identity for themselves is socially acceptable. Being blessed with white privilege, those adopting native identities don't seem to know or care about the racialized histories of their actions. Seeing themselves as rebels, and feeling good about identifying as tribal in opposition to the non-tribal industrial civilization, white shamanic practitioners are unaware that their appropriation of IK can *"stereotype, homogenise, objectify, commodify, distort and invalidate"*[96] indigenous cultures. In the belief that their shamanic practice *"celebrates other cultures"* they are unaware that their privilege isa direct benefit fromthe*"power dynamics that have been in place from centuries of imperialism, racism, exoticism, capitalism and colonialism. They may choose to believe that they are disconnected from any form of oppression, but even their sense of entitlement to have an experience of the 'other' is symptomatic of white supremacy."*[97]

The modus operandi of New Age or Neo-Pagan spirituality based on the appropriation of First Nations IK, has been to ignore the fractured histories and contemporary lives of actual indigenous people. It must be the very definition of immorality to strip away the IK of an indigenous tribe, then a few generations later move in and lay claim to those same IK practices, all the while professing to have a better spiritual focus than the original IK holders (certainly with cuter outfits, drums and jewellery anyway). Considering the history of systemic ethnic cleansing in the Americas, the appearance of a white person all decked out in native regalia must appear ghastly, macabre even to an indigenous person. Understanding the direct connection between imperialist domination and the activities of

---

[95] Winona LaDuke (Anishnaabe), *The Winona LaDuke Reader: A Collection of Essential Writings*, Voyageur Press, 2002.
[96] Harshbrowns, "The Kreayshawn Complex: Cultural Appropriation as Counter-Cultural Expression," *Harshbrowns*, (blog), March 7, 2012 (http://harshbrowns.wordpress.com/).
[97] Ibid.

pseudo-shamans practicing their own fabrications of Turtle Island IK, should activate the moral code of any thinking human being. If we genuinely love and respect First Nations culture(s), we must relinquish our privilege and find ways to act in solidarity with them as allies. This means relinquishing all claims to the spiritual practices and tools of indigenous peoples, as those groups continue to engage in "survivance"[98] and their much-needed recovery from social disorganization.

> *"I'm not here to burst your bubble of unity and friendship – but I am here to remind you that while you want to be our friends and ignore cultural differences, you can't ignore the history and current-day presence of colonialism and racism. I don't need to list the statistics of health disparities and poverty in Native communities to prove this to you – just consult the facts. I don't want to be the angry Indian, so do me a favor and when you talk about your "right" to participate in whatever culture you want because we're all human, know that there is such a thing as cultural protocol. Many of us are in crisis on how best to protect our IK."*[99] (Jessica Yee)

To understand our own Euro-colonial history and transform our relationships with First Nations, African-descended cultures and other people of colour, we need to face the inconvenient truth of our paradoxical past and shake off the complacency that comes with white privilege and power. The decolonization process, what many are now referring to as "unsettling the settler within," requires us to identify our unconscious privileges as well as the invisible ways in which we comply with the dominant hegemony. Our struggle, as the descendants of the original Settler Society, is to shift from unconsciousness, racism, denial and guilt about our history to the righteous anger of

---

[98] "Survivance," a term highly relevant to First Nations experience, was coined by visionary and scholar Gerald Vizenor (Anishnaabe).
[99] Jessica Yee, "Feminist Intersection: On Hipsters/Hippies and Native Culture," *Bitch Media*, April 27, 2010 (http://bitchmagazine.org)

critical thinking, reflection and social activism. As we come to an authentic recognition of our shared history with the First Nations and Afro-Americans of Turtle Island, and explore the myths and misconceptions we have had about each other, we can become empowered to use our new awareness as a catalyst for change. There is much that we can do to eliminate institutional racism, and to contribute as Allies to the anti-oppression, human rights and land claims struggles of our First Nation or Afro-American neighbours. Attending anti-racist training and learning about white privilege from reading or videos is our first step.

The white supremacist drivers of manifest destiny ("whites only") and the myth of progress that founded the Americas has created an illogical, unsustainable quagmire, destructive to all beings and ecosystems that share the planet. As we continue to learn about and embody our beloved Pagan worldview(s) and reclaim our diverse earth-connected communities, we also need to examine and deconstruct our "whiteness," and take responsibility for the white privilege we automatically hold as members of the dominant society. Our mission, if we are indeed evolving toward a new paradigm of ecological civilization, is to synthesize our moral code and critical thinking skills with our heartfelt social consciousness. Can we commit ourselves to the theoretical and practical work it will involve, and take the responsibility to learn what is truly valuable and worth rekindling in our own ethnic-based earth-wise traditions? As lost to time and impossible as it may seem, to be in alignment with one's own ancestral roots, to stand tall in one's own neo-indigenous knowledge, is to find empowerment and actualization as an authentic human being, and it may not be too late to establish the peaceful co-existence that the colonial powers denied us all.

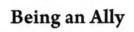

Being an Ally

Newly Revised List of Things I Wish White Pagans Realized

Xochiquetzal Duti Odinsdottir

When I first wrote this list up, I was coming off the tail-end of a big surge of top 10 style lists from other areas in my life around allyship; it was a heady time in the tumblr-verse and it was helpful for me to put the list together and so for this anthology I have decided to look back on the list and see what has changed and what we still need some growth on (and even items that I now wish I had said instead!)

So, here's my revised list of things I wish white Pagans realized when PoC (Pagans of Color) join the circle, (all of these are written in the first person singular, because these are things I WISH they realized, each PoC's list will be different by a little or a lot, that is part of the joy of dealing with people NOT as a single voice for their ETHNICITY OR RACE, but as the INDIVIDUALS they ARE):

1.When I talk about marginalization, I want you to imagine an onion, and all the layers an onion has, how thick or thin they are as they get down to the core, that's what marginalization is like for me. The more intersections I have, the more layers to my onion. I am a married, genderqueer, queer, kinky, poly, Pagan, female-presenting, AFAB (assigned female at birth), Mexican-American, lower socioeconomic status upbringing, working class person. My onion is nice and thick. When white Pagans complain about how demeaned they feel by the majority society and their tendency towards being Abrahamic Christian and the assumption that they are too, that's a layer on their onion. But, they have the opportunity to be heard because their whiteness grants them that chance to state that they aren't Abrahamic Christian. If I stand up to say that, it is automatically assumed that I must be a Santera, or some other derivative of that and therefore still have reverence for Catholic saints, etc. because I'm "Mexican so that's what you do, right?". I have layers to my onion added, because of what people assume about me by seeing me on the street, in the circle, and at Pagan gatherings, not REMOVED.

I still think this is a valid metaphor for my life as a person of marginalized groups. Don't get me wrong, I am proud of my upbringing and the struggles I learned to fight against because without that backbone I don't think I'd be standing before you working as hard as I do for change. But sometimes, I wish that I could honor my struggle by having less of it. Just as I hear people say that nonwhites shouldn't make such a big deal about racist comments because "they didn't mean anything by it", I wish white pagans wouldn't make such a big deal about being called on their racism. Or their homophobia. Or or or.

2. When I say that I want a separate space for marginalized groups within paganism, I'm not just talking about PoC (Pagans of Color), I'm also talking about groups that don't normally get lots of exposure or attention. The second generation, the older women, the young women learning their sexuality, the men who want to explore in safe space the feminine within (dressing, acting, taking up roles traditionally considered female and not allowed or accessible in normative society), the Christo-Pagans who have a need for sanctuary to practice their particular faith without getting the side-eye from 'true Pagans'... All those voices and experiences deserve a space they can carve out and call their own to feel *safe in*, not just from the rest of a 'con or gathering, but for themselves. It's not about self-segregating, it's about self-care. When I am asked if I would be okay with someone making a space in a Pagan gathering that was 'whites only' and how that would affect me, I honestly didn't have an answer because the majority population at a Pagan event tends towards white, so why do you need another room when there's a whole conference/space/gathering area where you can see each other?

This is one of the biggest markers of how great the change has been in the last few years. With the continued success of the PoC Hospitality Suite at Pantheacon and the willingness to engage in questions of access, and inclusivity the Pagan community overall is starting to ask itself the questions that get to the heart of the matter of invisible groups; groups that are marginalized in society in general and how that can be rectified.

Here is where I feel like I pin a lot of hope some of the time. Not all of it, but definitely a big chunk of it.

3. Using questions like how I feel about any and all forms of racism as a way to goad me into stating that some racism is worse than others is just plain tacky. At worst, it shows that you're grasping at straws for an argument. At best, it's a blind statement to how you might think you're being attacked when someone questions the privilege of your whiteness.

This one still holds true. Please, don't be the kind of person who goads another into trying to create a value system that places one oppression over another; that's not how the game that pits marginalized people against each other is rigged in the first place, so why try it? It is a derailing technique and doesn't further discussion, it effectively shuts it down because instead of focusing on the true issue, we are left arguing nuances.

4. Declaring that you are upset by people choosing to have a space that marginalizes you because you're white, is hard (for me) to take seriously. Do you actually HEAR yourself when you say these words? Do you realize how hard it is to hear this because that's what it's like for me and other PoC and marginalized groups for a few moments in a hypothetical situation? Our marginalization happens in our day to day. We are marginalized, othered, and shamed for things we have NO control over, just going about our day. I wish I could feel for you, I really do, and part of me does; but the part of me that does, is sardonic in its response because you have now been afforded a *taste* of what my life is like, CONSTANTLY.

I still hear this one though not as often or with as much conviction. Somewhere along the way, it was decided that the plight of nonwhite people in the US or abroad really wasn't as bad as we may think it to be in that moment or in the recounting of our experiences. But these intervening years have proven to me time and again that nonwhite lives don't matter as much as they should (if at all) to the power structure that keeps us all more concerned with the Kardashians than our neighbors, and our community, and the ills that infect these institutions.

5. My silence does NOT mean my consent. Silence means NO. My silence and what it means, does NOT get to be defined by you. By deciding for me, what my actions mean, marks me as the one needing to have my mind made up for me, and clearly,

you as the white person, know my mind better than I do. No, you do not, therefore you should NOT ever be allowed to do that. It's just another tactic that has been used in the past to drive home just how marginalized PoC are, and is plain bad manners.

This one is still difficult to believe happens but it does. Anytime that an ally or someone struggling against these sorts of injustices goes quiet in a debate (or flaming conversation) the moment they go silent (for whatever reason, for choosing to back out of the "debate" in order to stay sane, for work, for anything else that might take someone away from a keyboard for longer than 5 minutes)...the other person (usually extremely combative) will take it to mean that the other person is admitting defeat to their arguments. We're not. We have lives that require that we not always be online defending certain actions, calling out specific behaviors and being anti-racism educators. Google exists, books on activism and anti-racist work exist, we are not the only speakers on this topic, but we are expected to be on call to any sort of thing that happens. It can be exhausting, day after day, looking at the things going on in our world and having to be ready to answer to these issues. We're not automatons, our lives matter to us and we have to live them. We have to be given the same expectation of humanity that we are trying to give to the person on the other side of the screen, no matter how extreme their prejudice. The onus of being the "better man" always falls on the person doing social justice work and any deviation from that assumed blissful willingness to engage just destroys our points. This is the worst kind of derailing (to me) because instead of focusing on the strength of our arguments it becomes about who we are as people and only the worst light of that, never the totality of our humanity. Just that we're not "willing to give the benefit of the doubt".

6. One of the things that makes this hard for me is this commonly used phrase in Paganism, "in perfect love and perfect trust". A friend of mine and I were discussing it; I see it as part of the agreement I consent to by doing magic with a circle of people, not just with my deities. And this is the one that suffers the most every time I have to defend the need for space; the more I hear claims that people who are Pagan CAN'T be racist, the more I hear that this is self-segregating, separatist, etc. the less I feel I can trust being in sacred space with you. Paganism

isn't immune to these issues, if it were there wouldn't be the need to hear from one Heathen group after another distancing themselves from their more stringent contingents (the ones who claim that only Northern European descendants have the right to worship the Norse deities). We deal in interesting areas of life; we worship g*ds that are from a time that's not ours, a people we may have no actual genetic connection to, and have experiences that science can't explain but that feed our souls. Part of the experience within humanity is remembering that we all have walked a path long before we walked this Path together. I read a lot of talk about how each person's path is different and the destination looks similar even if it's worlds apart, but part of that is the fact that for some of us, the path has been thornier than just people not understanding the CHOICE to be Pagan.

The main thing I wish white Pagans realized: I'm not any more different from you, just because I have a skin color that is darker than yours. The g*ds called us both, even if the way we are called looks vastly different. I ask to join this circle because I want to have that moment of perfect love and perfect trust with you, with the group, with my g*dden. If you can't have me there because you hold onto some antiquated notion of what being non-white means, then tell me, before I enter into the circle with you. Don't waste my time with your issues; I have enough of my own.

I still stand by this. We are all of us called to this path in myriad ways. I would never imagine telling someone that their path is incorrect. I may be willing to argue about the actual practices that we engage in, how to maintain authenticity or innovate ways that we do worship, faith, practice, and the joy inherent in our diverse religious practices; but I also want a place at this table that allows me to sit and not have to feel as though I am on the edge of my seat. I want to be able to enjoy this sumptuous feast with compatriots and contemporaries, sharing our stories and finding ways to connect and engage. To truly feast of this life and all its bounties bestowed by the g*ds I serve, for the work of showing up each day, with all my joys and disappointments and eat my fill.

Racism is a Pattern

T. Thorn Coyle

[author's note: I wrote this as a white person, mostly aimed toward white people. I hope others also find the thoughts useful]

It is hard to examine racism, both personally and collectively.

What does it mean to look at racism? It means to look at ourselves, at our assumptions, at our patterns, at the people we surround ourselves with, and the ideas we return to again and again. It means to delve even deeper: to look for that which is hidden, and slowly bring that forth into the light.

We are not colorblind. We are not unbiased. We are not unbigoted. We have kneejerk reactions. We forget what inclusion looks like. We forget to make space for one another.

We make assumptions.

Here's one example: I was in a group gathered to read through Michelle Alexander's book, "The New Jim Crow: Mass Incarceration in the Age of Colorblindness". I noticed that the white activists in the group were always quick to speak when our venerable leader – a radical Methodist minister and a Black man – asked for comments or questions. The other members, many of them Black church-goers, were not so quick. Whether it was out of respect for the minister leading our group, or whether they generally give one another more space and time to think before speaking, or whether there was some other cultural difference at play, I don't know. But the result was: white people took up most of the talking time in a group that was pretty evenly split between Caucasian and African American.

I had to look at this in myself, the impulse to speak without making space. I brought it up to the small Interfaith group I was attending with. Several times. The behavior grew slightly better, but not by much, over the weeks we met.

To examine racism is not only to look to ourselves, but requires examining at the systems we live within. We need to notice the patterns that are so ubiquitous we barely ever notice they are there. If we notice them at all.

In the study group, we were so used to operating one way that noticing what was happening was difficult and shifting it was even more so.

This happens in Pagan groups, too. Despite all of our work at expanding awareness in our lives, there are always ways of being that our awareness falls just short of seeing.

Many of us are trained to read patterns, yet we can easily miss those that are most familiar to us: The way we run ritual. The way we hold meetings. Where we hold meetings. How we listen. How we speak. The ways in which we commune with one another. The ways in which we waste time. What is considered "wasting time." Culture around sharing or withholding information.

We could draw up lists regarding human interaction and always assume that the way we do things is the default and therefore correct. It isn't the default. And while it may feel correct for the group as it is, it may also be inadvertently keeping other people out.

Some of us in Pagan or magical communities work hard to develop our skills at seeing, sensing, hearing, and tasting that which ordinary senses cannot apprehend. We work hard to train ourselves to these subtleties. Yet just as we can fail to see or hear what is in front of us, because it is too familiar, we can also fail to notice that which is not of our lived experience, that which is outside our boundaries.

There are ways in which culture or habit has caused us to not recognize all the times when our professed values are not being reflected in our words or actions. Things slip by.

If we can become clairvoyant and clairsentient – if we can read the fall of cards and runes, or the way birds move across the sky, or how serendipity shifts events our way – we can train ourselves to see beyond what our lives are like, and open our senses to our brothers, sisters, and siblings whose lives are different because of the brutality of chattel slavery and lynching. Whose lives are different because of systemic racism or misogyny. Because of rape culture. Homophobia. Transmisogyny. Cultural assumptions and differences. Because of the prison industrial complex and a drug war that stacks the deck against brown and Black Americans, turning them into permanently lower caste citizens despite white people using and dealing drugs in greater numbers than Black or brown people in the US[100].

As white people, we can educate ourselves so that when our brothers, sisters, and siblings show up at a ritual, festival, or conference we don't assume that their experience is just like ours. We take the time to listen. To watch. To sense. We don't act like we can be "colorblind" which really has become a code for "I am blind to the daily injustices this culture dishes out to you and I don't want to know, to see, or to hear."

Shutting down our senses shuts people out, too.

We can pay better attention.

We can examine the ways in which our sub-cultures may not feel welcoming. For example, in allowing racialist Pagans a voice at the common hearth in the name of inclusion, we run the risk of pushing our comrades of Black, Mexican, Native, Southeast Asian or any other "non-White" ancestry further toward the edges.

To foster true diversity, we would do well to look at where oppression enters the systems we are building together. To foster diversity, sometimes we have to learn to draw a line. To be truly hospitable means setting common agreements for engagement. We have to keep re-centering and work to uphold the values that drew the boundaries and agreements in the first place. This does not always feel easy.

There are people who feel excluded from our rituals, gatherings, and conversations not out of malice, but because we just don't notice there isn't a place set for them at the table. We didn't think to look. Not thinking to listen or look is what helps give rise to the more heinous violations of body, mind, and spirit that occur every day. Exclusion—even the unconscious kind—gives rise to xenophobia because "the Other" has been created.

Racism exists in our overlapping communities in ways that are so subtle that those of us who are used to "white is the default" can simply fail to notice it. Whiteness as the norm, or the default, is the core of white supremacy. No one is immune to

---

[100] See "The New Jim Crow" by Michelle Alexander

the systems of racism, even as we try to root out personal bigotry from our own lives.

There are ways we are not welcoming. There are ways we shy away. There are ways in which we refuse to become educated. There are times we just grow tired of trying to learn yet another thing. There are times we get tired of being asked to examine our privilege when we see all the ways privilege feels absent from our lives. There are times we can grow tired of being called out for making mistakes when we were just trying to be kind...

Think of how tiring it must be to show up at a discussion in a hospitality suite and have people mistake you for a maid.

Think of how tiring it must be to attend a festival and find that there are only a handful of others that share your racial background out of several hundred.

Think of how tiring it must be to be put in a position to educate others about privilege, racism, or inclusion when you just want to enjoy the ritual like everyone else.

Think of how tiring it must be to have co-religionists assume you only honor a pantheon from Africa or Mexico, despite the fact that your Jewish-raised friend is a dedicant of an Irish God.

Racism runs in the systems we build, even the small systems such as groves, temples, or covens. We make a mistake when we think racism exists only in race hatred and blatant bigotry. The racism that is most toxic in our culture is not the surface stuff. The toxins permeate our institutions, large or small. Systemic racism is what we are up against in the overculture[101]. Systemic racism is what we are up against in counterculture.

We have the skills to listen, to notice, and to change. We can practice them in our immediate lives. Then we can turn our gaze upon the systems we create with others.

When we invite Gods and Goddesses into our spaces, we study their stories and seek to listen to their ways. We figure out the proper offerings and greetings. We treat our Gods and Goddesses with respect. For our human family, we can learn to

---

[101] Overculture is a word I coined to describe the dominant cultural paradigm.

do the same. We are all Gods and Goddesses in potential[102]. To honor one another is a sacred act.

Can we set our intention to learn how to best honor one another? That alone will go far in helping to bring about changes that will foster greater harmony and deeper alliances.

Once we have invoked honor amongst ourselves, we can then invoke our Gods and Goddesses of Justice and ask them to help us come to a deeper understanding of what exactly that might look and feel like. We can figure out what exactly Justice might mean. Once we can imagine Justice, we can set intention, engage our wills together, and begin to build the communities we desire.

---

[102] this paraphrases Feri Tradition founder Victor Anderson

Facilitating Inclusive Rituals and Events

Shauna Aura Knight

One of my values, as a Pagan leader, is to offer workshops, rituals, and events that are as accessible and as inclusive as possible. And it's often a difficult prospect--the more work that I've done in the Pagan community, the more I've seen how easy it is to be exclusive, even unintentionally.

I hesitated to write an article for this anthology. I'm a white, heterosexual, cisgender female, and basically a physically able person. What could I possibly offer to the discussion of Racism in Paganism, or about any discrimination? Yet, when I look at the different ways that I've worked to offer more inclusive events in the community work that I do, I believe that some of my experiences as an event planner and ritualist may offer some tools and ideas that would be of use to many Pagans.

There are some areas where I feel completely out of my depth as far as how to offer rituals and events that are more inclusive to people of color. In the past years I've done a lot of work to offer rituals and events that are more inclusive of transgender, queer, gay, lesbian, and bisexual community members. I've also work to make events accessible for people with various levels of physical ability. In both areas, I have room to grow, but I'm excited for the potential and I look forward doing more of this work.

What motivated me to make my work more inclusive in those areas — and why I want to help make a safe space for people of all colors, genders, sexualities, and abilities — is because I have compassion. I will never have the experience of growing up as a minority and facing that particular discrimination. I didn't grow up afraid of being beaten up because I'm gay. However, I do know what it's like to be abused by my peers, to be rejected for being different, for being the fat kid, and for having bad skin. It's not the same — but it's given me empathy for what others have gone through, and that's helped me to try and see Pagan event planning from outside the boxes that sometimes lead to discrimination.

There are many ways that Pagan events and rituals can unintentionally discriminate against people of color, as well as many other minorities within our community. I think it's important to look at the ways that we organize our events and our rituals, and instead of just going with rote patterns and almost dogmatic practices, actually look at how we might be excluding people, even if that wasn't our intention.

From there, we can work to change some of those patterns. There's a saying in the field of visual and strategic design that the solution is inherent within the problem, and that you can't *solve* the problem until you understand the actual nature of the problem.

For someone raised the way I was, the problem can be hard to see. It's too close to me. I don't see it, I don't feel it, until it's pointed out.

Unintentional Racism

In the past years, I've become more aware of how much "ambient" racism I was raised with and how at times it has bled into the work as I do as a leader, largely through 1. my assumptions and 2. my language. I have found so many things that I say or assume, and I've worked hard to identify these so that I can change them in myself. I hope that it will continue to make me a better ally.

It's like ambient noise in my head; I don't even know it's there, until I hear how my words have impacted someone and I look back and see how often I may have used those words. And then I think, where did I learn those words? How did I come to use them? Did I even know what those words meant?

I was raised in an almost all-white town. I was taught that the N-word is impolite…and yet, I was also taught to lock my car door if a Black person was nearby. I was taught that it's polite to try and be "color blind" and not make judgments about someone based on their skin color. And yet, there were jokes and phrases I heard at family events and at school that I only really later understood were offensive.

I recall hearing white people say "Yes, Mass'ah," as a sarcastic way to indicate that they felt put upon by someone asking them to do a task. One older family member was fond of saying, "I's a-shufflin," as a sarcastic way of implying he was hurrying, but at the pace of a lazy slave. I also recall lots of jokes that were basically saying things the way a Black person might say them, or with a Mexican accent, to make them sound funnier — and people would laugh. And I would laugh. Because, if there's one quick road to an easy joke, it's making fun of someone for being or sounding different.

I knew that overt discrimination was wrong, but a lot of it was stuff I literally couldn't even "hear," it was just stuff people said when I was growing up.

I look back and I cringe. I wonder about how many dumb things I have said that might have made a person of color attending one of my events think, "Wow, I feel totally unsafe here, I'm never coming back."

What I have greatly appreciated are, for instance, articles I've read about microaggressions. Microaggressions are "brief and commonplace daily verbal, behavioral, or environmental indignities, whether intentional or unintentional, that communicate hostile, derogatory, or negative racial slights and insults toward people of color," as defined by Columbia professor Derald Sue (with the term coined by Dr. Chester Pierce). I've included a link to a Buzzfeed article and the Wikipedia page in my resources at the end of this article, but a Google search on the term will help you find other articles. Those have helped me to see some of the places where I haven't at all intended to be offensive, but my words or actions could be perceived that way.

I will continue to seek out resources to try and better understand what the actions and words are that are background noise, which I'm doing that might be offensive. But I also appreciate support in that area, and I welcome more articles and resources that can help me to understand the words and actions that are offensive that I might have no idea I'm doing. I know that when I first began supporting Transgender activism, I was scrambling to understand more about what was offensive to someone who was Trans so that I could better communicate with people who wanted to be allies. I stumbled a lot in the beginning and probably said a lot of stupid things, however, ultimately I learned a lot and I became a better ally.

Racial and Religious Assumptions

I don't recall when I first heard white Pagans suggest that Black people weren't interested in Paganism. "It's European Pre-Christian religions and they have their own, like Voodoo." At the time it sounded reasonable, and I just went with the assumption that most Black people wouldn't be interested.

Years later I began supporting more local community events and I had the opportunity to support several Vodou rituals. And yet, some of these were Vodou rituals being put on by white people, some who trained in Haiti, some who didn't. There was literally a fight going on in my head.

A.In the one corner, the idea that offering public rituals working with African Diasporic traditions might be more inclusive and honor the traditions of people of color....

B. In the other corner, my concern that those traditions were being appropriated.

Yet, if that's the spiritual tradition that deeply inspires someone, isn't a divine calling more important than genetic ancestry? Honestly, the question is way above my pay grade.

What I'm clearly grateful for with the experience I had of supporting those rituals was being exposed to the African Diasporic traditions and learning more about them so that when I meet people who spout off about Vodou and animal sacrifice or other assumptions, I can actually speak to it just a little bit.

What was the most useful for me about attending those rituals was the hands-on exposure I got to Vodou. I, and most of the other participants, had only really heard stories about what Vodou was. Seeing and experiencing it firsthand was a potent, valuable experience I couldn't have learned from reading about it. I'm always for education. In fact, how I ended up supporting a Vodou ritual in the first place was that I used to help host rituals from as many different Pagan traditions around Chicago as we could find in order to help those groups do outreach and education.

This is an area where I really hope to be a better ally, but I admit it's another place where I'm not sure that I understand how to host something like that in a respectful way vs. an offensive way.

Typically for the public rituals I offer, I'm working with an ecstatic ritual style in a format similar to the Reclaiming tradition and Diana's Grove. In other words, the ritual "shape" largely comes out of Wicca. There's a circle, elements, deities. I might work with deities, or heroes from myth, or archetypes...basically whatever story inspires me. I've worked with Celtic, Norse, Greek, Sumerian, Egyptian, a few fairy tales and other archetypal/hero's journey types of stories.

I haven't yet worked with deities or archetypes from the African Diasporic traditions for the reasons stated above—I wouldn't want to work with these in a way that's offensive. One time someone asked me something like, "Wouldn't people of color be more interested in coming to Pagan events if we honored their ancestral deities and traditions too?" And I have no idea what to say to that. I sometimes feel like there's no good answer, and that no matter what I do, I'm guaranteed to offend someone. Thus, I stick to my strengths and I work with the pantheons that I know—but I'm also aware that in doing so, I am probably unintentionally excluding people.

Fear: Alone in the Room

When I was dating a Pagan man who was mixed-race, he told me how lonely or even how afraid he often felt when attending events where he was the only person of color. When he and I co-facilitated rituals in Chicago, I noticed that we had many more attendees who were people of color than I'd ever seen at a Pagan event where all the facilitators were white. A few of those attendees took the time to mention that they felt emotionally safer attending an event where there were people that looked like them, where they knew they wouldn't be the only person of color in the room. In fact, I've also heard similar feedback from Transgender community members who mentioned to me that specifically knowing I (as the primary event facilitator) was Trans-friendly made them feel safer being there, and seeing other Trans folks at my events made them feel more welcome.

And I get that. I had an experience of my own that—while it's a different experience—helps me resonate with that.

I've been asked on occasion to facilitate rituals for the Burning Man community in Chicago, and I have often found myself standing in a room full of people where I am fatter than

183

all of them. And not just a little bit. I'm standing in a room full of wiry-thin, totally fit people, none of them have a curvy build at all. I stand there watching them, and I know I don't belong. I know I'm not a part of their world. And I see the looks they are giving me, even some that are thinly-veiled disgust. It makes me want to leave the room, and it also makes me seriously reconsider returning to a future event, because I don't really feel like I'm one of them or that I'll ever be accepted there.

As someone who is white, I'm not sure how to make people of color feel safer in deciding to attend one of my events. I know what it's like to feel like you don't belong—but I don't know of a way to communicate that people of all colors are welcome. I used to put "People of all genders welcome" on some of my email promotions for events, for which several Transgender and queer people thanked me, but ultimately what GLBTQ folks told me was that my events themselves made them feel welcome.

And so that's largely where I have put my focus. I try to make people of all colors (among other things) feel safe once they arrive.

Ritual Techniques for Inclusivity

Aside from warmly welcoming everyone who shows up, there are a few specific techniques that I use in workshops and rituals that aid in inclusivity. One, for example, is related to physical accessibility. Before the ritual starts, I let people know what we're going to do and that I'll be inviting them to stand, walk, dance, or sing. But I also let people know that they are welcome to sit if they need to and that they have choice about how they participate. You'd be amazed what a difference this makes—I can't tell you how many rituals I've been to where people with canes are standing through a long ritual, obviously in pain, but they won't sit because nobody gave them permission to. That isn't making them feel welcome, and ultimately, that person's likely to decide that they just can't physically sustain going to public rituals like that.

That's what I hope to prevent.

In the rituals themselves, I use the technique that is sometimes called open-language trance. Instead of a guided meditation which tells you what you are seeing and feeling, open-language trance focuses on asking questions to let each person build their own experience of the journey, or of the divine.

A guided meditation might say, "You are walking along a path through the forest, you feel excited, you are going to the divine temple. There's a black pillar and a white pillar, and inside the temple is the Goddess. She has blue eyes and blonde hair, and she gives you a gift, it's a key." Etc, etc.

With open language trance, we might still take a journey to a sacred place where they meet with the divine, but I leave the details up to them. "Can you find yourself journeying to a sacred place? Perhaps you walk along a path, or perhaps you fly or move in some other way. How do you journey to this sacred place?" I build up the journey with questions, and usually with overlayered voices of several facilitators, or possibly a soft drumbeat. "And as you reach that sacred place, what does it look like here? What does it smell like? Can you find yourself in the presence of the divine? And what is that divinity, what does the divine look like? Or perhaps you experience the divine as a sound, or music....perhaps a scent? Is there a feeling in your body?" I keep asking questions that not only let people build the experience for themselves, but I help people with different learning modalities, not just visual.

I make space for people to shape the experience in the way that works best for them. They can determine skin color, gender, or even a form that isn't based on a human body at all. It's up to them. I'm facilitating the experience, but it's not so much about what I want the participants to see as it is about making space for them to shape what will be a powerful experience for them.

Over and over, the feedback that I get from participants is that they are able to have powerful, deep experiences. This approach to ritual—and to the spiritual work I offer—allows me to make my events, rituals, and workshops far more inclusive.

Challenges of Planning Events

One final area that I perceive offers some challenges to Pagan event planners is in the area of event planning itself, or rather, in the numerous difficulties that are inherent in grassroots leaders planning events on a shoestring budget.

Any Pagan event that's gone on for a while has reasons for why that event has ended up being run the way it is, largely around the particulars of event logistics and cost. And I can definitely see how Pagan events could end up excluding any number of people: People of color, people with limited mobility, people with limited income, or people with children. Perhaps in exploring the challenges event planners face we can begin to look at ways to make those events more inclusive.

When I organize a Pagan event, I'm doing so on a shoestring budget. I highly value everyone being able to attend that event regardless of ability to pay, and, I still have to cover the rental fee for the venue. I work hard to find event venues that are physically accessible, as well as close to public transportation and to parking. In Chicago, that's no mean feat.

I don't think I can adequately express the frustration of the hundreds of hours I've spent researching venues online and going on venue visits. Every once in a while I will have to use different venues because one of my main venues isn't available, but ultimately, there are a couple of venues that I return to because they solve most of my problems.

However, any time I choose a venue, that means that I'm inherently choosing to host an event in a particular neighborhood in Chicago—and thus, I'm unavoidably choosing to *not* host an event in those other neighborhoods or suburbs. People are welcome to come in from other neighborhoods, suburbs, or even other states, but whenever an event planner picks a neighborhood to host an event, there's a perception of discrimination and exclusion.

Here's a quick rundown of Chicago neighborhood politics. There's a North Side and a South Side. Well—there's also a West Side, but the main disgruntlement you'll see is between North and South. The North Side is perceived as white collar and white. The North Side perceives of the South Side as being primarily Black and minority neighborhoods, and bad, unsafe areas.

Chicago's very much a patchwork quilt. There's bad neighborhoods everywhere, and there's people of all skin colors everywhere, but in general the South Side tends to have poorer neighborhoods, worse public transportation, and more minorities. Both the South Side of the city, and the South

Suburbs, are more blue collar. The South Suburbs, however, are more predominantly white and blue collar. The North Suburbs, as you've probably guessed, are even more white collar, and more affluent.

Now — the venue I use most frequently is on the North Side, though it's fairly close to downtown and is in fact just west of downtown. It's a community center in a warehouse district, and it's perfect in so many ways for the work I do. It's affordable, there's free parking, it's not too far from public transportation, and it's accessible. It's not in a pretty area, and there are homeless people who make their homes in and around some of the warehouses.

However, here are some of the complaints that I've had over the years at different venues:

1.Can't you do that event up on the North Side (meaning, the far North Side)?

2. Do you do events up on the North Side anymore? (meaning, the upper-class North Suburbs)

3. Why don't you ever do events on the South Side? (meaning, the South Side of the city)

4. I'll come to an event when you do it on the South Side, I don't drive in the city (meaning, South Suburbs, unavailable to public transportation)

5. Why can't I bring my kids?

6. I can't afford your event.

7. Can't you just do women's rituals? I don't want to attend if you're invoking the God.

8. I wouldn't come to your event, I can't park my car there.

9. You're hosting an event near a homeless shelter, it's not safe.

The list actually goes on, but this is sufficient to pull out some patterns. The North Side folks won't go to the South Side. The South Side folks don't want to go to the North Side. The Suburbs folks hate the city. City people without cars can't always get to the Suburbs.

I have hosted and attended events all over Chicagoland and its suburbs. And there is no way to please everyone, so at a certain part, I stopped trying. I found that my life as an organizer is far easier when I work with what I know. In this case, that's going with a venue that has worked for me time and again. It suits most of my needs, and even when the price went up, it's still the most affordable venue for what I need.

And that's ultimately why Pagan events end up the way they do—because at some point, cost and feasibility are the pressures that shape how an event is run.

Using that particular venue allows me to keep my costs fairly low so that I can host my events on a sliding scale with no one turned away for lack of funds. I do ask for a suggested donation—usually $5-$25 for a ritual or for a day-long event with workshops and then a ritual. But keeping the costs low allows me to include people regardless of income.

Some people tell me they can't afford bus fare to get there, and I wish I could help more of them. I'm willing to arrange carpool for people I know, but I have a general policy that I'm not going to ask someone to pick up a stranger. I also don't have the time to manage complicated carpooling when I'm running an event. My hope is that over time, as more community members get to know each other, I'll not only have more people to help manage something like that, but more people with resources like cars who can help each other out.

It's difficult, as a Pagan event organizer, to take every single person's needs into account. Honestly, if I did, I'd never be able to offer an event. There's just no way to make an event that is inclusive of everyone.

As a volunteer organizer, there are some accommodations I don't have the budget or staff to make. Sometimes, I have to go with the cheaper venue that had stairs and wasn't accessible or that had terrible (and expensive) parking.

I have sincerely regretted it when I have hosted an event that, by the location or logistics, excluded someone who wanted to attend. The difficulties I face include a hard time raising funds that would give me better options on venues, and also there's only so much I can do as an organizer with a volunteer staff.

While most of the vocal complaints that I get these days are from people on the North Side or the suburbs, that doesn't mean that my choice of event venue and location doesn't inherently exclude people of color.

Discrimination and Exclusion

There are so many ways that I, as an event planner, might be unintentionally excluding people from an event. There are ways I might be discriminating against people of color in ways I can't even see. I can only speak for myself that it is not my intent. However, it is my continued hope to find more ways that I can offer events that are inclusive, and to help others do the same.

Resource:

http://www.buzzfeed.com/hnigatu/racial-microagressions-you-hear-on-a-daily-basis
http://en.wikipedia.org/wiki/Microaggression

Note: Some content for this article was adapted two blog posts written by Shauna Aura on her leadership blog:
http://shaunaaura.wordpress.com/2013/07/20/planning-pagan-events/

And on the Pagan Activist blog:
http://paganactivist.com/2013/07/21/ritual-physical-accessibility-transgender-inclusion-and-more/

How to be an Effective Ally

Taylor Ellwood

At Pantheacon 2013, Crystal Blanton sat me down and said, "I don't think you know the impact you've had on my community." I looked surprised and asked what she meant. She proceeded to tell me that the anthology *Shades of Faith* had started conversations and helped her launch the Daughters of Eve blog. I reminded her that she'd edited the anthology and that I had not done much at all, but she disagreed and told me that I was the one who came to her and told her of my vision to have an anthology published that examined Paganism from the perspective of people of color. I'd been the one to ask her to be the editor of the *Shades of Faith* anthology, recognizing (as I'll share in moment) why I wouldn't be the appropriate person to edit that anthology. Certainly what Crystal told me is true and so I told her that I felt I had played a small part in starting up some much needed conversation, but insisted that she, moreso than I, has been the one to have an impact on her community.

I'm a white male, in my late thirties at the time of this writing. I come from a middle class background, and I'm self-employed. While I've faced some challenges in my life, it's fair to say that I've lived a privileged life. I haven't always been aware of that privilege, or how such privilege is institutionalized and set up to favor certain types of people over others, but as I have become more aware of privilege over the years and come to recognize racism in its more subtle forms, I've also felt called to combat it in my own way.

I feel that to be an effective ally to a person of color, or for that matter to be an ally to any person requires certain skills, which many people may find hard to grasp because they require a humbling that can be hard to swallow. Nonetheless I share these skills because I hope that readers of this anthology will ponder them carefully and apply them as needed, and not merely in matters of race, but also in any other situation where it becomes apparent that a person has a level of privilege greater than another person has, and has an opportunity to address that inequity.

The first skill is probably the hardest to learn. You need to learn how to listen and stop reacting. That's right. You need to listen and stop reacting. I've written that twice, because it can't be said (or written enough). The majority of white people, when confronted with racism or privilege or other such topics that cause squirmy feelings of discomfort, tend to react in one of two ways. They either argue that racism is gone and that there is no such thing as privilege, or they start talking about how guilty they feel for being white, which just takes away from the actual conversation that needs to occur. I'd argue that both responses are actually subtle forms of racism in their own right, because both responses, in their own way, are really about reinforcing the status quo and keeping each person where s/he is. Yes, even the admission of guilt applies precisely because it focuses on the white person and his/her plight in response to having to face the realities of racism and privilege head on.

Listening, really listening, involves putting your own thoughts, feelings and reactions on hold and actually making the effort to really take in what someone else is saying. It involves accepting that some hard things will be said, but that if we want to have a genuine conversation, then it's important for white people to actually listen without bursting into guilty apologies or arguing that racism doesn't exist. White people just need to listen and if they want to give a response, let it be an informed response, which leads to the next skill.

The second skill involves getting out of the white bubble of privilege as best as possible. It's pretty hard to do, if not impossible, but there are ways to get a glimmer of perspective and such perspective is necessary if we are to have constructive conversations on racism and privilege. One of the ways to get out of the bubble or at least see beyond it involves getting curious about other people and being open to listening to what they say (see skill one above). For example, when I was a Resident Assistant (RA) at a dorm in Clarion University, one of the other RAs was a fellow by the name of Brian. Brian would get together with his friends in his room and they would play games and talk about their experiences. I asked if I could visit, and join in, and they let me. I was the only white person in the room and I got to hear a lot of things that made me uncomfortable, but I sat and I listened and I didn't argue. I just listened and let it open my perspective. And yes I was still in my white bubble of privilege, but it opened my eyes a bit.

Later on, I would date a girl by the name of Maryam for a few years, and conversations with her opened my eyes further as I learned what she, and her family, had experienced just because of skin color. Those conversations forced me to recognize my white bubble of privilege, on some level, though it would still take some time for me to really get it. In fact, in all honesty, I'm still recognizing it. That might seem odd to say, but I don't think you ever stop recognizing the privilege you have, not if you want to genuinely have conversations with people that actually involves changing the system.

Since then I've continued to put myself into situations where I can see that bubble of privilege I'm in and also see how it affects other people. Sometimes it involves reading up on critical race theory (or something to that effect, because it's not just racism I'm examining) or having conversations where I listen to people tell me about their experiences. I do it because I realize that if I am to really understand what other people are going through I have to get perspective, gain awareness, and then in turn I can apply that awareness, not just to myself, but to other people, which leads to the third skill.

The third skill involves using your privilege to level the playing field. Now realistically I can't change the systems of racism and privilege all on my lonesome, but I genuinely believe they can be changed. Such change is slow and takes a lot of work and a lot of people, but it can happen. What's important is that each of us asks ourselves, "What can I do, in conjunction with others, to help create change?" For myself that has involved leveraging my position as a publisher to facilitate conversations around issues involving race, privilege, disability, and gender. I realized some time ago that there were certain topics not being discussed in the Pagan community (not overtly anyway) and I thought to myself, how can I stir the pot and get some of those conversations to happen. The solution involved deciding to find editors who could coordinate and publish anthologies on social issues in Paganism that need to be addressed, but haven't been addressed. I knew, that as a white male, I couldn't be the editor for some of the anthologies I wanted to put out, because I wasn't the right person and didn't have the necessary perspective. I also didn't have the connections and recognized that my privilege might cause me to offend people. The best action I could take involved finding someone who was qualified to be the editor of a given anthology. That person would know who to contact and would be able to edit the anthology, as well as promote it. I could help set up the stage, but then what I could do was step back and let that person and the people s/he found say what needed to be said.

To be an ally to any type of person that is marginalized on the basis of gender, skin color, or other attributes is a choice that involves continually taking action that truly speaks to leveling the playing field, but also recognizes that part of how you do it involves knowing how to support without getting in the way of the very people you want to help. Being an ally means you don't speak for the people who are marginalized, but instead stand with them as they raise their voices to be heard. At times, you may need to speak up, in order to pave the way for their voices to be heard, but even in that situation, you should recognize that you are helping to make their voices be heard, as opposed to being a spokesperson for them. An ally can be an opener of doors for people to whom those doors are shut. Being an ally also means that you learn how to own your feelings of discomfort and place them into the proper context, which is the last skill I'm going to mention in this article.

When an issue like racism or privilege is brought up, it makes white people feel guilty and nervous. I think that for most white people, the first thought that goes through their mind is, "Am I going to be called out for being white?" That thought is uncomfortable, because white people typically aren't called out on being white, but what they're really thinking about is: "Am I going to be called out for what my ancestors did?" or "Am I going to be called out on my privilege?" or something else to that effect. This thought is a bit self-indulgent, in my opinion, but it occurs precisely because issues of race and privilege have not been brought up or dealt with in a way that honestly and critically examines how those issues are sustained by our culture and the institutional systems that are part of our culture.

The feelings of guilt and discomfort that a white person feels can all too often take up the bulk of the conversation around these issues. It is not the responsibility of people of color to help white people deal with these feelings. Instead, white people must learn to come to grip with these feelings, and through that begin to critically examine and engage the issues of racism and privilege that pervade our society. Part of how white people come to grips with these feelings involves employing the skills I've mentioned above, but it also involves confronting our history and our own role in the systemic support of racism and privilege.

But, you protest, I am aware of the history of slavery and the civil rights movement. Yet how aware are you really? The history we are taught is white-washed by white people and fails to address the continuing issues of race and privilege that pervade our culture. It also fails to examine recent events, or when those events are brought up in mainstream media, rarely do we see race and privilege critically examined. Instead such issues are portrayed by the media in a way that attempts to sweep them under the rug, or portray the people who bring them up as conspiracy theorists. Additionally, the majority of white people are ignorant of the realities that people of color face each day including police profiling, an education system set up mainly to help white kids, and the subtle and not so subtle forms of racism they deal with each day, simply because their skin color isn't white. And white people perpetuate these issue everyday by refusing to critically engage them.

How do we critically engage these issues? First and foremost, we must recognize the color of a person's skin and how perception of race, according to that skin color, affects the level of privilege that person has access to. If a person has a darker skin color, s/he will often be treated differently in society because of the perceptions attached to the skin color. Instead of trying to opt for a colorblind approach, we need to acknowledge that skin color plays a role in how people are treated, and also occurs as a result of the history of racism and privilege in this country.

Secondly we need to call out and admit when skin color is an issue. Only by repeatedly calling it out and bringing it to the attention of people around us can we effectively start to address the white bubble of privilege and the racism that still pervades our culture and society. There are times, where a white person, as an ally, can use their privilege in ways that are supportive to people who have less privilege. Sometimes a person of color (or someone who doesn't have privilege in a different way) will not be heard without having the support of an ally to call out the privilege for what it is. But after the ally has done that and the person who doesn't have the same privilege is actually being listened to, the ally needs to support that voice and remember that s/he is not a spokesperson (Yes I wrote this above, but it bears repeating.)

Third, white people need to own our history and accept as well that we have likely played a role in perpetuating the privilege and racism issues that are part of our society. At the same time, we also need to make a conscious choice and choose to break the cycle of racism and privilege by critically examining our choices and actions and then changing them to address the issues of racism and privilege, instead of ignoring them or supporting them.

Finally we need to take consistent action in supporting diversity by making sure that their voices are heard in regards to these issues. If white people can do that, then we will have taken a step toward redressing the wrongs visited on people of color. It will not solve all the problems or make everything right, but it will be a step in the right direction, and one that all of us need to take if humanity is to evolve.

Conclusion

I started this article out with the story of how Crystal was thanking me for the impact I had on her community. In truth, I feel I have only played a small role that is nonetheless supportive of her and her efforts, as well as the efforts of others. I feel the same way with any of the other anthologies I have helped to publish. If anything, I am thankful to Crystal, Brandy, and Tara for their courage and their willingness to speak up and have their voices be heard, as well as help others speak up. I hope that those efforts continue to create the conversations we need to have for not only the Pagan community to evolve, but also our society as a whole.

Removing My Color-Blind Glasses: The Journey from White Liberal to White Ally

Kat Bailey

Introduction

Racial discrimination has always been a mystery to me. I have never understood why the color of a person's skin should have any bearing on how they should be treated. The only way I know how to approach this topic is through my own personal experience, for I can only share my own perspective with accuracy. Before I could become a white ally in racial equity work, I had to accept how the privilege I have as a white female and my belief in being "color-blind" were perpetuating racism-the complete opposite of my intent. I share my own difficult journey with the hope that others will see reflections of themselves and join me to reverse racism in our communities.

Background

This metamorphosis has required me to examine the origin of my beliefs. Much of the mystery around racism occurred for me because I have never been comfortable in the white skin I occupy. As a toddler, reincarnation was simply a reality, for I was plagued by nightmares in which I relived violent ends from three different lifetimes; lifetimes spent in different shades of skin. Those bodies seemed more familiar to me than my own pale existence and I felt out of place in this time and space.

In addition, my childhood was filled with the influences of different cultures. Our next-door neighbors, my extended family, were Chinese-Canadian, and I accepted the rich cultural traditions and food in which I participated as my own culture. One of my Chinese "sisters" was bound to a wheelchair and would only visit a few times a year, as in those times children with severe disabilities were institutionalized. Her soul shone out of her body through her eyes and I understood that bodies were housing that didn't accurately reflect the intelligence within. I simply looked past her race and disability, treating her as my sister.

Just as influential was the time I spent on the Tuscarora reservation, for my grandfather was an honorary member of the tribe. I still remember the excitement of having a Tuscarora Chief and Princess come over to my house for dinner, and how in awe I was of the beautiful culture they shared with our family. I was envious of their customs and traditions, for they flowed together like a beautiful melody compared to the strict cultural guidelines my mother had brought as an immigrant from Germany.

As I grew spiritually and learned to assimilate my past lives I realized my body is just a temporary vehicle, a tool to support further spiritual development. I learned both positive and negative experiences were opportunities for growth. I gravitated toward the field of education and received training that matched my belief system, training that reinforced looking past one's physical appearance and acknowledge the presence within. Multiple professional development opportunities built on my early experiences and taught me to be color-blind, and I continued to deemphasize shades of skin in my personal, spiritual, and professional lives with the hope that emphasizing who was in the skin versus the skin itself would make the world a place of acceptance for all.

White Privilege

This illusion of racial harmony came to a grinding halt when I accepted a job in southern California. As I began to settle in I realized racial tensions were high, and nine months later I experienced the Los Angeles Riots. As the fires finally began to go out and attempts were made to try and return everything to normal, I decided, as part of my spiritual service, to join a group of volunteers and help clean up the aftermath. I felt great compassion for the neighborhoods hit by the waves of violence during the Riots, neighborhoods where residents already had so little. As I arrived at the rendezvous point I saw National Guard troops along the streets and sidewalks with their guns drawn, as well as tanks in the middle of major intersections. When I asked why the troops were there I was told that snipers had attempted to shoot anyone coming into the neighborhood, including volunteers. I was dumbfounded and couldn't understand why anyone would want to shoot people who were coming to help.

I was further shocked to see that all of the businesses that had been vandalized were Cambodian, whereas businesses with Spanish or English on their signs had been left intact. Volunteers were directed to board up those businesses as well as paint over graffiti in the neighborhood. I remember residents watching the volunteers, all of whom were white from outside neighborhoods, from behind their curtains or blinds. Despite my desire to help I knew our efforts were unwanted and were raising up feelings quite the opposite from the gratitude I had expected. I left conflicted and confused, unsure as to why communities of color would target each other and why my help wasn't appreciated. I thought I could connect to the people in that community because I came from a background of poverty, not realizing that race and ethnicity make a parallel circumstance like poverty a very different experience.

That answer didn't come until a few years later, when I discovered one of my friends had lived in the neighborhood where I had volunteered. When I asked him about the businesses targeted and the need for protection from the National Guard, his response surprised me and completely changed my attitudes about white liberals doing community service for "those in need." He explained the Cambodian businesses had been targeted to send a message to the Cambodian population, who were the "new kids on the block" according to the pecking order assigned based on amount of time spent in the United States. He said it was typical for new immigrant groups to be hazed by other communities of color who had to establish a territorial foothold.

In regard to people being resentful about a bunch of white people cleaning up their neighborhood, his community viewed it as hypocritical that white people acted as though they cared about such conditions when white systems are the reason people of color are forced to live in those conditions. I walked away with the perspective that community service is an illusionary way for people to feel good about themselves, when in reality it's a poor substitute for doing the harder work of disrupting racism. I resolved to try and do more to set things right.

Color Blindness

Afterward I made a conscious choice to work with adolescent and teenage gang members in a program that supported their return to the school system after serving time in the juvenile detention system. I decided I would unconditionally love and accept each person as a fellow spiritual being, regardless of race, ethnicity, or crimes committed. One concept I have always believed based on my past experiences and spiritual beliefs is that the way a person looks on the outside doesn't matter. I was convinced what is important is to honor what is inside each person.

I have since learned this assumption is not only wrong, but a manifestation of white privilege. I can decide to ignore the racial or ethnic background of people I encounter, but the reality is each person always has some awareness of the skin they are in as part of their basic identity. Ignoring a person's race or ethnicity by pretending I don't see it isn't honoring the whole of that person as an individual. I soon learned that the shade of one's skin meant everything and that the concept of color-blindness was as much an illusion as the unwanted community service in which I participated. For the youth I worked with color-blindness was an illusion held only by white people. The color of their skin was literally a matter of life and death depending upon what neighborhood they walked or drove through. Regardless of their actual race or ethnicity, they were judged based on the race they were *perceived* to be. It became apparent that gang lines were primarily drawn using a race as an identifier, and all my sweet-talk about ignoring race and looking at the person within became insignificant as I realized I needed to be keenly aware of racial background and gang affiliation in order to keep myself and those in my care safe.

The idealism that inspired me to take the job was quickly stripped away by raw reality. Everything I had learned was rendered absolutely useless and the color-blind glasses were ripped away. I had no choice but to begin seeing how people are treated differently based on their skin tone or last name. Other disparities related to housing, education, and the legal system soon began to rise to my attention; things that had been there all along, but which I chose to ignore due to my naïve dreams of everyone becoming one big happy community.

I realized the illusion of color blindness was reflected not only at work but in my personal life. Despite all of the hype about race not mattering, others have had different experiences than me simply because of their *perceived race*, and many of those experiences have been unpleasant. I have two examples of how the racial perceptions of others affected people in my life.

A black female co-worker and friend is married to a white man. The two have children from previous marriages, but also had a son together. While this young man is biracial, his skin tone is closer to that of his mother. As a result, he has had an educational and social experience that is very different from those of my own white son, who is only one year older. Teachers have had low expectations for him academically and behaviorally, and when he is out in public he is aware that he is sometimes perceived unfavorably even when he hasn't done anything wrong. When the Trayvon Martin incident occurred in Florida, my friend's son asked her, at the age of ten, if it was safe for him to go out in public with a hoodie on. As my co-worker told me about this conversation I discovered that she had already had multiple conversations with her son about how he might be treated differently because of his skin color despite the fact that one of his parents is white. In contrast, I have had similar conversations with my own son to explain how differences should be celebrated, but I have never had to warn him about how he might be treated differently and unfairly because of his skin color.

The second example is closer to home for me, for it involves my own sister. My sister looks nothing like me and inherited other aspects of our genetic line. As a result she had olive colored skin, dark eyes, and long dark wavy hair. In the South, she is sometimes mistaken to be Mexican and feels like people talk down to her, are less likely to help her, and give her judgmental looks. Sometimes she is directly asked her ethnicity. She has two white parents, but when she is perceived to be a person of color she has very different experiences.

These experiences have shown me that actual genetic makeup is less important than the perception others have of you. It has also shown me that color-blindness is an aspect of white privilege. Even with the best intentions it is no more than a luxury held only by those in white skin- the dominant culture in our society. As I sought ways to turn my intentions into more conscious action, I began to study the implications in my spiritual practice.

Implications for the Pagan Community

I began to look at my own Pagan community and those around me. When I attended Pagan classes and events I generally saw white faces looking back at me despite the fact that I was living in southern California, one of the most racially diverse areas of the country. I became puzzled as to how something so meaningful for me- my spirituality- could only be appealing to others who look like me. I decided to throw out a broader net and began attending events beyond local boundaries, but encountered a similar lack of diversity. There were a couple of groups at each convention composed of people of color, but I saw very few groups with any diversity at all.

This led me to do some deep reflection about how Pagan groups draw and welcome others. A number of groups practiced Reconstructionist magic based on ethnic traditions. Many of the group members were from that particular ethnic background, but that wasn't a steadfast rule. The tradition I was involved with at the time was Stregheria, or Italian witchcraft. A number of people in my group were Italian, but about a third, including myself, didn't have a drop of Italian blood to our knowledge. I had pursued the tradition because it was the closest thing I could find to the hereditary Germanic tradition in which I was raised. I had looked for something tied to my ancestral roots, so I began to wonder if the lack of ancestral connection was what kept Paganism so white.

I compared this to the Zen tradition I had practiced for the twelve years preceding my entry into formal magical practice. I realized our temple, up in the wilderness of the San Jacinto Mountains, could only be reached by driving up a mountain on a winding road with treacherous curves. Yet, somehow it drew people from all ethnicities, very few of whom were Japanese. The Zen organization did not advertise in magazines or have membership drives. People simply found their way there through a number of seemingly coincidental experiences, much as Pagans find their way to a group. This blew my theory about the need for connection to ancestral knowledge as the key factor in drawing White practitioners out of the water. I wondered what my Pagan group and others were doing differently. Why didn't our gatherings better represent the population of our communities?

I began to wonder if the deciding factor was wealth. Pagan events cost money, as does Pagan jewelry, magical tools, and spell crafting materials. I knew in my magical group the majority of our members lived paycheck to paycheck, but I thought perhaps that was a result of living in an area with a high cost of living. I began to observe carefully at bigger events and listen to conversations around me. What I saw and heard verified the majority of the Pagans I encountered had some disposable income, but had to save up or use credit cards in order to attend events and purchase goods. Many of the Elders I knew in the community lived month to month and were often brainstorming ways to try and increase their income in order to have better financial security and be able to afford health benefits. Having disposable income did not seem to be a large factor in preventing people of color from joining the magical community.

I examined how we draw new people into the Pagan community. How do people find out about Pagan classes and groups? Is it all through word of mouth, by seeing a flyer at a shop, or through the Internet? How is Paganism and magic presented, and why does it draw people primarily from European descent even though it has deep roots in other parts of the world? I realized the problem may not be what we are doing, but how we are doing it.

Becoming a White Ally - From Color-Blindness to Color Consciousness

These questions mirrored the research I was doing on a professional level in the field of education, and I began a journey where my spiritual life and professional life began to closely intertwine. In the professional arena I took racial equity training and was introduced to critical race theory and the concepts of color- blindness and white privilege, concepts I didn't initially feel applied to me because of my eclectic background and open views. I started meeting with racial affinity groups and hearing the stories of my brothers and sisters of color and really hearing them without forcing their words into my own constructs. Having learned those lessons I continue to face the challenge of finding ways to be an ally to racial equity work. While I have much more to learn, three lessons have made a deep impact in my life:

Awareness of Non-Verbal Cues

One thing I have heard repeatedly is how whites use non-verbal cues to show a lack of acceptance toward people of color. I have not done this intentionally, but after hearing these comments I began to track by own actions. I discovered I unconsciously gravitated toward people who looked like me, and sometimes avoided eye contact. On a spiritual level I realized the energy I was sending out wasn't always consistent, especially when I was in a group of strangers. I found that I was more open and welcoming to people who looked like me, and while I was welcoming to some people of color, I began to notice a difference in that exchange- one where I patted myself on the back for being welcoming to people different than myself. Upon deep reflection I realized how condescending that was, and how people pick up intent even if on the surface your words and actions appear positive.

It is a difficult thing to track your thoughts, physical actions, and energy output at the same time. I found that the more regularly I meditated or did internal work, the more aware I was of the subtle changes in my body and mind. This improved even more when I did spiritual work that was grounded in my body. Much of Western spirituality is focused on visualization of some type, but there are practices outside of sex magic that involve using your body as a magical tool. I highly recommend such practices for their benefits transfer over to mundane life, especially in the area of self-awareness.

Receptivity

Two aspects of white culture is to process things out loud verbally, and to immediately go into problem solving mode when others share a concern. In my experience, I have seen people of color shut down by whites who talk over them. I have been guilty of this myself as an assertive, outspoken person. Sometimes though, we just need to listen, especially when a person of color has an opportunity to share their perspective. Plainly said, we just need to shut up and listen.

There are plenty of programs out there that teach receptive or active listening. Many of us have had such training as spiritual leaders. We need to apply these skills in all aspects of our lives so that all perspectives can be heard without us having to offer a story that shows we connect, or offer a solution. I have found that when I am in a group where people of color are sharing, my white guilt kicks in and I get the urge to prove I'm not like the white people they're discussing. Ironically enough, I'm exactly like the people they're discussing when I do that. Again, this is where internal work can help untangle those urges and where that feeling of guilt is really coming from.

Just a note- one of the worst possible things we can say as a way to "connect" is that our ancestors didn't participate in slavery or other forms of racial genocide- for even if we weren't directly involved, we reap the benefits of white privilege every day. The way to really connect is to be present and receptive without any defensiveness.

Courage with Grace

As someone with white privilege, I am able to speak up about racist remarks or situations and be heard differently than if a person of color raises objections. As such, it is my responsibility to open the door not only so my objections can be heard, but so that perspective of color can be received. Sometimes as white allies we simply need to prop open the door for that alternative perspective, especially if we are in a position of power in our spiritual or professional lives.

However, that being said, it is important that we make our best attempt to model respect and grace during such interactions. There are plenty of reasons to justify being "in your face" when expressing frustration and inequality in a culture that has been systemically racist for over 250 years, but I have found my strongest impact is when I'm bold, but don't turn off the people with whom I'm interacting. I feel we have to approach this work as a joint initiative that is part battle and part "sneak attack." Where aspects of it are presented in a loud and powerful way but is also embedded in everything we do so that it gradually permeates the actions of others. Our most powerful messages are sent through our actions. Some people will be turned off no matter how it's presented, but I view them as acceptable losses- they're in their own little world and can't be changed no matter what they experience. I believe though that most people though can be reached by seeing examples, through discourse, and through the energetic resonance we emanate as spiritual people.

These are the lessons I have learned during my journey, a journey that is far from over. It's a journey that requires humility and hard work because I'm working to correct something that is embedded in every aspect of our society. As spiritually aware people, we have the responsibility to work to reverse the effects of racism in our professional, personal, and spiritual lives. I have learned how my best intentions were actually compounding the problem, and have begun unlearning what I thought was right. It's a difficult path, but I urge each and every person who comes across this book to join me in this work in some capacity- whether in the Pagan community or the world as a whole. Social justice is its own spiritual path, and as Pagans who have all felt discrimination at some point, we have a responsibility to create a world of acceptance.

Do I See Color?

Lisa Spiral Besnett

I was born and raised in suburban Minnesota. Land of lily white Swedes. I grew up in a time and a family where "All people are the same and deserve the same treatment.". It was easy to see "everyone is equal", because in my household everyone was.

You'd think that I was isolated from actual issues of color, beyond the theoretical and what we might have noticed on our black and white TV. My family was happy to include anyone, regardless of race creed or color. In many ways rather than being isolated I was immersed.

My family's interaction with racial inclusion is multigenerational. On my father's side are French fur trappers out of Canada. The voyagers, are mythological in a line that has clear paper records only as far back as my Great-Grandfather. He was on the Police force when "Joe the Frog" (as he was called) was a racial slur and Frogtown was St. Paul's slum. My Grandfather claimed that there was native blood in our line. That was an unusual statement from someone of his generation. It's likely true, but what it means and what those relationships actually were is anybody's guess.

My Mother's Grandparents were mostly immigrants directly out of Sweden. "Not the painted horse Swedes", I was told, "but the black Swedes". There's no clarity about what that means. I have reason to strongly suspect that they were displaced Saami. My Grandmother was raised in a household along with two Native American girls. Again I'm not clear on why, or what the relationship was. Maybe they were borders while they went to school. I do know that when my Grandmother lost one of her children she asked those girls, who had passed, to take him into their arms and care for his spirit.

When I got to an age to start dating my Mother made it clear that race wasn't what was important. She told me she dated a black boy for a while when she was in high school. My Mother's graduating class might have been 15 people on a good day. She lived in the middle of nowhere in the county with the largest KKK population in the 5 state area (Minnesota, Wisconsin, Iowa, North and South Dakota). Where on earth would she have found a black boy to date? I don't know if this is family history or a story designed to illustrate a point.

I know that growing up I got along better with the kids from very ethnic families than I did with the middle class whites. The family friends were Jewish or Italian, the neighborhood kids I ran with were from a mixed race family adopted by their foster parents.

I was exposed to the politics of race from a very early age. I marched in solidarity with Martin Luther King. In later years I rode the city bus regularly, late at night, through those same neighborhoods. I attended fundraisers supporting the birth of AIM. I railed against the perpetuation of the Jim Crow South, election laws removing people's rights, and the disproportionate presence of blacks in the military and in prison. I was scared when while driving through Southern states I saw people with Confederate flags on their cars and guns hanging in racks on the back window. I knew they wouldn't like "people like us."

Because I am bright, well educated, well traveled, have a good ear for language and a dark olive skin I pass. I pass as white. I pass as Native American. I pass as a light skinned black woman. I pass as Jewish. I pass as Italian. I'm good at reflecting what people expect to see. Because I was raised with inclusion, I simply expect to fit in. I'm surprised when I don't. That's privilege.

It wasn't until I traveled in the Orient that I understood what it was like to never see another face like mine. I experienced never fitting in. I could not pass as anything but a gaijin, a Japanese slang term for "outsider". I was too white, too tall, too fat, too American. In India even the non-verbal cues were off. They do a head bob that looks to a Western eye like "I don't know" or even "no" but it means yes. I began to recognize that inclusion only goes so far.

I'm not a visually oriented person. I remember people's stories before I remember what they looked like or what they were wearing. When someone cuts their hair or shaves their beard I might notice something is different, but I probably won't be able to place what it is. When I say someone reminds me of somebody else, they never look alike. They may move the same, or share a cadence in their voice, or have similar backgrounds. In that same way I don't SEE color.

We had a meeting in our home, when my son was small, for a political committee. We spent a good two hours talking over issues that we wanted to prioritize in our agenda. A lot of our conversation revolved around the importance of early childhood education. I spoke vehemently about the need to support parents of children with special needs.

Another woman in the group talked about the support welfare mothers need to provide their children with educational opportunities not available in the home. We both shared our stories along with our passion for ensuring early childhood education was a priority for our community.

After they left my husband commented on how I seemed to really connect with the black woman. My response? "Was one of those women black?" Apparently she was, but her story was more important to me than her color. Now I wonder if her story wouldn't have been more powerful if I had acknowledged her color.

As we explore privilege and culture I hear black people saying "if you don't see my color, you don't see me." I didn't used to believe that was true. I've always seen culture. I've always listened to the stories, to the history. My context has been place, environment, even ethnicity, but never color. But I live in a visual world, and color does make a difference. These people walk in a world where they cannot pass. They walk in a world where "passing" means rejecting everything that came before.

By acknowledging color I acknowledge that there are places I cannot go. I acknowledge a history I can find resonance with, but never share. I acknowledge that even if I'm family, I don't get a share in the inheritance - good or bad. I acknowledge that I can walk away, and they cannot. By acknowledging color I acknowledge my own privilege.

It's high time I take ownership of my own color. I may never claim it or relate to being white, but being seen as white carries an implicit acceptance from white people in power. These people see themselves in my face. It's time to start seeing color.

Shoop!
Transforming Stereotypes with Love

Erick DuPree

"Don't know how you do the voodoo that you doSo well it's a spell, hell, makes me wanna shoop shoop shoop" - Salt-n-Pepa

I was 13, the first time I heard that line from Salt and Pepa's award winning hit, "Shoop". It was a big song, and to this day I think every person probably knows the lyrics. I had a yellow Sony WALKMAN and it played all Hip-Hop all the time. But it was more than the music; in my mind, I was living Hip-Hop in the urban jungle of my adolescent experience. I grew up in the heart of urban community, sometimes in the projects when my father was between jobs and sometimes in pastor houses next to great big churches where my father served as minister. I spent all my teen years with Taehynna, her father and my father were co-pastors of a mostly black, Pentecostal church. Let me tell you, I can sing a riff into any song and turn it gospel!

Courtesy of Taehynna, I know more about weaves, perms, and lace-front wigs than any white boy should. And no matter where life takes me, she always finds a way to remind me that the man I lost my virginity to wore Timberland boots, chains, and baggy jeans. I am not quite sure exactly when I realized it, but at some point, the white man told me *I wasn't black*! My black community never really cared either way, or if they did, I never knew. I was just the pastor's kid, who got a perm even though my hair is already stick straight.

Despite having been raised conservative Christian, "alternative spiritualities" like Voodoo and Santeria were very real in my neighborhoods and I felt special attraction to those mostly female practitioners. Imagine my surprise about four years ago when I saw a Voodoo practitioner who was not black at a Pagan event. He had a fanciful New Orleans style name, dressed all in white, and doing his *voodoo*. It seemed everywhere I turned, a white person was having a lucid dream waking up with titles like "Docteur So and So" and 'Mambo Such and Such". Even people whose magic I had respected had jumped on the Voodoo Express. I suppose this wasn't a new phenomenon, this alleged cultural appropriation. Throughout the late 80's and 90's, plenty of white men had worn South Western style jewelry, had adopted Native American inspired names and published Shamanic Ritual books, CDs and such. But for some reason, my emotions ran deep and a bit out of control. I mean, who were these people to come along and appropriate Voodoo?

For a good 6 months, I sat steaming mad at the white privilege all over indigenous cultural magic. Someone needed to stop this cultural insensitivity and I was determined I would expose it! While visiting Taehynna in Atlanta, I went on a real rant, as I am occasionally known to do. When I finally took a breath, she looked up from her drink and said, "This reminds me of that time a white boy was singing 'Take My Hand, Precious Lord' like he was Mahalia Jackson herself!" Leave it to a best friend to *shut it down.*

******

We live in a world of stereotypes and prejudices that, in addition to affecting the day to day lives of million upon million of people, on the job and in school, affect our magical community as well. Western society loves to project on to other races and cultures their own assumptions, opinion, and ideals. Stereotyping has become so ingrained in the fabric of our culture that often it happens without so much as cognition until the trauma is deeply manifested.

You just read a narrative about my experiences growing up within urban community, about my best friend and I, and more recently about my experiences with Voodoo. It is a story laced with stereotypes. Can you spot them? It assumes that all people must listen to hip-hop, especially the song "Shoop" and that hip-hop is the Black community's sole music. That if you are 'urban' then Urban must mean 'black' over African American, and that the urban community is poor. It assumes that Pentecostalism is a traditionally African American religious community, which it is not, and that to be part of a black spiritual community one needs to have a black best friend, sex with black men, and sing gospel. It assumes that all African

American women wear fake hair, that all African American men wear chains, Timberland boots, and baggy jeans.

It also assumes that people who are not black cannot or should not apply the practices of Voodoo into their lives. And that the authentic experience of others is in some way not valued and therefore not legitimate. It assumes Voodoo must be afrocentric, and you must be black to practice it. In a few paragraphs, I stereotyped not only an entire race and community of people, but in the process of trying to support a thesis *that white practitioners were in some way not worthy to practice "that kind" of magic,* I also used my white privilege to align myself as 'black" to validate my outrage. In truth, I wanted to set the stage to get my point across and I wasn't even cognizant how greatly I was appropriating culture and stereotyping until it was already written. This glaring lack of mindfulness is a form of cognitive dissonance.

Cognitive dissonance arises when we hold two contradictory thoughts (technically "cognitions: ideas, beliefs, values or emotional reactions"). For example, "all humans are created equal" and "slavery is okay." These two thoughts don't go together when we enslave fellow humans, so we experience cognitive dissonance. Most of the time, we dissolve the dissonance by changing one of the beliefs – or adding a third. In the example, we might add the belief "colored people are not full humans," which dissolves the dissonance because now "colored people" are no longer created equal because they are not fully human. Many probably feel some kind of visceral response to this pretty extreme example, considering in the dissolution of the cognitive dissonance we have chosen another option: *Slavery is not okay.* To come to this dissolution however, required a lot more mental effort and also behavioral changes, which might be why it's a choice many don't gravitate to automatically.

It is because the dissolution of cognitive dissonance is so challenging that more often many, including me, reach for stereotypes. Even when seemingly innocuous, some of the most mindful will err on the side of stereotyping. Stereotyping makes life easy, offering an opportunity to turn a blind eye to systems of oppression, privilege, and power. Like in the example, about 'colored people.' But what exactly are stereotypes, how do they play out in our magical and ritual community, and how can we choose not to become Sorcerers of Stereotypes?

Stereotypes are essentially assumptions that are made about a person or group's character or attributes, based on a general image of what a particular group of people is like. It is the assumption that all Voodoo practitioners are ethnic, while all Wiccans are white or of European descent, and giving value judgments to both parties. In reality, some magic workers that might be called Docteur and Mambo are of ethnic heritage and practice Voodoo, while there are Wiccans of many races. Stereotypes are generalizations that are further oversimplified and wrong, and are especially likely to be wrong in conflict situations. We find ourselves in conflict situations, speaking and acting from places informed by stereotypes when we feel threatened and have something to prove, like defending personal truths, as I did.

Stereotype assumptions don't just happen, but rather typically come from the appropriation of cultures and communities. We call this cultural appropriation. The phrase means literally, "one culture taking parts from another culture", for example, the idea that the origins of Voodoo are solely of African origin and thus as afrocentic must look, feel, and be applied with afrocentric characteristics. Anything that doesn't fall in line with that assumption is thus wrong. This is not dissimilar to the idea that *all* shamanism must be derived from the indigenous peoples of America, and as such, tomahawks, feathered head dresses, and peace pipes are in order. Or conversely, the belief that by solely wearing the clothing of indigenous people, it validates who you are.

Cultural appropriation has the power to make stereotypes of cultures of origin, by creating a version of 'culture' that is mostly invented by those who are not from that culture, and often times, is not actually true. This is rampant in Pagan communities where syncretic traditions blend, and weave, to create new religious truths.

This can cause people to see the other cultures as "strange" and "exotic" because they only see the other culture through their eyes and not from within the actual culture. This usually happens when a dominant culture takes things from a less powerful culture, and stereotypes them or creates their own ideas about them, which typically erases the truth behind original cultures.

So how do we develop this negative into a positive picture? How do we grow out of a culture of cognitive dissonance, stereotyping and cultural appropriation which inevitably becomes a tool of oppression, into beloved community? The first step is to become grounded in fact over feelings and assumption. As we have seen, if stereotype is most typically based in assumption and assumption is fed by cultural appropriation; being grounded in fact is the magic key.

It starts with how we approach what we want to know? When we study other cultures, be mindful that we come to the study from original sources, from those within in that culture. I find that sometimes that even seemingly grounded scholarship is using writings by 'outsiders' and is biased and vast with stereotypes. It is really about the details, and important to explore more than one aspect or a few things, before you decide that you "know about the culture". Cultures are large, glorious living traditions. Often we purchase a book on a topic as the entry point, like a book on voodoo, but one book is what I call "small study" When cultures and communities are approached with "small study" we are treating that culture like a shallow thing.

As we grow to understand the culture of our community, we become aware of our tendencies to lean into assumption, and we can begin making conscious efforts to correct the inaccuracies. When study in books or blogs, leads to study in a directly experienced way, we increase person-to-person contacts between people from different groups, everything changes when we meet each other, talk together, and/or work together. Soon we learn that the 'opponents' we had made assumptions about are not nearly as awful as we had earlier believed. Just think, how bland our magical community would be if we didn't have this diversity to grow, learn and share experiences with? We have to make a choice, the choice to breakdown stereotypes to build the spiritual community that fosters Love.

****

The blessing of Paganism is that there is no litmus test for belief entry, our community holds varied beliefs, but with this is the tendency for all to want or feel they must be right. Stereotyping finds itself the star player in the "I'm right, you're wrong" game. When we are engaged in a conflict, the image of our opponent tends to become more and more hostile. In these situations communication gets cut off, and many people make generalizations and assumptions about opponents based on very sketchy and often erroneous information. A personal favorite example of this would be when women of color are defending the right to own their heritage, and how that often becomes interpreted as the "angry black woman." What is really happening is that we see faults in ourselves and then "project" those faults onto our opponent, preferring to believe that we are good and our opponents are bad. Eventually, opponents develop a strong enemy image, like the "angry black woman."

This type of enemy imagery runs throughout the Pagan community, across a wide variety of platforms. Part of this is because the right to self-determination is a sacred rite to the Pagan community. "Nobody is going to tell me what I believe." We see stereotyping within our community on every topic from Heathens being racist, to Caucasians appropriating cultural magic. From calling oneself warlock vs. witch and the assumption that to self-identify as "warlock" makes you an oath breaker. All black people worship afrocentric deities. All transgender women are not "women born women" and that "all acts of love and pleasure", as quoted in the Charge of the Goddess, means all Pagans are pansexual, open and polyamorous. The list is exhaustive and the countless essays, bloggings, and Facebook postings that support this kind of stereotyping continues to grow in a discursive current.

Magic is an interconnected experience, and when we choose to provide support for rather than against each other, we build a place where people from various magical experiences and traditions can be part of our gathered community. An inclusive community works together to break down stereotypes, and encourages a dialogue where people are safe and free to explore each other's magical truisms. That deep dialogue connects us through the divine spark in all of us, regardless of whom or how we define that spark.

When we choose to encourage discussion and understanding among varied paths and wisdom, we discover that we learn through the stories we tell each other. There are stereotypes about every single magical group. But people are people. And as we get to know each other as individuals, not just a stereotype or label, we can break down barriers and form relationships. That guy who calls himself Warlock actually isn't an 'oath-breaker', but rather an awesome magic worker who just taught you the Feri Tradition's Iron Pentacle. The witch whose been labeled "Angry Black Woman" actually has a right to be angry, as she recovers her sisterhood and confronts her enslaved past. From her we learn to recognize the racist world is still very much alive. And those Voodoo workers who are white, maybe it isn't cultural appropriation, after all. But a genuine appreciation and cultivation upholding folklore in their approach to magic.

Recently, I was hungry for more practical applications of magic in my life. I wanted to learn, engage, and become a better magic maker. Most of the traditions I'd been affiliated with (Feri, Reclaiming, and Dharma Paganism) mostly dealt with "the self" as access to magic. And so I sought wisdom from a dear friend. This person recommended I read about rootwork and folk magic. I thought, hmmm maybe? I began to interview root workers, Docteurs, and Mambos, professors and untitled workers. I came into the dialogue seeking wisdom and from a place of inquiry. I made the choice to make the connection and build relationships, rather than walls of opinion.

This approach lends itself in cultivating a cultural exchange over appropriation. Together we gave and received an exchange of information from direct sources to deepen understanding. Quickly, I discovered that there was more to these practitioners' stories and entry into Hoodoo, voodoo and rootwork than I had ever imagined. I realized that I was wrong in perpetuating the stereotype that there was a gross cultural appropriation. While some were certainly misappropriating, the majority had a deep desire to document, hold up, and rebuild a sacred tradition. In fact these were skilled practitioners that, like me, had walked many paths that lead them to folk magic. Over the course of months, I got to know intimately their practices, and fell in love with their love for what they do. They too, were of Goddess and the only thing that held me back from them was stereotype. I chose to enter on a path to study hoodoo.

I came to this realization by making authentic connections, and connecting back to the sacred within us all. I choose to lean into Goddess, and away from stereotype. Goddess, in Her many emanations created these paths to wisdom, power, and love, and our diverse community. Within each of our diverse viewpoints, we can offer comfort and ways of forming the loving connections that most of us yearn for in the world. When we embrace facts, over stereotypes, our different traditions help people to find what resonates within each soul and community. Learning about and understanding our diversity, is part of that sacred rite to self-determination and helps us to broaden our perspectives and can actually deepen our own spiritual beliefs. Together we can find answers all around us to the deep questions of life. By understanding and respecting all, we release ourselves from discursive stereotyping, and can come into our beloved community's greatest potential that celebrates life and love as we honor the divine spirit.

In the end, because I choose to turn stereotype into Love, I came to know *that the voodoo that they do*, was the choice I too could make. I choose to get with love and shoop!

Paula Dean Syndrome

Lydia M.N. Crabtree

I am, despite my sincerest desire to deny titles, a High Priestess. There is no coven or tradition, other than my own, which stands behind my ordination. My oaths were made alone in a sacred grove on land borrowed from a dear friend. The sword placed upon my breast was braced by the good earth and my witnesses were the Lords of the Watchtowers, the Elementals, and the Gods and Goddesses that I called upon and came to me.

However, before my third degree ritual, before my entrance into the mysteries of Wicca and modern Paganism, before leaving the Catholic Church because I couldn't proclaim their oaths in my heart, before leaving Protestantism for Catholic worship, before being excommunicated from the Presbyterian Church of America for blatant disobedience, before long walks with my grandmother covering herbal remedies and spiritual mediumship held together by oral traditions steeped in American Indian folk magic, before my baptism as a Southern Baptist, I knew I was called. It is a distinctly Southern thing, to be called by God. Certainly not something most Southerners believe can happen to a girl.

I have always thought differently than the people in this Southern landscape I call home. I have always looked differently at things like race and sexual orientation. As a child, I would check out and hide the sermons of Martin Luther King, Jr., and read them in my room after lights out, devouring the words of a man of God who taught things I could wholeheartedly agree upon despite what I was taught at my own church Sunday mornings. The God who called me was not just a man or one color. Most assuredly I understood Jesus was not white. God was the Great Spirit, an American Indian warrior looking over my grandmother's fields. God was Mary in blue robes in the vestibules of Catholic Churches I would sneak into because their doors were always open. God was the fox in the wood and the deer on the table. God was in everything and of everything and had chosen me to do what God commanded. I was called.

Being called is not a privilege or honor, it is a responsibility. It makes me responsible for the spiritual questions and questing of those I come into contact with. It makes me painfully feel when I betray the oaths and promises I can never remember not knowing I had to uphold. On this journey of being the vessel, as my grandmother might say, I have learned that there is much I didn't know or understand, especially as it refers to race and the South. It is part of my quest to uphold the oaths of my calling that has driven me to seal the cracks in the vessel that I am; the cracks through which racism permeates my life and seeps into the pure offering Divinity tries to fill me with.

It has been a strange turn of events that led me to meet someone who challenged everything I thought I knew of race and racism. A chance meeting online, a deep and abiding friendship that grew into something that defines me as a woman, sister, daughter and high priestess. It has been one woman's willingness to discuss race and racism that has shed a growing light of understanding into why Southerners are so often thought of as being racist.

Being a Southerner, I suffer(ed?) from what might be called "Paula Dean Syndrome" (PDS). A belief that I am a good person, proud of my Southern heritage. Good people aren't racists. I do good things for the black community. I have friends, generally cursory friends, who are black. I read Martin Luther King, Jr.'s sermons and speeches and give to the King Center. These things mean I am not racist. So what if I secretly cherish the Confederate flag or think with pride and fondness about the era before the Civil War or even the Civil War itself; that is just ancestral pride and you can't make me ashamed of that. I am not racist.

PDS is most insidious in the South because the thoughts behind the disease are not fully formed. It is as if Southerners live in a fog created by a unique set of factors not found anywhere else in the United States, the world or history. Here, with a conflict in our history that existed during a time of great progress and prosperity without the exposure created by media that included video clips, the South is left to revel in the idea of the past with a fairy tale like quality to it.

The inability of outsiders to understand our stubborn refusal to acknowledge or even comprehend the extent of the damage slavery caused and slavery's continued pervasive effect on America today is tied inexorably to a nationalism that rises far above the taint of the history of slavery, Jim Crow and current racial tensions. The South of the pre-Civil War era had more in common with itself than with its neighbors to the North[103]. The South were a people then, and is a people now, that were not immigrants. We were born with red dirt and pine needles flowing through our veins. We were galvanized by a common evangelical Protestant belief system. We were prosperous and of one class, the white upper class, where if you were white, then you were wealthy[104]. Seeped in our clearly delineated social norms, moral and religious doctrines, we were a Nation within a Nation. The only thing Paula Dean did was expose the world to what Southerners already knew. That Nation did not die when the South lost.

When I say we were not and are not a Nation of immigrants, I can best explain this by my own experience. When I was in tenth grade, I moved from the urban setting of the suburbs of Atlanta to Dawson County, Georgia. A county set against the foothills of the Appalachian Mountains where nothing but Bill Elliott's auto shop for his NASCAR business was located. In my first days there a strange feeling of otherness developed about me. I was southern. I had been born in Georgia as my biological mother had been. I remember being introduced to students who had grown up together, literally. People who had known each other from Pre-K to 10th grade and whose prospects were to remain in Dawson County and be laid to rest in the family cemetery plot. I'll never forget how this was driven home when I was introduced to a popular girl on the cheer leading squad.

---

[103] Thomas, Emory M. "Editors' Introduction." Introduction. *The Confederate Nation: 1861-1865*. New York, NY [u.a.: Harper Torch, 1998. Kindle Print.
[104] Woodard, Colin. "Chapter 7, The Founding of the Deep South." *American Nations: A History of the Eleven Rival Regional Cultures of North America*. New York: Viking, 2011. N. Kindle Edition Print.

"She's not from here either," the teenager making the acquaintance said with an air of conspiracy. Almost, *look here is another outsider like you,* she seem to be saying.

"Really? How long have you lived here?" I politely inquire.

"Oh," the from-Dawson-County girl interrupts, "She moved here when she was in second grade." The girl in question turned a pretty shade a red, as if to apologize for her inherent lack of roots in the county.

This is my South. There is a lot of talk by Western and Northern Americans about how Atlanta is the new melting pot. Our climate and industry are attracting people who were not born in the South. This is seen as some progress toward altering our backward thinking. However, if you are FROM the South, you keep score. You excuse their radical ideas as being Northern brashness because they were not raised to the more genteel and proper ways of the South, which is obtainable only by being bred for generations in the same Southern place.

We are a people of church. Unlike our neighbors to the West and North, we are a people of *one* church, the right church. The churches which are deemed appropriate are like antebellum houses, large and ostentatious in presentation or old, well-kept and seeped in hundred year old roots. The really old ones are kept alive by the families who founded them, tending the family plots adjacent. When new churches spring up, they are born with a surprisingly Southern ideology. This ideology harkens back to that calling I previously discussed. Our evangelical rules, and despite Southerners not recognizing it, our long standing history of refusing to be ruled over by any person or belief, allows us to know that the Holy Spirit in Its infinite wisdom can ordain anyone. In ordination, the Holy Spirit is clear only about a two things.

> 1.Those who are called and have the spiritual gift to rouse a church with their preaching always have a penis.
> 2. The King James Bible is the ONLY Bible permitted and is always translated in accordance to the strictest and often the most right-wing conservative

view available in the time period which the preacher preaches.

Evangelical, which I have always understood to mean, refusing to be governed by any over sight, denomination or opinion, except the Word of God as received those called. Pastors have learned with time to slowly moderate opinion and views and translations of the Good Book to remain successful and allow for the continued influx of those pesky "others." However, the underlying belief is still there.

The most important thing to remember about the South? We are a conquered Nation, not "were," not "was," not "at one time." Today, families of Southerners whose roots are as old as the pecan and dogwood trees, have a generational feeling of being defeated, robbed and invaded by ideas, laws and a people that are not their own. Not in some war hundred plus years ago, today, in this moment. For us, we never recovered.

To understand this, you must understand that before the Civil War, the families who were already generationally entrenched in the area, were prosperous - not moderately wealthy, extremely wealthy. By the eve of the American Revolution the per capita wealth in the Charleston area was six times higher than New York or Philadelphia.[105] This wealth did not permit for any class but a wealthy one. Colin Woodard in *American Nations: A History of the Eleven Rival Regional Cultures of North America* galvanizes this ideaby quoting a 1773 resident of the South Carolina region, "We are a country of gentry, we have no such thing as Common People among us."[106]

Of course, as Woodward quickly points out three-quarters of the white population were not so fortunate to say nothing of the population majority, enslaved blacks who outnumber whites nine to one in some areas.[107] To keep the supermajority under

[105] Woodard, Colin. "Chapter 7, The Founding of the Deep South." *American Nations: A History of the Eleven Rival Regional Cultures of North America*. New York: Viking, 2011. N. Kindle Edition Print.
[106]Woodard, Colin. "Chapter 7, The Founding of the Deep South." *American Nations: A History of the Eleven Rival Regional Cultures of North America*. New York: Viking, 2011. N. Kindle Edition Print.
[107] Woodard, Colin. "Chapter 7, The Founding of the Deep South." *American Nations: A History of the Eleven Rival Regional Cultures of North America*. New York: Viking, 2011. N. Kindle Edition Print.

control, the slave codes from other slave nations, particularly Barbados, were imported. Whipping, branding, maiming by cutting off ears, slitting nostrils or severing an Achilles tendon, and castration were all punishments used within the daily course of maintenance over the slave population. White masters who withheld these punishments were severely fined. Punishments for whites who helped slaves could include whipping, fines and death.

If these punishments meted out for escape, maiming or disabling a white person and stealing, seemed extreme, even more austere punishments were given to runaways who "attempted to go off from this province in order to deprive his master or mistress of his service."[108] In short, death was given to black slaves who sought to keep their virtue.

Although it is true that slavery was not a condition monopolized by Southerners, the mortality rate of our supermajority slaves necessitated a constant replenishment of slave labor. This kept the machine of the slave trade sailing to Africa and Caribbean islands, forcibly removing and transporting natives back to the Deep South for a life of indentured cruelty.

In this land of wealth for nearly three centuries (1670 to 1970), the Deep South is characterized by Woodward as a Caste system. A system where there were poor and rich whites, as well as rich and poor blacks, living within the bounds of social system designed to keep them separated. Living, working and praying in unofficial areas created not by boundaries of state, county or country but by color and money. Within the Caste system you are born to certain expectations, or not. You were given certain rights or not. To hold this Caste system in place an organization of barbaric ritual was utilized from social ostracization to death by lynch mobs. Rape, torture, maiming and quiet backwoods punishment kept fear as the greatest motivator for those, white or black, who may question the status quo.[109]

---

[108] Woodard, Colin. "Chapter 7, The Founding of the Deep South." *American Nations: A History of the Eleven Rival Regional Cultures of North America.* New York: Viking, 2011. N. Kindle Edition Print.

[109] Lauer, Matt. "The Today Show; June 26, 2013." *Paula Dean Interview.* NBC. WXIA, Atlanta, GA, 26 June 2013. Television.

So what does all this have to do with Paula Dean or Paganism? Everything. There is a disconnection between the attitudes of our generational ancestors and our behavior today. Because, for us, in the fairytale Kingdom of Dixie, life is about the destruction of mint juleps on the porch, antebellum dresses and a simple innocent time when all whites were wealthy and all slaves cherished and cared for properly, as befitting their caste.

The destruction of the Kingdom of Dixie has left a generational bitterness which flourishes. With no Northern Army to persecute, the resilient Southerners turned to the only whipping post they could find, Jim Crow and poor whites. Admittedly, blacks have gotten the worse end of Southern ire. This bitterness has galvanized the Southern battle cry with every federal intervention since the Civil War.

With this backdrop, looking at Paul Dean's apology on the *Today* show may paint for the outsider a better view of where Dean was coming from. Her first statement was that she was recovering from a "state of shock." For most, her shock seems to highlight a willingness to deny racism and the sudden high wattage spotlight that exposed her secret hatred of blacks. Her shock was actually a response to someone suggesting that the Kingdom of Dixie is not all antebellum dresses, grand parties and a gentile South, filled with cotillions and sweet tea. There was brutal slavery in that Kingdom which is not something she really even thinks about. Don't call it ignorance, call it blissful un-acknowledgement of un-pleasantries.

She continues her apology with tried and true Southernisms.

> I believe that every creature on this earth, every one of God's creatures was created equal. No matter who you choose to go to bed at night with, no matter what church you go to pray. I believe that everyone should be treated equal and that's the way I was raised and that is the way I live my life.[110]

To a Southerner this initial statement speaks to the things that Southerners hold most dear: God, sex, church, hospitality. Everyone is God's. That white Protestant God worshiped in an

[110] Lauer, Matt. "The Today Show; June 26, 2013." *Paula Dean Interview*. NBC. WXIA, Atlanta, GA, 26 June 2013. Television.

old Protestant church. Sex is sacred between a man and a woman; however, we always tolerate a fruity uncle or butchy aunt with love and the cautionary tale that their soul will die and go to hell. Love, however, and loyalty are always there. Even though the white Protestant God is the right God, most Southerners, in the face of true heathens like Muslims, Sufis, Hindus and even modern Pagans, have agreed to embrace any church that fundamentally professes a belief in the Judeo-Christian God. We prefer you wouldn't go to a Catholic Church and if you do, we can find it in our hearts to pray for your hell bound soul. Hospitality is an innate state of being in Southern society. Having a cake ready for unexpected company and a clean house ready to receive at a moment's notice is still considered the sign of either a wealthy home or an efficient woman, usually both. The idea that we would turn away anyone, not treat anyone like they are equally important once they present themselves on our door, is mortifying. Growing up the story of *The Stranger*[111] was told every Christmas, Easter and family gathering. It left us with a deep sense that God would test our hospitality at any time by showing up at our door steps as an indigent woman, down-on-his luck man and a sick or wounded animal. To suggest to such a deeply rooted Southern woman as Paula Dean that her hospitality wouldn't extend to someone of color is to propose she would deny God.

Matt Lauer spends time trying to get Dean to focus on the business aspect of her verbal indiscretions. Dean does the typically Southern thing of deflecting the conversation again and again to her perception that her character has been attacked. Because money may come and go for Southerners, but an attack on the heart of a human is forever. It is the stuff of gravestones and family legend. Finally Lauer, capitulates and asks her if she is a racist.

"...is Paula Dean a racist? So I'll ask to you bluntly, are you a racist? ... By birth? By choice, by osmosis? You don't feel you have racist tendencies?"

To the non-Southern viewer, this question seems to give Dean a chance to admit that the South, by definition, is filled with

---

[111] Wilson, Todd. *The Stranger*. South Bend, IN: Familyman Ministries, 2009. Print.

racism. To a Southerner well versed in the denial that permitted Jim Crow and maintains those invisible dotted lines of caste to continue, the question will get nothing but a denial. Dean reinforces this by recounting what her Daddy taught her.

"As a child I was raised in a home that my father tolerated bad grades, he would tolerate maybe me breaking a curfew. But he told me, he said, "Girl if I ever find out that you have behaved in a way where you think you are better than others or have been unkind, your butt is going to be mine."

Again the outside observer takes note that Daddy didn't say anything about being racist, just behaving better than others or being unkind. Southerners understand the omission is not one of deliberate subversive racism. For Dean, racism has become equated with hospitality and kindness. Racism is blatantly unkind and being inhospitable is unthinkable. Dean would never dream of being either of those things.

She later is quoted as saying that you "...can't, myself, determine what offends another person", as part of her deposition when asked if telling jokes about niggers is offensive. True to her Southern sensibilities she explains that most jokes are aimed at a group of people: Jews, rednecks (read poor whites) or blacks. As a woman these crass jokes would not be told in her company or by her or her Southern white female friends. The ways and means of southern white men is a world unto itself, one where off color jokes are told over after dinner drinks and cigars while the women clean the dishes or take tea on the veranda.

This isn't some idealistic painting of a fantasy realm. This is how many Southerners live today. Dean was raised to be truthful and kind. She isn't a man, so how can she possibly know what men might find funny. Couple this type of thinking with the subtle shifts in societal norms and the picture Dean paints is much more complex than you could imagine. For example, no one, man or woman, would dare discuss gay politics when the fruity uncle comes to call. That would be unseemly. When he is out of the room the conversation will be completely different and in no way diminishes the true love and affection for Uncle. There is a disconnection that the words spoken out of earshot of said Uncle has any real impact upon him. He is given the same hospitality as others so what if talk disparages him behind his back. It is said with a genuine concern for his soul, after all.

Paula Dean's most fatal mistake is to turn her use, excuse or feigned ignorance of racial slurs back on the "young people in her kitchens." What the educated viewer immediate understands is that the place Dean mostly interacts with blacks is in a boss to hire relationship, a horrible correlation to the plantation owner and slaves. Her kitchens seem to be described as some other place separate from where she actually lives, where she goes to work with people she doesn't really understand. There she encounters young people who seem to lack the genteel raising by a good Daddy to be kind to others and never hold yourself above another. They call each other those N* words and the affect is confusion to all the white bosses in the room. If they call each other that name then is it acceptable? If it isn't should they get to use that word and white people not?

What this portrays is the remnants of that Caste system being vividly painted for us. As times have moved forward, poor whites, blacks, and increasingly Hispanics who do menial labor aren't raised to the same standard as wealthy whites and blacks and Hispanics. Wealth brings with it the genteel breeding and nature afforded only by money which makes room for less time cleaning one's house or making dinner and more time tending the rearing of children properly.

Dean ends her apology with a typically dramatic Southern plea:

> *"I am heartbroken...I've had to hold friends in my arms while they sob because they know what is being said about me is not true. I am having to comfort them and tell them it is going to be alright. If God got us to it, he'll get us through it. I have had wonderful support from Rev. Jackson. I have had wonderful support. I'll tell you what, if there is anyone out there that has never said something that they wish they could take back. If you are out there please pick up that stone and throw it so hard at my head that it kills me. Please, I want to meet you. I want to meet you. I is what I is and I am not changing. There is*

*someone evil out there that saw what I worked for
and they wanted it."*

To most this seems melodramatic and largely overdone.
However, not enough can be made of the affront to her standing
as a Southern woman by this widely publicized racial issue.
Dean, from my Southern view, is sincere. She doesn't
understand why one racial slur, said one time after a traumatic
life event, could lead people to judge her as racist in all her
business and personal dealings. She cannot comprehend the
ways in which her life's structure and work are tainted by the
pervasive invisible chains of chattel slavery morphed into
acceptable racism, homophobia and elitism.

This is the crux of the Paula Dean Syndrome. In the once
isolated Kingdom of Dixie, racism is not something easily
identifiable or understood by bred and born Southerners. It is in
the water, you could say, an underground spring most
Southerners do not recognize that we drink from daily, weekly,
monthly, yearly. There has to be a retraining of thought patterns
that are subtly reinforced at church, school, in polite society and
at large extended family gatherings. Choices have to be made
about when and how to confront the insidious nature of racism
in the South. In order to accomplish this the famous Southern
pride has to take some hits. We have to mourn the Kingdom of
Dixie, acknowledging that our romanticized view of the pre-
Civil War era is built upon mass graves filled with chattel slaves
treated worse than most cattle. We have to come to understand
that the Confederate flag instills fear into the hearts and minds of
blacks because it suggests that nothing was learned from the
lynch mobs and people who terrorized black voters at the polls.
When we raise a beer glass to the South rising again, we are
saying we would like to see blacks working our fields for no
compensation and reinstate a caste system that divides poor
from rich regardless of color.

And I would assert that, at least in the South, this
subversive racism continues into the sacred circles of Paganism.
How odd that I can clearly remember seeing my first black
woman at a Pagan gathering drum circle. She was gorgeous and
to my not yet awakened mind, almost more offensive in her
beauty. She was deep black, almost that purple black of someone

who has little taint with white breeding. She wore these beautiful velvet panties that showed off a woman's figure that was fit but not thin. Her breast were bare as she drummed rhythms that are most assuredly Pagan and yet steeped in African tradition with the djembes and cone drums.

It was obvious that she was used to the outright gawking that occurred in her presence. She would catch someone's eye and hold their gaze, often while the person in question found a way to shut their gaping mouth. She was never far from a Craft sister or brother with whom she had traveled to the gathering and I remember them touching her kindly and often, as if to somehow make up for the lack of immediate acceptance. She was braless and her breasts fascinated me because the deep purple black was stretched around her enticing and young globes, causing the fire to reflect upon her heated skin demonstrating how many colors black really is. I saw her nudity as defiance. As if she was saying, "If you going to look, then look at all of me and know that I reflect the Goddess too!"

After my awakening to Paula Dean Syndrome, I took note while in California how few minorities were there and fewer still were actually teaching. I wander around discussing things with my sister and feeling painfully aware of the fact that she was one of the few showing any shade of color upon her skin. I also noticed that even when it came to the HooDoo, VooDoo and VooDaun houses, it was a plump white woman dressed in a cross between antebellum and Stevie Nicks' style that ran the proceedings during the Pomba Gira. There were no black persons drumming or singing. Even here, miles from the South, the South that had shown up was still homogenous – white – well off and stealing their spirituality from another race with little thought or acknowledgment of such.

Eventually, I was blessed with my brother Nathan. A Pagan man and mixed race southerner, we met under trying circumstances that often bind people more surely than blood can. He was the beginning of real change in my Paula Dean world. He was the first minority to circle intimately with me outside of my sister, mother and their family. As I threw open my heart and worshiped with Nathan, my spiritual world opened too. I found myself at gatherings in the South wondering where the Hispanics, the blacks, Indians and American Indians were at Pagan events. The more I wondered about this, the more of the same seemed to start coming to our circles. It was easier to find the gay, lesbian, bi or other gendered, maybe because Paganism offers a spiritual outlet not given them anywhere else. I can remember my son asking me years ago at gathering why there weren't any blacks.

"Oh, honey," I said, "Well African Americans in the South go to ecstatic African American churches. They are known for their singing and dancing and for having a deep tradition of church and family. I guess that is why."

I cringe now because it never entered my mind that Nathan existed and was going to a Southern white church where skin color was a daily reminder that he didn't really belong. They were probably wondering why his mother didn't send him to the black church down the road. These broad statements about people of race were steeped in my own Paula Dean Syndrome. My PDS symptoms were infecting the circle I found so sacred.

As the years have gone on, I have ended up in a community in the South that I am inordinately proud of. Our web guru is a wonderful black HooDoo practitioner who is well versed in herbs and magic. Nathan is running our open classes and serves as the Summoner to our inner circle. Our moons and Sabbats are often attended by a Cherokee man who came from the reservation in Oklahoma.. He is hard working and found sympathy and help when he couldn't get hired because of his cinnamon skin and long, straight, black warrior's hair he assures me he binds up when he is job hunting. He told me potential bosses were always upset that he didn't have a second language.

"Cherokee," he said to me, "I guess doesn't count. They always want me to speak Spanish."

Recently my Ojibway sister moved back to the reservation in Michigan with her white husband. On a recent visit he confided in me how different and back woods it was. He explained how little he fit in. He was having a hard time finding work and the spiritual tides at the reservation didn't seem to really allow for his blended Pagan background.

"And they aren't friendly," he tells me, a true Southern gentleman. "I can count on one hand the number of times people wave back at me when I pass them on their porches."

I make appropriate sounds of Southern disdain for the obvious lack of manners taught to Northerners. I understand acutely, however, that what he is experiencing is uncomfortable because he is having to face his own Paula Dean Syndrome and isn't yet aware of it. He is already talking about moving "home" to Georgia.

On my last trip to California I was startled when a man asked me how my community managed to attract and keep such an eclectic group of Pagans in skin color, class, education and spiritual background. I was startled because when you begin to attend to the symptoms of your PDS, the idea that you wouldn't attract an eclectic groups such as the one I worship with is unthinkable.

Lamely, I tell the man that our community has no dogma of practice as one of our foundations. This means that we do not tell people which gods or goddesses to worship or what quarters or elements to call and how. We have a ritual standard we adhere to but ultimately we strive to make any spiritual path welcome. I think this is true, however, my inquisitor was not satisfied.

"I mean where did you FIND the minorities?"

Now I was truly baffled. Nathan and I met at the local metaphysical book store. He was brought by another member. Our web guru found us through Facebook. I met my Ojibway sister at the laundry mat when my dryer quit before my laundry was finished. My Cherokee brother came through the store as well, as did a younger African American who infrequently comes. My first thought was how do you go about your day and NOT meet minorities and then eventually find a minority who shares a common spiritual belief system?

Of course, if you liberally apply the Paula Dean Syndrome to Paganism it is quite easy to understand. Like the Kingdom of Dixie, Pagans are a defeated people. The Burning Times is our battle cry whenever we are persecuted legally. However, we cannot fathom those burning as anything other than white Europeans. The common misconception is that the only Pagans who were persecuted were White Europeans or only olive complexion of the Spanish Inquisition. The Burning Times as the focal point of our defeat by definition excludes our brothers and sisters of other color, cultural background or sexual orientation. I will never forget my gay circle brother telling me where faggot came from during an ongoing rant by another circle member about the Burning Times.

"Faggots were the kindling used to burn witches. Often times this included sodomites who were used as kindling upon which witches were burned. Of course you won't hear that in a song about the Burning Times."

I was stunned and did not know what an appropriate reply was. At the time I was years from understanding my racial Paula Dean Syndrome so I had not context with which to apply my coven brother's obvious bitterness.

Now, I know, this is where the root of Paganism's Paula Dean Syndrome lies. It is in the assumption that only whites who were Pagan were/are persecuted. The European Pagans were assimilated by the church from Rome and eventually Paganism was stamped out. That is why there are no snakes in the Celtic Isles, the Pagan beliefs were the snakes and St. Patrick was the priest who took away the remnants of Pagan holidays and transmuted them to Christianity.

We do not think about chattel slavery destroying the spiritual fabric of the blacks taken from Africa. We give no thought to the abuse by the English over those in India and other provinces conquered by Great Britain, much less to the spiritual toil this took upon those peoples. Little is said about the American Indians who whites decimated by disease and conversion so that entire tribes and spiritual ways of life were made extinct. No attention has been paid to the many Pagans who at one time or another were a part of the Christian church and gave to Christian missionaries whose sole purpose for travel was the conversion and assimilation into Christianity of conquered peoples at the expense of the native beliefs and spiritual knowledge.

Sometimes there might be a post or two about people being killed in Africa or South America by stoning because they are accused of witchcraft. There is no thought given to how the rise of the occult has helped lend an air of urgency to the missionaries who travel to those places.

Generally, we dismiss it as a one off, an unclear thing that has no correlation or inter-relation on our private practice at home. If the church wasn't so zealous then they wouldn't be stoning witches. Forgetting that evangelicals are the most prolific when it comes to conversion and in their deep seated faith, Pagans are very close to the devil. In these new bastions of Christian lands, making sure that the mistakes made in developed countries aren't repeated elsewhere is a priority. So harsh punish for homosexuals and lesbians are enacted along with the killing of people who make waves, branding them witches. When asked about this the missionaries adopt their own Paula Dean Syndrome stance of gross indifference grounded in a belief that these minorities are getting what God wants.[112]

Pagans, unlike Southerners, haven't had hundreds of years to wallow in despair over their being conquered. Nor are the majority of Pagans in a situation where they cannot fight back without risking death, dismemberment or maiming. Which is what we do, through *The Lady Liberty League* and *The ACLU*, laws suits are brought and won in the name of religious freedom and no thought given to the global and spiritual implications that these decisions have. Nor is there any thought that even in these legal battles the plaintiffs are still mostly white and mostly upper middle class. Nor is there concern that our circles are homogenous and significantly focused on white practitioners with distinctly European spiritual leanings. All of this opens the door for radical Paganism which says only those defined by specific racial characteristics can practice as Druids or Heathens or Asatru. After all they are only revealing in words and beliefs what is actually already reflected in the circles in which we worship.

We just don't want to hear it. Because in the hearing, we must seek understanding and in the understanding we must confront our own prejudices against the minority practitioners who are gay and Pagan, black and Pagan, or other culturally oriented and Pagan.

As with all magic, I attempted to explain to my inquisitor, thought proceeds action, intent draws to you what you believe.

"I think you set the intent first," I reply delicately, "You make sure your energy says that you WANT other backgrounds, races, sexual orientations and perspectives in your group. You

---

[112] "Roger Ross Williams." *The Daily Show*. Comedy Central, Atlanta. 13 Jan. 2014. Television

want to learn from them and grow with them, not just tolerate them as a novelty to boost your self-portrait."

"Do you do that in some ritual?" he immediately inquires, "Or is that a spell?"

Dumbfounded again, I gape at him trying to find the courage to say, "It comes from the heart and soul of each person in ritual space."

As the time ticks on I cannot find the strength of will to say it and lamely end with, "You could do a ritual I suppose."

My querent makes a noise that says clearly I am holding back and dismisses me, disgruntled by the conversation. I am not much better. How much happier would he have been had I told him the truth. That unless white Pagans start looking for the subtle and insidious ways that Paula Dean Syndrome is part of our spiritual practice, no amount of ritual or spellwork would draw minorities or those with minority orientations to our sacred spaces?

For me, it has been nearly seven or more years since meeting my sister and my mother. Seven years of discussing race, talking to my mother about race and discussing my own PDS with my white husband. Seven years of a slowly answering why pride in the Civil War South could not be extracted from the horrors of chattel slavery. Seven years of working in a highly skilled labor force for my husband to identify the inherent sexism and racism in his own field. Seven years to be appalled at a company dismissing the only black engineer because he was a Rasta, complete with wonderfully kept dread locks. Seven years of coming to understand that exposure and interaction, true intimate interaction with other Pagan paths and minority orientations and skin colors was the only way to address my own PDS.

How can I explain this to a random white guy I just met?

Looking back, I am wondering how could I not? If it is true that the ripples of my spiritual freedom are having an impact in countries and people hundreds of miles from me in cultures I cannot begin to fathom, then I have a responsibility as part of my calling as a high priestess to fight and secure sacred circle space for everyone. I must be willing to say the hard things to people and speak the truth. This isn't my sister's fight around racism, this is my fight around inclusion and spiritual fulfillment. I teach that the Gods and Goddesses are like a multifaceted gem. When the light strikes it I can see very clearly the Morrigan whom I worship with deep devotion. However, my sister sees Yemaya, and how much time have I tried to spend seeking her out in meditation? As I cling to the very fabric of my spiritual practice the energy says, "If you are Celtic and worship the Morrigan be drawn to me."

I do not think that this is the way it should be – or indeed the way the Morrigan would have it be. Recently I was crafting my personal prayer book, making changes and updates. I had placed within it a Pagan rosary crafted by Tirgereh. This beautiful piece of liturgy clearly demonstrates the depth of our cultural Paula Dean Syndrome.

Tigereh compares the Celtic Goddess he is praising to Greek or Roman Goddesses. The reader gets the sense that the author is trying to help the practitioner connect. Why not African American Goddesses? Or Hindu? Or any other connection that isn't based upon a white European background.

It is, however, the last stanza that really made me frown.

> Hail, our beloved Ladies of the Celts,
> To You, we honor and worship,
> In the Old ways when Woman was the Center
> Woman was the Creatrix of the World
> And Ireland, Gaul, Wales Your own,
> Our hearts in Your hands, our will is Yours
> Keep and protect our children as you do all Celts,
> Your chosen people, in Your prayers. So Mote It Be![113]

It was the "keep and protect our children as you do all Celts, Your Chosen people…" that stopped me. This is exactly how the racism that has slowly begun to sink into Pagan Culture began. Clearly, if this liturgy is the only explanation of these Goddesses, then Cerridwen, Bridghe, Morrigan, Epona and Blodeuwedd are only concerned with Celts who are white Europeans. These Goddesses aren't concerned with the spirituality of anyone who does not reflect their own white nature and comes obviously from that Celtic white Culture.

---

[113] Celtic Goddess Rosary. *The Sacred Grove*. Tirgereh. Accessed 08.15.2014. Internet. www<dot>sacredgrove<dot>com

To be sure, I do not believe that Tigereh means this liturgy to reflect the idea that blacks or Hispanics or other culturally raised Pagans cannot worship these Celtic Ladies. However, the idea is there in that subtle Paula Dean Syndrome way. Tigereh is only being proud of his spiritual path. He is only owning spiritually who he is. It is only a mistake if that comes off elitist or limiting to others. Tigereh only means not everyone is drawn to worship these Celtic Goddesses.

Which leads me to my challenge, to you, Pagan practitioner. If you want your circles to reflect the various manifestations of the Gods and Goddesses we worship, then start in your own heart confronting your own Paula Dean Syndrome. Read your liturgy and ask yourself if all the goddesses and gods you mention are always white? Do you even know or can you even fathom what a correlation to them might be in a non-white culture? Does your liturgy subtly suggest that only those who are white or with obvious spiritual roots in a white homeland can worship with you? In the Charge of the Goddess, is she always white when she speaks her words of wisdom? Do you even know who all the goddesses the charge lists are? Are they all white?

This is when and how we address the Paula Dean Syndrome taking over our Pagan culture. The only question that remains is: are we, any of us, brave enough, to do the inner work that will alter forever the growing climate of subtle racism in Paganism?

> Hail, my beloved Ladies,
> To You, I honor and worship, in the Old ways
> When Woman was the Center of the Earth, the Creatrix of the Universe
> Spiritual Quencher of the Soul's Thirst
> I am Your own, My heart is in Your hands, My will is Yours to keep
> Protect my children as You do any who worship You,
> As I honor and protect You through my prayer. So Mote It Be![114]

---

[114] Celtic Goddess Rosary. *Lydia M N Crabtree's Personal Prayer Book.* Lydia M N Crabtree adapted from Tirgereh. Private Collection.

Works Cited

Thomas, Emory M. "Editors' Introduction." Introduction. *The Confederate Nation: 1861-1865*. New York, NY [u.a.: Harper Torch, 1998. Kindle Print.

Woodard, Colin. "Chapter 7, The Founding of the Deep South."*American Nations: A History of the Eleven Rival Regional Cultures of North America*. New York: Viking, 2011. N. Kindle Edition Print.

Woodard, Colin. "Chapter 7, The Founding of the Deep South."*American Nations: A History of the Eleven Rival Regional Cultures of North America*. New York: Viking, 2011. N. Kindle Edition Print.

Woodard, Colin. "Chapter 7, The Founding of the Deep South."*American Nations: A History of the Eleven Rival Regional Cultures of North America*. New York: Viking, 2011. N. Kindle Edition Print.

Woodard, Colin. "Chapter 7, The Founding of the Deep South."*American Nations: A History of the Eleven Rival Regional Cultures of North America*. New York: Viking, 2011. N. Kindle Edition Print.

Woodard, Colin. "Chapter 7, The Founding of the Deep South."*American Nations: A History of the Eleven Rival Regional Cultures of North America*. New York: Viking, 2011. N. Kindle Edition Print.

Lauer, Matt. "The Today Show; June 26, 2013."*Paula Dean Interview*. NBC. WXIA, Atlanta, GA, 26 June 2013. Television.

Lauer, Matt. "The Today Show; June 26, 2013."*Paula Dean Interview*. NBC. WXIA, Atlanta, GA, 26 June 2013. Television.

Wilson, Todd. *The Stranger*. South Bend, IN: Familyman Ministries, 2009. Print.

Celtic Goddess Rosary. *The Sacred Grove*. Tirgereh. Accessed 08.15.2014. Internet. www<dot>sacredgrove<dot>com

Celtic Goddess Rosary. *Lydia M N Crabtree's Personal Prayer Book*. Lydia M N Crabtree adapted from Tirgereh. Private Collection.

Reweaving the Web:
Pagans, Privilege, and Solidarity

Claire "Chuck" Bohman

In her book, *Belonging: A Culture of Place*, bell hooks tells of her experience as an African-American woman growing up in Kentucky. She speaks of the safe haven that the earth provided her and her community in the face of racial violence and oppression, "The hills in the back of our house were the place of magic and possibility, a lush green frontier, where nothing man made could run us down, where we could freely seek adventure."

hooks dives into the ways that her childhood relationship with nature allowed her to escape racism and white supremacy. She says, "Nature was the place where one could escape the world of manmade constructions of race and identity." Through this articulation, I have been able to find words for a key dimension of my own relationship with the land. For me, nature has been the place where I can escape the world of human constructions of gender and sexuality. When I am in the woods, swimming in the ocean, connected with nature, I have felt more at home in my body than I do anywhere else. As I sit with the plants while I am planting, tending, or harvesting, the constant struggle of how I fit into the societal boxes of male/female and straight/gay melt away and I am *just me*.

Sometimes I wonder how this was for my German ancestors, who tended the land as sustenance farmers for generations in Germany until poverty and drought pushed them across the ocean to a land of promise in North America. They walked across the Canadian border and settled in Ohio, where they retained their German identity, traditions, and dialect for over half a century until the world wars drove them to shed because this identity made them a target of discrimination. On this side of my family, I hear stories and see pictures of tall masculine women who worked the land and loved their god. I dream of these ancestors sometimes, wondering how their relationship with the land allowed them freedom from 'traditional' notions of womanhood that my modern city life has enforced.

Brazilian eco-feminist theologian Ivone Gebara explores the way that religion has played a role in our movement away from listening to the wisdom of the earth and the wisdom in our bodies, "Often we turn traditional religious statements into 'truths' that are somehow above and beyond our bodies and our personal histories." She and other eco-feminist and eco-womanist authors emphasize the importance of the body and lived experience. In our modern world, dominant culture shames and stigmatizes the importance of the body and the importance of our own inner knowing.

A core teaching in most Pagan traditions is the deep connection between our bodies and the earth. Our bodies are the physical manifestation of the earth. We are the earth through the bodies that we inhabit as we walk along her skin. The more we can inhabit our bodies, the more we move towards right relationship with the earth. The more connected we are with the earth, the closer we become to the liberation that is possible when we can hear the "truths" that are within our bodies.

Each time we encounter another being, a thread of connection is created. The deeper the encounter, the stronger the thread. These threads create a sacred web of relationships and these threads hold our universe in balance. We are living in a time when many of us weave strong threads with only a few. We are living in a time when dominant culture teaches us only to care for ourselves and the people closest to us, even if it is at the expense of many others. Most of us have forgotten how to weave those threads with the non-human world. Most of us have forgotten how to weave those threads strongly and sustainably with each other. Or as Chan K'in Viejo, spiritual leader of the Lacandone people says, "What the people of the city do not realize is that the roots of all living things are tied together."

Feri ancestor Victor Anderson speaks of weaving webs of energy through connections between humans. In an interview before his death he names this process, "When you shake hands with a person the mana [energy] from the Unihipili [Fetch] forms fine etheric threads connecting you with that person." We weave the web of the universe and sometimes the threads we weave are healing and sometimes they can be hurtful. If you have ever spent time in practice cutting cords you are probably intimately aware of the ways in which these threads can be out of balance. I believe that we also weave these webs in a larger collective context.

Just as we are all related and interconnected, so are the systems that cause oppression. As we move towards solidarity with one another we can begin to see the ways in which the imbalance in our lives creates dysfunction in the web of the universe. Christian womanist theologian, M. Shawn Copeland, drawing upon the work of Iris Marion Young, speaks of this web when she writes how, "Oppression assaults (materially rather than formally) our connectedness to one another by setting up dominative structural relations between social and cultural groups as well as between persons."

The word solidarity has been a part of my vocabulary since I was a child. My father works in the labor movement, and my mother has always been an activist. Some of my earliest memories are looking out at the masses of human legs before me in crowds of large marches. I remember attending "Solidarity Day" in Washington, D.C. with my family in 1991. A snapshot of memory that has always stuck with me is looking around the crowd through my ten-year-old eyes. I remember feeling the power present there in the spaces between us as we marched for workers' rights. Even as a child, the power of the collective was clear to me there in the streets of D.C.

Solidarity is many things. One dimension of solidarity is the moment of becoming aware of the web of connection between us. M. Shawn Copeland speaks of solidarity emerging from a place of needing to go deeper in the struggle for right relationship saying, "We sense a need for something deeper and beyond the moral attention that social justice accords to the distribution of the material and cultural conditions for human living. That something deeper and beyond, I suggest is solidarity." Solidarity is refusing to turn away from the suffering of another and instead turning towards it and asking the questions, where am I in relationship to this suffering? Have I participated in this suffering? How can I work to eliminate this suffering? Solidarity is feeling the impact of injustice on the sacred web of life. Solidarity is ultimately rooted in love.

Political scientist and ecowomanist theologian Shamara Shantu Riley speaks of the need for solidarity between human and non-human beings. She says, "There is no use in womanists advocating liberation politics if the planet cannot support peoples' liberated lives, and it is equally useless to advocate saving the planet without addressing the social issues that determine the structure of human relations in the world. If the planet as a whole is to survive, we must all begin to see ourselves as interconnected with nonhuman nature and with one another."

I would argue that this is true not just for womanists, but for all of those advocating liberation politics, liberation theology, environmentalism, and environmental justice. What is the good of human liberation if the earth is destroyed in the process? And it is not possible for humans to live in balance with the earth if we are exploiting each other because *we are the earth*.

In the words of bell hooks, "Until we are all able to accept the interlocking, interdependent nature of systems of domination and recognize specific ways each system is maintained, we will continue to act in ways that undermine our individual quest for freedom and collective liberation struggle."One of the key ways that we can begin to be in solidarity, as bell hooks suggests, is to see the ways in which the oppression of another is interconnected with our experience of brokenness in the world.

Solidarity extends beyond our human relations. In her book on the feminicide in Ciudad Juarez and the stories of the women of Juarez' resistance to these atrocities, Nancy Pineda-Madrid discusses the importance of community and relationship in the struggle for collective liberation, or in her words, salvation. She offers a frame for community that I believe is critical in our Pagan understanding of solidarity. She says,

> *Community is forged by a commitment to others, particularly to the most vulnerable, and from a commitment to see our lives as inherently connected to those who live now, those who lived long before our lifetime, and those who will live long after we are dead. They teach us that community comes into being through a process whereby we understand our*

present moment in light of the past, with an eye
toward the future and in relationship to others.

Pineda-Madrid evokes the wisdom of the women of Ciudad Juarez in their struggles to respond to, resist, and eliminate feminicide. She explores the importance of building community not only with our human relations, but also with those who have lived before us and those who will live beyond us. In a Pagan context, I would suggest that Pineda-Madrid is pointing to a dimension of solidarity that builds community with our ancestors and descendants. I believe that the wisdom of the women of Juarez and their struggle against the violence of feminicide is important learning for all of us who are on the spiritual journey of moving towards right relationship with one another. We must build community, not only with our human relations in this world, but also build community with our ancestors and the descendants of life.

I have been studying plant medicine and healing traditions with a Choctaw elder for a number of years. One of the first assignments she gave me was to research and study a healing tradition of my ancestors. I remember thinking that I would study the runes, an ancient system of divination and healing in pre-Christian Germanic tribes. I assumed that my assimilated family would be so disconnected from any indigenous traditions that it wasn't worth the effort. Still, I followed her instruction and spoke with the elders in my family. It was through this process of connecting with the elders of my blood that I learned of my Great Great Grandfather.

My great uncle remembers this ancestor as a gifted farmer and a healer. He had a "German remedy for every ailment and a German saying to go along with it." I was shocked to learn that my assimilated white family had such a recent history of a deep connection with an earth based healing tradition. This teaching, that each of us has traditions in our families and in our blood that are earth based has been fundamental in my journey as a healer and as a witch.

I wonder what is possible through reconnecting with the ancestral roots that have been erased or stolen from us in the process of assimilation. How can creating spaces to deeply listen to our ancestors serve us in the journey of moving towards right relationship so often haunted by the "culture vulture", hungry to snatch up the culture of others. Spiritual misappropriation is a dangerous extension of the legacy of colonization. Guarding against the "culture vulture" does not mean that we should only engage with spiritual traditions or practices of which we are ancestrally connected. Quite the contrary, we need to celebrate the many manifestations of divinity in its multiplicity of racial, gender, and cultural manifestations. However, I believe we must always consider the ways in which our privilege plays out in our spiritual journeys and be mindful of the impact that these practices may have on those who are from positions of less privilege.

This connection with the ancestors is a fundamental dimension of solidarity, resisting spiritual misappropriation and dismantling white supremacy. We must know the threads we came from and the threads we carry if we are to weave threads that heal more than hurt.

As I see it, we must continue this weaving through building community and solidarity with our non-human relations. Many eco-feminist and Native American theologians assert the ways that an expanded understanding of community and relationship with non-human beings challenge dominant understandings of the world around us. In the words of Ivone Gebara, "In what ways do the feminist and ecological issues change our understanding of our own reality?" Gebara poses a fundamental question in Pagan cosmology and invites the question of how solidarity with human and non-human beings compels us to live our faith differently.

Our world is broken. We struggle against oppression and we benefit from the ways in which others are oppressed. If we are serious about justice and serious about healing then we must begin to see the ways that our lives impact the lives of others and the world around us. Having grown up in a UU Pagan community and spent the overwhelming majority of my life on this earth in Pagan circles I have deep love for these ways. I offer these words with heart full of love because I know that earth based spiritual traditions have much healing to offer this earth and her people. We can weave spells that hurt and we can weave spells that heal. May we stay connected with the earth and deepen in our connection with each other. May we always move towards healing ourselves, our communities, and the Earth. Ashe, Aho, and Blessed Be.

Works Cited

Baruch, Inni. "Speaking with Victor Anderson."*Connections Magazine* 9, no. 4 (Winter 2001): 6. http://www.lilithslantern.com/article02.htm (accessed March 28, 2013.

Copeland, M. Shawn. *Enfleshing Freedom: Body, Race, and Being.* Minneapolis, MN: Fortress Press, 2010.

Gebara, Ivone. *Longing for Running Water: Ecofeminism and Liberation.* Minneapolis, MN: Fortress Press, 1999.

Gottleib, Roger. *This Sacred Earth: Religion, Nature and Environment.* New York, NY: Routledge, 1996.

Halifax, Joan. *The Fruitful Darkness: a Journey through Buddhist Practice and Tribal Wisdom.* 1st Grove Press ed. New York: Grove Press, 2004.

hooks, bell. *Belonging: a Culture of Place.* New York: Routledge, 2009.

hooks, bell. *Outlaw Culture: Resisting Representations.* New York: Routledge, 2006.

Pineda-madrid, Nancy. *Suffering and Salvation in Ciudad Juarez.* Minneapolis: Fortress Press, 2011.

White Feminism is Part of the Problem

Lasara Firefox

When I first heard the term white feminism, I had to take a breath, center, and check myself. My brain was full of the garbage that pollutes the thought process of any of us, in the spaces that need examination. The alarms bells of the defensive, "Not *all* white feminists..." response was clanging behind the more reasonable thoughts, like, "Ok, just listen. There is obviously something to learn here."

Thankfully, it only took me one moment of true misstep to realize that just listening was the best action I could take; after Miley twerked her way into infamy at the VMAs (video music awards) in 2013, I wrote a response to the slut-shaming aspect of the roar of critique.

I was checked.

A facebook friend asked why I wasn't addressing the cultural appropriation and racism angle. So I looked for writing on the web in order to get a deeper understanding of what the issues were, and found very little in the way of critique by women of color.

Instead, I found articles by black men saying things were as they are, as they have been, as they always will be. They shrugged off the cultural appropriation angle. And articles by white feminists saying all kinds of things. And by "family values" bloggers saying Miley was going to ruin America for all of us.

I came back to the conversation on my facebook and said that I hadn't found anything on the subject, and that maybe it was not as big an issue as my friend thought.

I was wrong. I was directed to previously hidden areas – internet cul de sacs full of commentary from marginalized voices - that held the teeming, pained response to the use of black women's body as props, the cultural signifiers as faulty "cred", the anger over the "But I have black friends!" nonchalance of Cyrus's response to criticism, the appropriation and misuse of the word *ratchet* and by extension the further stereotyping of women of color, and the prevalence of the legacies of slavery; story upon story about black women's bodies being treated as community property - hair touched, breasts grabbed, asses nonconsensually fondled, white women and men alike treating black women's sexuality as a dangerous and exotic door prize for getting drunk enough to cross the colorline at closing time.

The testimonies were nauseating, and the anger palpable. I dug deeper. I looked up words I didn't understand. I read scholarly articles, activist blogs, twitter feeds, and tumblr posts. I followed, friended and fanned as many women of color as I could find, and I read, listened, and learned.

What I have come to understand as I lean into the process of self-education - reading, listening, witnessing - has been life changing; Challenging and illuminating at once. And humbling. Vastly, vastly humbling.

Here I offer a distillation of a few things I have learned so far. I offer this as an opportunity for other white feminists (and white people in general) to streamline the process a bit, and also to challenge us to become part of the solution. Because until we do, we are individually and collectively part of the problem.

Blind Privilege

Like marginalization, privilege is something we experience by degrees. It's easier by far to see where we're lacking in privilege than where we are operating from it. Our degrees of marginalization loom as stumbling blocks; physical or mental disabilities, poverty, sexual orientation, and gender identity. Even being Pagan or otherwise 'alternatively' religious may show up as a factor for marginalization in our lives.

You may envision each of these elements as degrees of marginalization. Most of us experience at least a few degrees of marginalization.

Conversely, privilege is something that works to your advantage. We are often unaware of our advantages because they are not "in our way". Rather, we experience them as part of the underpinnings that make our lives run smoothly. Thoughts like, "What's the big deal?" or "Of course people of color are welcome at this festival!" come from privilege. Instead of asking

"What can I do to make this festival more accessible?", we allow ourselves to sit in the assumption that because we are comfortable, everyone must be.

Privilege is not something that will just go away. It's not even something we would want to give up. Rather than anyone losing privileges, wouldn't it be better if everyone had access to what should be considered basic rights?

What if everyone had the ability to reliably cover monthly bills, put food on the table, keep a roof over one's head, have access to higher education, or even access to a high school education in a safe environment that offers the same educational standards as schools in more affluent neighborhoods?

However, while this is a lovely dream - and we know that dreams are important! - it is not the reality we live in.

Privilege is an issue most intensely when it we are blind to it. When we are blind to our privilege we are not able to take into account issues of access, inclusion and exclusion, representation, and safety of marginalized populations.

White feminism does not take many of these issues as central to the aim of mainstream feminism. We focus on closing the gender wage gap, but most of us are not aware of the fact that the wage gap between Latina women and white men is the widest gap in the American economy. Hispanic/Latina women make about .59 on the white male dollar.

White feminists are most surely not malicious in this blindness, but not being malicious is not enough. For feminism to become part of the solution, feminists need to educate ourselves, and become aware of how people of color experience layer upon layer of marginalization.

Intersectionality

One of the most important elements of finding our way to an inclusive feminism is the concept of intersectionality. The term, coined by feminist theorist Kimberlé Williams Crenshaw in 1986, allows for a view at the matrix of domination[115], and a language with which to discuss the interactions of different aspects of marginalization, oppression, and discrimination.

---

[115]http://en.wikipedia.org/wiki/Matrix_of_Domination

In other words, issues of relative levels of wealth and poverty, sex, levels of education and more *coincide* with issues of ethnicity. While issues of race, religious belief, sexual orientation, and gender expression are not seen as implicitly feminist issues, they can't be separated out.

When taking intersectionality into account and integrating it as an essential element of a more egalitarian and inclusive feminism, equal access to funds for educational services across different regions and neighborhoods, access to varied food choices in poor neighborhoods, and even police brutality, prison reform, and putting an end to the drug war can be seen as feminist issues.

It doesn't take much to realize that these issues affect different populations with different levels of severity. Yet as a white feminist, you may not understand why it's a feminist issue that while 12% – 13% of the American population is African American, African American men represent 40% of the prison population. A young black man has a one-in-three likelihood of being incarcerated[116]. Two thirds of all people in prison for drug offenses are black men.

When men are taken out of families, out of homes, out of communities, women and children are left behind to pick up the pieces.

And it doesn't end there; one in eighteen black women will serve prison time. And two-thirds of women in prison are mothers to minor children.

As it stands, white feminism defines the terms of mainstream feminism, thereby excluding women who have different life challenges, hold different values or are working toward different goals from the movement.

When we look more deeply into the intersections of privilege and oppression, it is clear how much more complex the requirements on an inclusive feminism are.

Paternalism in White Feminism

Another misstep that white feminists make is thinking that we know best. We know what the most important issues are. We

---

[116]http://www.sentencingproject.org/template/page.cfm?id=122

know how to best sway public opinion. We know what freedom and liberation look like, consist of, require.

White feminism has had serious splits in the movement since the beginning of the American movement. The core of the suffrage movement believed that the right to divorce, and equal property rights to men, were too fringe to take into consideration. The right to divorce, and basic sexual and reproductive agency, was considered "free love". It was felt that taking those causes to the banner would cause to further marginalize the movement, and push the dreamed of right to vote off the table.

Many women were ostracized from the movement because their politics didn't fit in the narrow width of the agreed upon aims of the first wave of feminism.

That split has never gone away, but has instead shifted. In the 2nd wave, the spilt was about sex positivity and sex negativity. With the reach for egalitarianism being focused on the ERA (equal rights amendment), "personal" issues such as sexual orientation, gender expression, and many more basic elements of identity were pushed to the edges.

In the 3rd wave, again sexual and identity aspects were a point of contention. For the first time, sex workers were claiming a voice within the feminist millieu.

Feminism now solidly recognizes sexual orientation as part of the feminist struggle.

But white feminism does not have room to support Muslim women when their right to agency in religious dress is challenged.

In fact, white feminism is responsible for some of the most harsh words spoken to hijabi activists. Again and again women of color are told by white feminists that they don't know what liberation is, that they are oppressed, and worse, self-oppressing.

The white feminist conversation holds fast to the banner topic of "choice", but only so far. The conversation has little room to talk about things like eugenics[117] and forced sterilization[118] in communities of color. Or disproportionate

---

[117]http://en.wikipedia.org/wiki/Project_Prevention
[118]http://www.policymic.com/articles/53723/8-shocking-facts-about-sterilization-in-u-s-history

arrest rates for women of color for nonviolent offenses. Or who has the *choice* to wear what.

When a woman of color brings up a concern that goes against the "conventional" feminist reasoning, they are often asked, "Aren't there bigger issues you could be focusing on?" As if the issues that affect women of color – issues that affect them on the ground level, all the time, every day – aren't valid issues just because they aren't issues that white women have to think about as often, or at all.

White feminism decides how a woman must present, what their values must be, and how they behave in order to be a feminist.

It's no wonder that strong women of color are claiming other terms to define the movement they are building.

If that weren't enough, instead of being graceful and apologizing when we get called out, and trying to learn from the situation and do better, we have apologists.

Another big moment in the intersection of feminism and race happened in 2013 when a disastrous incident involved "the little folksinger", Ani DiFranco. Ani, long heralded as a champion of human rights, a strong feminist, and a relevant voice for certain groups of people (me amongst them), was going to have a singer-songwriter camp. It sounded awesome, with one hitch; it was going to be held on the largest former plantation in the South.

The vast majority of white feminists could not understand in the least what the big deal was. But those of us who were ready to listen got a crash-course in how to *not* create unity in the movement.

Adding insult to injury, DiFranco took too long in getting her head around canceling the event and making an apology. And when she finally got to it, her first try was an exercise in whitesplaining – aka an excuse for one's racism or white bias, instead of an actual apology[119]. (Her second one[120] was better.)

---

[119]http://www.righteousbabe.com/blogs/news/11177617-righteous-retreat-cancelled

[120]Ani DiFranco

January 2https://www.facebook.com/anidifranco/posts/10153721862335226

everyone, it has taken me a few days but i have been thinking and feeling very intensely and i would like to say i am sincerely sorry. it is obvious to me now

Yet if that had been the height of the damage, we could shrug it off as the actions of one person. The true depth of the split between lefty white people – many of whom called themselves feminists – and people of color was written out in stark relief. The name calling, paternalism, defensiveness and lack of understanding, empathy or compassion were unbelievable.

Unbelievable if you are a white feminist, at any rate. I learned quickly just how believable women of color felt the situation was, because women of color deal with having their feelings, needs, concerns, and requests not only ignored, but belittled, shouted down, and shamed regularly.

As white feminists, we have to get past the idea that all the good intentions in the world don't give us the corner on righteousness.

How to Be An Ally

So how *do* we create an inclusive feminism? While it's bound to be a long road, but here are some relatively simple steps we can start with.

1.Recognize your privilege. There has been so much written about this already, and I encourage you to read as much of that writing as it takes for you to realize what I mean when I say, recognize your privilege.

We all have some level of privilege. Literacy is a privilege. Being able to buy books, own a computer, and drive a car are all markers of privilege.

If you are white, you have white privilege. Being poor doesn't take white privilege away. Nor do physical or mental health concerns.

Don't argue it. Accept it. If you can't get this one, you aren't going to be able to do the rest.

---

that you were right; all those who said we can't in good conscience go to that place and support it or look past for one moment what it deeply represents. i needed a wake up call and you gave it to me. it was a great oversight on my part to not request a change of venue immediately from the promoter. you tried to tell me about that oversight and i wasn't available to you. i'm sorry for that too. know that i am digging deeper.-ani

2. Educate yourself. Racism is as pervasive as sexism. There are many kinds of Othering that are operating at any given time. Learn about intersectionality. Learn about marginalization. Learn about the elements of racism that you may not have yet come into consciousness of. Read blogs. Read books. Watch documentaries.

Remember that it is no one else's job to educate you.

If you reach out to your friends who are people of color and bring up something you just read, know that they may not want to have a conversation about that thing. And that's OK. Realize that your friend may have already had that conversation a billion times, and you are not being an ally – or a good friend – by pushing them to talk about something they don't want to talk about.

3. Make room for marginalized voices. Support people of color when they raise an issue, even if you don't understand why it's an issue. Listen. If you disagree, listen with even more dedication. If you listen for long enough, with enough openness, you will come to understand issues that are new to you, and their relevance to the feminist struggle.

4. Reach out to those who are under-represented in your community, and ask how you can help create room for collaborative thinking.

5. Finally, speak up when it's called for. Ask questions that need asking; who's not here? Why are they not here? Intervene when people are being threatened in any way. Explain the concept of microaggressions to those who aren't aware. Share language and consciousness with those who are ready to listen. Speak up when people say hurtful things.

But never let your voice eclipse the voice of those you are attempting to be an ally to.

Revisioning Feminism

What would it be like to have a feminism that held all women's struggles to be the core of the feminist movement? Can you imagine a feminism that is multiethnic, age inclusive, culturally aware, and that holds true choice at its heart? Can you imagine a feminism that is collaborative and co-creative? A feminism that is built upon the concept of equal rights for all women?

Many of us may imagine we are living that feminism. If that is you, I encourage you to think deeply about who is not represented in your circles. I encourage you to consider what ideologies you hold that may alienate women who need feminism just as much as you do. I encourage you to see what parts of reality don't yet fit up with that dream.

And then change them.

Biographies

Clio Ajana (Dr. Carla-Elaine Johnson) is a queer Hellenic Orthodox High Priestess, scholar, teacher, writer and member of the Lodge of Our Lady of Celestial Fire, Hellenic Alexandrian tradition.She is deeply passionate about numerology, astrology, herbalism and writing as a spiritual practice. She writes for the Patheos blog*Daughters of Eve*and her writing can be found in the anthology, *Shades of Ritual: Minority Voices in Practice.* Her current projects include a work on the individual's quest for a spiritual home and a second work on the intersection of racism, homophobia, and religious non- acceptance in modern Paganism. Her life in the Twin Cities of St. Paul and Minneapolis, Minnesota includes writing, teaching, translating, dancing, collecting comic books and enjoying craftwork. She considers everything in her life to be touched by her religious practice and spiritual beliefs. You may follow her blog at: www.clioajana.com

Lasara Firefox Allen is the internationally published, best-selling author of *Sexy Witch* (Llewellyn Worldwide, 2005). Lasara's work is widely published in anthologies, magazines, and on the internet. Lasara is a teacher, coach, and activist. She has a thriving coaching practice, and offers ongoing programs and courses online. She regularly teaches in person in her home region, and at conferences, festivals, and other events on the west coast. Married to the love of her life, Robert Allen, and mother to two amazing kids, Lasara lives in the wilds of northern California. She and her family surround themselves with a community of loving, like-minded souls. Find out more at www.lasarafirefoxallen.com.

Racial equity is a central focus in **Kat Bailey's** professional and personal life. Kat views internal work and magic as integral to reversing the effects of racism in our society. Kat, a white woman who has practiced magic for over forty years, descends from a Germanic hereditary tradition. In addition to exploring her ancestral roots she spent twelve years formally studying Zen Buddhism and was later initiated into a Stregherian tradition. In recent years she has been working in the Inner Temples Inner

Convocation tradition facilitated by R.J. Stewart and Anastacia Nutt, as well as practicing magic with her wonderful husband, Taylor. She is happily married with two teenagers and six cats.

Lisa Spiral Besnett has been involved in social justice issues all her life. As a writer on spirituality (*Manifest Divinity* and *When Gods Come Knocking: An Exploration of Mysticism from a Deity Based Perspective*) she makes a conscious effort to be inclusive in her perspective and examples. She considers herself an ally. Lisa Spiral Besnett understands that part of being supportive is actually listening to the issues that are distinct to each community. This is especially true when support is offered from a point of privilege.

Stephanie Rose Bird is an eclectic Pagan, Hoodoo and Green Witch who practices magickal herbalism. She is a writer and visual artist. Bird the author of five books:*The Big Book of Soul: the Ultimate Guide to the African American Spirit: Legends and Lore, Music and Mysticism and Recipes and Rituals,* (2010, Hampton Road Publishers), *A Healing Grove:African Tree Medicine, Remedies and Rituals*(2010, Chicago Review Press), *Light,Bright, Damn Near White: Biracial and Triracial Culture in America and Beyond*(2009, Praeger Press) *Sticks, Stones, Roots andBones: Hoodoo, Mojo and Conjuring with Herbs*(June 2004, Llewellyn Worldwide Publishers) and*Four Seasons of Mojo:an Herbal Guide to Natural Living*(Llewellyn Worldwide Publishers, 2006). Her sixth book and debut novel, "No Barren Life," will be published by Lodestone Books in 2015.

Crystal Blanton is an activist, writer, priestess, mother, wife and social worker in the Bay Area. She has published two books (*Bridging the Gap* and *Pain and Faith in a Wiccan World*), and was the editor of the anthology *Shades of Faith; Minority Voices in Paganism* and *Shades of Ritual; Minority Voices in Practice*. She is a writer for Sage Woman and Patheos'*Daughters of Eve* blog. She is passionate about the integration of community, spirituality and healing from our ancestral past, and is an advocate for true diversity and multiculturalism within the Pagan community.

Claire "Chuck" Bohmanis a lifelong lover of magic and the land. Claire is an Ordained InterfaithMinister and a Priestess in the Reclaimingtradition. Her spirituality has played a critical role in her decades of activism and she is deeply committed to the work of justice with roots in spiritual practice. She currently serves the Bay Area community as a Clinical Herbalist and a hospital Chaplain. She blogs regularly atwww.sacredplanthealing.comand is a guest blogger atwww.tikkun.org.

Janet Callahan is a priestess, wife, and mother of two complicated former preemies living near Detroit. She has a day job as an engineer, but has finally decided that she wants to be a writer and artist when she grows up. You can find all of her projects at http://www.janetcallahan.com

T. Thorn Coyle is committed to love, justice, and liberation. Pagan, mystic, musician, teacher, and activist, she is author of *Make Magic of Your Life: Passion, Purpose, and the Power of Desire, Kissing the Limitless, Crafting a Daily Practice, Evolutionary Witchcraft* and the novel, *Like Water*. Thorn hosts a podcast and video series and blogs regularly on her website and at Patheos Pagan. Head of Solar Cross Temple and Morningstar Mystery School, she lives near the San Andreas Fault and the San Francisco Bay. For information on her books, classes, CDs, and social justice work please visit www.thorncoyle.com. Thorn is also active on Facebook and Twitter.

Lydia M N Crabtree is a daughter, sister, wife, partner, mother, musician, a person challenged with disability and a writer. She writes on ideas around Paganism as it intersects with the disabled, families, persons recovering from PTSD and Major Depression. Her writing reflects a life filled with a wide range of different experiences. Currently, Crabtree writes on her own blog*Confessions on Being....*and *Birthing Hereditary Witchcraft*on Patheos Pagan Portal. Her first book, *Family Coven: Birthing Hereditary Witchcraft*is due out in 2015. Crabtree travels with Alice the Pagan Service Dog and both can be found on Facebook and Twitter or through lydiamncrabtree.com.

Lilith Dorsey M.A., hails from many magickal traditions, including Celtic, Afro-Caribbean, and Native American spirituality. Her traditional education focused on Plant Science, Anthropology, and Film at the University of R.I, New York University and the University of London, and her magickal training includes numerous initiations in Santeria also known as Lucumi, Haitian Vodoun, and New Orleans Voodoo. Lilith Dorsey is a Voodoo Priestess and in that capacity has been doing successful magick since 1991 for patrons, is editor/publisher of Oshun-African Magickal Quarterly, filmmaker of the experimental documentary *Bodies of Water: Voodoo Identity and Tranceformation*, author of *Voodoo and Afro-Caribbean Paganis*and *The African-American Ritual Cookbook*, and choreographer for jazz legend Dr. John's *Night TripperVoodoo Show*. She can be found on her blog *Voodoo Universe* and at her website www.blackbrigit.com

Erick DuPree is a writer, teacher, earth activist, and lover of Goddess. His studies in magic include Working Within a Reclaiming Collective, Soul Work with T. Thorn Coyle, Tantra with Dr. Douglas Brooks, Occult Magick with Ivo Domingues, Jr. and Dharma Paganism with Yeshe Rabbit Matthews. He writes the popular column *Alone In Her Presence*, and is author of*Alone In Her Presence: Meditations on theGoddess, Weaving Moonlight: Lunar Mysteries,Meditations and Magic for the Soul*(Circle Within Press), and the anthology *Finding the Masculine in Goddess' Spiral: Men in Ritual, Communityand Service to the Goddess"*(Immanion Press).

Taylor Ellwood is the managing non-fiction editor of Immanion Press, as well as the author of the books *Magical Identity, Space/Time Magic* and many other titles on magic. He is also a business coach by day. He also works in the Inner Temple Inner convocation tradition, as well heading up a group for magical experiments with his wife Kat. To learn more about Taylor's latest work visit his site at http://www.magicalexperiments.com

Pegi Eyers is a visual artist, writer and cultural visionary, occupied with smashing icons, contributing to the paradigm shift and working with the decolonization process in herself and others. A Celtic idealist who sees the world through a spiritual lens, she is a devotee of nature-based culture and all that is sacred to the Earth. Author of *Ancient Spirit Rising: Reclaiming Your Roots & Restoring Earth Community*, she examines cultural appropriation, the interface between Turtle Island First Nations and the Settler Society, rejecting Empire, anti-oppression activism, social justice work, cultural reclamation, earth rights, sacred land and the holistic principles of sustainable living. She is an advocate for our interconnection with Earth Community and the recovery of authentic ancestral wisdom and traditions for all people. Pegi Eyers lives in the countryside on the outskirts of Peterborough, Ontario, Canada, on a hilltop with views reaching for miles in all directions. www.stonecirclepress.com

Lou Florez is an internationally known speaker and lecturer of folk magic traditions of the South. He is a deeply rooted Spirit Worker, Priest, and Medium who has studied with indigenous elders and medicine holders from across the globe. In 2008, Lou was confirmed as an Olorisha and Priest of Shango and is a Tata Nkisi in the Bacongo Tradition. Lou also holds the titles of High Priest through Wicca and he has studied and apprenticed with Curanderos and Hoodoo Workers throughout the South.

AmyHale, PhD is an anthropologist and folklorist whose academic interests are primarily focused on modern Cornwall and British esoteric culture with specializations in ethno-nationalism and research methodologies. She is the co-editor of *New Directions in Celtic Studies*, *Inside Merlin's Cave: A Cornish Arthurian Reader* and *Journal of the Academic Study of Magic* 5 in addition to over 30 articles ranging from Druidry to Celtic cultural tourism, and sits on the editorial board of the Black Mirror Research Network. She teaches in the Liberal Studies department of Golden Gate University, where she is also the Undergraduate Director of Instructional Technology and Teaching Excellence.

Shauna Aura Knight is an artist, author, ritualist, presenter, and spiritual seeker. Shauna travels nationally offering intensive education in the transformative arts of ritual, community leadership, and personal growth. She is the author of *The Leader*

Within, Ritual Facilitation, and *Dreamwork for the Initiate's Path.* She's a columnist on ritual techniques for CIRCLE Magazine, and her writing also appears in the anthologies *Stepping in to Ourselves: An Anthology of Writings on Priestessing, A Mantle of Stars,* and *Calling to our Ancestors.* She's also a fantasy artist and author of urban fantasy and paranormal romance novels. Her mythic artwork and designs are used for magazine covers, book covers, and illustrations, as well as decorating many walls, shrines, and other spaces. Shauna is passionate about creating rituals, experiences, spaces, stories, and artwork to awaken mythic imagination. http://www.shaunaauraknight.com

P. Sufenas Virius Lupus is a metagender, *Doctor, Magistratum, Mystagogos, Sacerdos,* and one of the founding members of the Ekklesía Antínoou—a queer, Graeco-Roman-Egyptian syncretist reconstructionist polytheist group dedicated to Antinous, the deified lover of the Roman Emperor Hadrian, and related deities and divine figures—as well as a contributing member of Neos Alexandria and a practicing Celtic Reconstructionist Pagan in the traditions of *gentlidecht*and *filidecht,* as well as Romano-British, Welsh, and Gaulish deity devotions. Lupus is also dedicated to several land spirits around the area of North Puget Sound and its islands. Lupus' work, (poetry, fiction, and essays), has appeared in a number of Bibliotheca Alexandrina devotional volumes, as well as Ruby Sara's anthologies *Datura*(2010) and *Mandragora*(2012), Inanna Gabriel and C. Bryan Brown's *Etched Offerings*(2011), Lee Harrington's *Spirit of Desire: Personal Explorations of Sacred Kink*(2010), and Galina Krasskova's*When the Lion Roars*(2011). Lupus has also written several full-length books, including*The Phillupic Hymns*(2008),*The Syncretisms ofAntinous*(2010),*Devotio Antinoo: The Doctor's Notes, Volume One* (2011), *All-Soul, All-Body,All-Love, All-Power: A TransMythology*(2012),*A Garland for Polydeukion*(2012),*A Serpent Path Primer*(2012), and*Ephesia Grammata: Ancient History and Modern Practice*(2014), with more on the way. Lupus writes the *Speaking of Syncretism* column at Polytheist.com, and also blogs at Aedicula Antinoi (http://aediculaantinoi.wordpress.com/)

Xochiquetzal Duti Odinsdottir is an organizer and speaker on a variety of topics that meld spirituality with social justice issues and strives for a world where the sorts of discussions that are currently uncomfortable to have become commonplace. An ordained Priest/ess within the Fellowship of Isis and a Pagan for over 5 years, Xochiquetzal works hard to honor and worship those referred to as the Fearsome Foursome. Xochiquetzal can be found at SacredProfanity.com.

Ryan Smith is a practicing Heathen and graduate student specializing in modern history. He is one of the founders of Heathens United Against Racism, has been a Heathen for eight years, and a Pagan for 17.

Reluctant Spider: While she had enriching experiences within Christian traditions growing up, Reluctant Spider sought a better spiritual fit early in life. After a few years of study, she joined a witchcraft coven in 1999 and continues in coven and magickal working groups to support her solitary practice. Her personal practice is heavily influenced by ongoing training in the Anderson Feri Tradition which works well with her mixture of influences that include relationships with LWA and Orisha from the African Diasporic traditions, Western Ceremonial magic and a framework of eclectic Paganism. Within the Pagan community, she was a part of the 2013 coordinating group of friends for a sold out Goddess based women's spirituality weekend in the St Louis area called Goddess Weekend. She is also at home in the Unitarian Universalist church assisting in finances, governance, teaching Adult Religious Education and scenting "G!D Fragrance" wherever she finds it. She and her husband live in St Louis, MO with 2 cats to round out the family.

Mathew P. Taylor, known to the Pagan Community as Khemet Raa, was born and raised in sunny Southern California. He has a Bachelor's Degree in Communication. He has previously been published in the Phineas, the literary magazine of San Bernardino Valley College. In July 2009 he wrote his first book *A Collection of Treacherous Thoughts and Ramblings.*He is currently working on various literary projects, the most recent of which is his second book of poetry*The Love, the Laughter, the Lyrics.*

Rhiannon Theurer is a polytheist and animist living in Northern California. She is grateful to the many writers, thinkers, mentors, and colleagues who have shaped her understanding of race and culture, ranging from Frederick Douglass to the women of the New College of California Counseling program. Special thanks to Rahula for early feedback.

Heaven Walker is a High Priestess, Scholar, Teacher, Writer, and a member of the American Academy of Religion. Heaven Walker is an Elder and co-founder of the Come As You Are Coven, and the founder of the Grove of Artemis women's moon circle. She is also a legally ordained interfaith minister who offers professional tarot card readings, spiritual counseling, wedding ceremonies, and rites of passage. However, Heaven considers her most sacred work to be motherhood and is the former leader of the "Sprouts" Pagan parenting and ritual group. She hopes to eventually create an earth-based, spirituality-centered children's scouting troop.

Cecily Joy Willowe is an eclectic solitary Wiccan of 10 years and recently became member of the Boulder Valley Unitarian Universalist Fellowship. After completing her Master of Divinity degree from Naropa University, she went on to work at the local homeless and domestic violence shelters. She is passionate about Eco-Paganism, African Diasporic spirituality, Spirit Guide communication and Womanist theology. You can find her blogging at virtualchaplain.tumblr.com

Bethie Jelen Vanderyacht graduated from the University of California, Santa Cruz with a degree in Literature and moonlights as a writer and editor. She lives in the Bay Area with herhusband.

Brandy Williams has been practicing and teaching magic for over 30 years.Her work spans magical orders such as Ordo Templi Orientis, the Golden Dawn, as well as Witchcraft and Pagan reconstruction. Her book *The WomanMagician* examines and challenges the Western understanding of women'sbodies, energies, and powers, articulating a new metaphysics which freesand empowers women to act authentically as women and as magicians. She isalso the editor of the Immanion anthology *Women's Voices in Magic*.

A long-time Thelemite and former O.T.O. member, **Zack Anderson** is anactivist for social justice from Minneapolis, where he works full-timeas a tarot reader at Eye of Horus Metaphysical in Minneapolis.

Get More at Immanion Press

Visit us online to browse our books, sign-up for our e-newsletter and find out about upcoming events for our authors, as well as interviews with them. Visit us at http://www.immanion-press.com and visit our publicity blog at http://ipmbblog.wordpress.com/

Get Social With Immanion Press

Find us on Facebook at
http://www.facebook.com/immanionpress

Follow us on Twitter at
http://www.twitter.com/immanionpress

Find us on Google Plus at
https://plus.google.com/u/0/b/104674738262224210355/

CPSIA information can be obtained
at www.ICGtesting.com
Printed in the USA
LVHW110801050620
657464LV00006B/686